LIBRARIES WITHOUT WALLS 7

Exploring 'anywhere, anytime' delivery of
library services

LIBRARIES WITHOUT WALLS 7

Exploring 'anywhere, anytime' delivery of library services

Proceedings of an international conference held on 14–18 September 2007, organized by the Centre for Research in Library and Information Management (CERLIM), Manchester Metropolitan University

EDITED BY
Peter Brophy
Jenny Craven
Margaret Markland

facet publishing

Published by
Facet Publishing
7 Ridgmount Street
Lomdon WC1E 7AE
www.facetpublishing.co.uk

Facet Publishing is wholly owned by CILIP: the Chartered Institute of Library and Information Professionals.

First published 2008

British Library Cataloguing in Publication Data
A catalogue record for this book is available from the British Library.

ISBN 978-1-85604-623-7

Typeset in 10/13 Caslon 540 and Zapf Humanist from authors' disk by York & Timberlake Partnership.
Printed and made in Great Britain by MPG Books Ltd, Bodmin, Cornwall.

CONTENTS

CONTRIBUTORS

Panos Balatsoukas, PhD student at the Department of Information Science, Loughborough University, UK

Moira Bent, Science Librarian, Newcastle University, UK

Christine L. Borgman, Professor and Presidential Chair in Information Studies, University of California, Los Angeles, USA

Peter Brophy, Professor of Information Management and Director of CERLIM, Manchester Metropolitan University, UK

Jayne Burgess, Library Services Manager (Art & Design/Special Collections), Learning and Research Services, Manchester Metropolitan University, UK

Geoff Butters, Research Associate, CERLIM, Manchester Metropolitan University, UK

Jenny Craven, Research Associate, CERLIM, Manchester Metropolitan University, UK

Robert Davies, Partner, MDR Partners, UK

Emmanouel Garoufallou, Lecturer at the Department of Library Science and Information Systems, Technological Educational Institution (TEI) of Thessaloniki, Greece

Bob Glass, Senior Lecturer in Information & Communications and Information Literacy Learning Area Coordinator for the LearnHigher CETL, Department of Information and Communications, Manchester Metropolitan University, UK

Nancy Graham, Subject Advisor, The Medical School, The University of Birmingham, UK

Jillian R. Griffiths, Research Associate, CERLIM, Manchester Metropolitan University, UK

Kirsi Heino, Information Specialist, Helsinki University of Technology Library, Finland

Cath Hunt, IT Liaison Officer, University of Salford, UK

Kay Johnson, Head of Reference and Circulation Services at Athabasca University in Alberta, Canada

Kara Jones, Science Librarian, University of Bath, UK

Sangeeta Kaul, Network Manager DELNET – Developing Library Network, Jawaharlal Nehru University, New Delhi, India

Margaret Markland, Research Associate, CERLIM, Manchester Metropolitan University, UK

Gill Needham, Head of Strategic and Service Development, Open University Library and Learning Resource Centre, UK

Jouni Nevalainen, Information Specialist, Helsinki University of Technology Library, Finland

Pauline Ngimwa, Senior Information Specialist, African Virtual University, Kenya

Bo Öhrström, Deputy Director, Danish National Library Agency, Denmark

Virpi Palmgren, Information Specialist, Helsinki University of Technology Library, Finland

Kamani Perera, Librarian/Research Officer of the Regional Centre for Strategic Studies, Colombo, Sri Lanka

Gwyneth Price, Student Services Librarian, Institute of Education, and Fellow of the Centre for Distance Education, University of London, UK

Graham Pryor, Project Manager, Source to Output Repositories, University of Edinburgh, UK

Susan Robbins, Liaison Librarian, University of Western Sydney, Australia

Kate Robinson, Head of Reader Services, Library and Learning Centre, University of Bath, UK

Marie Scopes, Skills for Learning Consultant and Teacher Fellow, Leeds Metropolitan University, UK

Jane Secker, Learning Technology Librarian, Centre for Learning Technology, London School of Economics, UK

Karen Senior, Head of Learning Support Services, University of Bolton, UK

Rania Siatri, Lecturer, Technological Educational Institute (TEI) of Thessaloniki, Greece

Maggie Smart, ISD Liaison Officer for the School of the Built Environment and the Salford Business School, University of Salford, UK

Helen Standish, e-space Project Manager, Learning and Research Services, Manchester Metropolitan University, UK

Sarah Taylor, Assistant Librarian, Electronic Services Development Team/e-space, Learning and Research Services, Manchester Metropolitan University, UK

Ioannis Trohopoulos, Director of the Veria Central Public Library in Greece

Sirje Virkus, Head of the Department of Information Studies, Tallinn University, Estonia

Anusha Wijayaratne, Senior Assistant Librarian, Open University of Sri Lanka

Caroline Williams, Executive Director of Intute, MIMAS, The University of Manchester, UK

1

Introduction

Peter Brophy

The seventh Libraries Without Walls conference, held as is the custom at Molivos on the Aegean island of Lesvos, demonstrated that 'anytime, anywhere' delivery of library services has become the norm. Only 12 years after the first Libraries Without Walls conference in 1995, when remote delivery of services was a niche interest in the profession, it is the library within its walls which is in danger of becoming the minority concern. Of course that library remains of vital importance, both for the preservation of information resources of all types and as the base from which to deliver an ever-wider range of services, but its centrality is under challenge. Speakers and delegates from many countries and from both the academic and the public library sectors came together to discuss recent developments and to try to map out future directions.

Our keynote speaker, Professor Christine L. Borgman of the University of California at Los Angeles, drew attention to the increasing need for libraries to consider their role in facilitating and supporting the use of research data, enabling scholars from disciplines as disparate as history and nuclear engineering to handle the 'data deluge' that increasingly characterizes leading-edge research. However, as yet only a few fields recognize the publication of data as a scholarly contribution in the same way as that of papers, books, etc. The immaturity of data curation is illustrated by a lack of coherence between the essential components of the infrastructure needed for long-term sustainability. In this developing scenario the roles of libraries, and indeed of other actors, are unclear. Many scholars would prefer to trust their precious data collections to colleagues with the necessary disciplinary knowledge rather than to generalist librarians. Librarians therefore need to promote the relevance of their existing expertise, while at the same time recognizing that they too are faced with a new set of challenges – they will need to change and adapt if they are to become significant players in the data curation field.

Bo Öhrström, of Denmark's Electronic Research Library (DEFF), has presented at previous Libraries Without Walls conferences and used this opportunity to demonstrate how national infrastructures for research information are evolving. Central to these changes has been the espousal of open access, with important international collaboration being realized in Europe through the Knowledge Exchange partnership. The following paper signalled a change in emphasis. The Libraries Without Walls conferences have always been concerned to explore library service development across the world, and Pauline Ngimwa contributed a fascinating insight into the problems associated with delivering digital library services to distance learners in Africa. Innovative use of satellite technology, together with carefully planned use of local digital storage, has enabled the African Virtual University to deliver services to a hugely dispersed student population. Much remains to be done, but Pauline has cogently described a viable way forward.

After these opening and scene-setting papers, Graham Pryor returned to the topic of research data and questioned whether academic institutions and their libraries were taking seriously the need for custodianship of the rich research data they produce. Furthermore, because so much of this data is produced through publicly funded research, it is in essence a public good – and needs to be treated as such. Project StORe (Source-to-Output Repositories) illustrates the work being undertaken to provide the essential middleware to enable bidirectional links to be created between research papers and the source data on which they are based. The reluctance of users to engage with curation services and processes presents real challenges, and StORe is attempting to bridge this gap by supporting researchers' desire to collaborate while protecting their interests in relation to data ownership. Quite apart from the technical difficulties, there is a huge challenge to achieve a major cultural shift in researchers' attitudes to data.

Margaret Markland, Jayne Burgess, Sarah Taylor and Helen Standish continued this theme with a paper on the cultural problems of achieving acceptance of institutional repositories. The evaluation of the UK's major initiative in this area, SHERPA (Securing a Hybrid Environment for Research Preservation and Access), identified the key inhibitors to repository use, reinforcing the need to encourage a change in higher education culture while recognizing the legitimate concerns of researchers. Broadening the theme of cultural change assisted by new technologies, Jane Secker and Gwyneth Price described experimental use of Web 2.0 technologies to enhance the use of library services for distance learners.

Information literacy has become a dominant theme in librarianship in recent years and it was no surprise that this was a major concern of presenters. Bob Glass and Jill Griffiths, Cath Hunt and Maggie Smart, and Sirje Virkus all focused on the issues surrounding this topic, illustrating both new ways in which information literacy tuition can be delivered and the inherent problems in securing its place in the mainstream. Virpi Palmgren, Kirsi Heino and Jouni Nevalainen showed how concept mapping tools can be used for structuring information search.

A recurring theme in the literature is the centrality of learning to libraries' roles and purposes. Rob Davies and Geoff Butters reflected on the policy framework within Europe and showed that considerable challenges lie ahead in the areas of learning management, the use of information and communications technologies (ICTs) to support learning, and the identification and testing of learning outcomes. In supporting such work, Kara Jones and Kate Robinson discussed the role of collaboration and specifically the use of recommendation and review to build communities and conversations, thus incorporating user-generated content into library services. Nancy Graham rounded off this theme by looking at the potential for the incorporation of reusable learning objects into information literacy courses.

Turning to issues of content, Rania Siatri, Emmanouel Garoufallou, Ioannis Trohopoulos and Panos Balatsoukas drew on experience of digitizing cultural heritage resources, using the example of VeriaGrid, to explore the critical issue of usability. Their conclusion was that new usability frameworks with direct applicability to this kind of resource are needed. Jill Griffiths then took up this challenge in a paper presenting the use of 'Quality Attributes' to determine not just usability but also impact.

The third day of the conference began by returning the focus to developing countries, with papers by Sangeeta Kaul from India and Kamani Perera from Sri Lanka. Both presenters showed how the challenge of working in countries where ICT infrastructures are only just emerging can be overcome by innovation and ingenuity, not least through collaboration and co-operation. DELNET in India, for example, already has well over a thousand member libraries, yet the government aims to expand networking to 25,000 libraries in the near future! The proceedings also contain a contributed paper from Anusha Wijayaratne, who was prevented from attending the conference in person because of visa problems. Anusha reflects on why developing countries need to embrace new technologies, on the challenges of training library staff and on the need to familiarize users with services which may be taken for granted in the developed world.

Shifting the emphasis to remote delivery, Susan Robbins described how the libraries at the University of Western Sydney in Australia had developed a single receipt and response point for all incoming queries, termed Information Central, and outlined the steps taken to evaluate its effectiveness. Moira Bent, Marie Scopes and Karen Senior turned the spotlight on international students, demonstrating that where students move from one country to another to study they inevitably face language and cultural barriers and very often find that the library experience is very different from that which they were used to at home. In an increasingly competitive global market for students, UK libraries are trying to make a concerted effort to address these problems.

An unusual workshop concluded the third day's morning session and is reported in the proceedings in a paper by the presenters, Gill Needham and Kay Johnson. This presentation was concerned with the question of professional ethics, specifically in the context of providing library services to distance learners. Ten ethical guidelines were presented, and delegates – having engaged in lively discussion – were given considerable food for thought in relation to their own service delivery.

The final session provided an opportunity to consider how services can be made truly inclusive, with a paper from Jenny Craven and Jill Griffiths reporting on an initiative to involve users in the assessment of accessibility. Using an iterative process, these studies helped to refine technical and service development in the European Internet Accessibility Observatory (EIAO) project.

The conference concluded with reflections on managing change in a complex, ICT-rich environment. Caroline Williams, Executive Director of Intute (formerly the Resource Discovery Network, RDN), shared lessons learned from the need to achieve rapid and deep-seated change in a national service with myriad stakeholders. One of her conclusions, that we 'are still learning as we look to our future', might stand as a fitting summary of the conference as a whole.

Libraries Without Walls conferences deliberately present a wide variety of perspectives and the 2007 event was typical. The view of library service delivery is not uniform across the world and we all learn from each others' successes – and our mistakes. Those from the academic sector learn from the experience of public libraries, and vice versa. It is hoped that this volume will give a flavour of the debate at the conference, and perhaps encourage readers to attend the next – where the lively discussions will be enhanced by the beauty of the location!

2
Disciplines, documents and data: emerging roles for libraries in the scholarly information infrastructure

Christine L. Borgman

Introduction

Libraries have long taken responsibility for maintaining the scholarly record by selecting, collecting, organizing, preserving and providing access to publications. As data become part of the scholarly record in their own right, libraries are confronted with a new set of responsibilities. Some research libraries are curating data, some are deferring to data centres and disciplinary repositories and some are ignoring data entirely. While improving the ability to use and reuse data is a central goal of e-research programs in the UK, USA and elsewhere (Cyberinfrastructure Vision for 21st Century Discovery, 2007; Hey and Trefethen, 2005), the best ways to accomplish this goal have not been determined (Lyon, 2007). Notions of what it means to 'publish' data are far less mature than notions of publishing journal articles and books (Borgman, 2007). Definitions of 'data' vary widely between disciplines and between individual research specialties. Librarians, scholars, funding agencies and publishers are entering a new conversation about which data will be of most future use to whom, and how to capture, preserve, curate and make those data accessible over the short and long term (Borgman, in review).

Use and reuse of data

Today's scholarship is distinguished by the extent to which its practices rely on the generation, dissemination and analysis of data. These practices are themselves distinguished both by the massive scale of data production and by the global dispersion of data resources. The rates of data generation in most fields are expected to increase even faster with new forms of instrumentation such as embedded sensor networks in the sciences, mass digitization of texts in the humanities and the digitized traces of human behaviour available to the social sciences. Digital scholarship is spawning its own new set of research questions about how to manage the 'data deluge', about the changing nature of scholarly practices and about economic and policy models to sustain access to research data (Borgman, 2007; Hey and Trefethen, 2003).

The scholarly value chain

Data can be reused to leverage research investments, whether by replicating or verifying findings or by asking new questions with extant data. Data are even more valuable if they can be linked to the resulting publications and to other associated objects such as field notes, grant proposals and software models. Finding technical and social means to make these links is among the great challenges for the next generation of scholarly information infrastructure. Technical developments such as the Open Archives Initiative (OAI) Protocol for Metadata Harvesting (PMH) improve the ability to discover scholarly documents and data on the internet (Van de Sompel et al., 2004). The Object Reuse and Exchange (ORE) project is building a layer on top of the OAI that will enable links between parts of compound objects (Object Reuse and Exchange, 2006; Van de Sompel & Lagoze, in press). These efforts, in turn, build upon earlier interoperability technologies embraced by the library and publishing communities, such as Digital Object Identifiers, OpenURL and CrossRef (Hellman, 2003; OpenURL and CrossRef, 2006; The Digital Object Identifier System, 2006).

Data can be viewed simply as 'a reinterpretable representation of information in a formalized manner suitable for communication, interpretation, or processing' (Reference Model for an Open Archival Information System, 2002, 1–9). Technical definitions such as this one tend to obscure the complex social environment in which data exist. Observations that are research findings for one project may be background context to another. Data that are adequate evidence for one purpose (e.g. determining whether water quality is safe for surfing) are inadequate for others (e.g. government standards for testing drinking water). Similarly, data that are synthesized for one purpose may be 'raw' for another (Borgman, 2007; Borgman et al., 2007; Bowker, 2005). Data do not become 'evidence' until someone makes a claim that some data are evidence of something (Buckland, 1991).

Online access to scholarly publications

The sciences were the first discipline to have online access to their journal publications, and their advantage continues. By 2003, 83% of science, technology and medicine journals were available online (Cox and Cox, 2003). Other disciplines have less online access to their journal publications, as illustrated by the citation indexes comprising the ISI Web of Knowledge. Bibliographic coverage in the Science Citation Index dates back to 1900, in the Social Sciences Citation Index to 1956, and in the Arts and Humanities Citation Index only to 1975. Scopus, the competing Elsevier product, indexes science, technology, medicine and social sciences literature only for the prior 10 years, and does not claim to cover the humanities at all (Scopus in Detail, 2006).

Notably, the use of scholarly literature by discipline is the inverse ordering of that available in the Web of Knowledge. Scientists have the longest time period of content available online, yet concentrate their reading and citing in very recent publications. Conversely, online coverage is the shallowest in the humanities, where reading and citing span a much longer time range. Literature in the humanities notoriously goes out of print long before it goes out of date. The social sciences fall in between the sciences and humanities in both availability and use of literature (Meadows, 1998; Tenopir and King, 2000). However, the mass digitization of books undertaken by Google Print, the Open Content Alliance and other international projects will benefit the humanities more than other disciplines (Mass Digitization, 2006).

Online access to scholarly data

Research data are more discipline-specific in form than are journal articles and books. Examples of scientific data include sensor readings, x-rays, protein structures, spectral surveys, biological specimens and records in laboratory and field notebooks. Scientists tend to use data that were created for research purposes, whether they generate those data themselves or use data acquired from collaborators or other scientists. Public repositories for scientific data also are important sources (Incorporated Research Institutions for Seismology, 2006; Protein Data Bank, 2006; Sloan Digital Sky Survey, 2006).

Among the many types of social science data are opinion polls, surveys, interviews, laboratory experiments, field experiments, demographic records, census records, voting records and economic indicators. Most social scientists collect their own data, but many also acquire research data from collaborators, other social scientists, or repositories of surveys or other data (Survey Research Center, Institute for Social Research, 2006; UK Data Archive, 2006). Social scientists differ from natural scientists by drawing upon data that were not produced by or for research purposes, such as government records, corporate records or economic statistics. Much additional effort and analysis may be required to analyse, interpret and compare these types of data (Berman and Brady, 2005).

Almost any record of human activity can be considered data in the humanities, including newspapers, photographs, letters, diaries, books and articles; birth, death and marriage records; church and court records; school and college yearbooks; and maps. An old book might be read as literature or might be treated as a source of data to be mined for names, places and events, thus blurring the boundary between data and publications. Humanists search libraries, archives and public records; acquire data from other scholars; and search public data repositories (Arts and Humanities Data Service, 2006; Beazley Archive, 2006; Mahoney, 2002; Perseus Digital Library, 2006). Being the most dependent upon external data sources, they tend to encounter the most intellectual property problems in access to data (Unsworth et al., 2006).

Creating and maintaining the scholarly record

Scholarship advances by sharing, exchange and access. The idea of 'open science', that scholarship exists only after being reviewed by peers and openly distributed, dates back to Francis Bacon (1561–1626). Incentives to publish journal articles, books and conference papers proceed from these basic premises. Scholars are judged by the quality of their publications for the purposes of hiring, tenure and promotion. Libraries are judged by the quality of publications available in their collections and through their services.

Access to data that were produced with public money is the highest priority for e-research, as these data are seen as a public investment to be leveraged for the good of the larger community. However, the means by which data are to be published or otherwise made available is not yet entirely clear, and considerations vary by discipline. Concerns for access to data are similar to those for publications; thus open access models offer a helpful comparison.

Scholarly incentives for open access to publications

Publication of articles, books and papers is still the primary means by which scholars' research is evaluated. Among the concerns that scholars balance in deciding where to submit their work are the accessibility, visibility and recognition of their research that a publication channel offers. Other factors include speed of publication and requirements by some universities and funding agencies to make their publications openly available within a certain time frame. Evidence is mounting that articles 'self-archived' on websites or repositories are cited more frequently than those accessible only via subscription-based journals (Harnad and Brody, 2004; Kurtz et al., 2005). University libraries are taking the lead in establishing repositories for scholarly publications (Crow, 2002; Directory of Open Access Repositories, 2007; Lynch, 2003; Lynch and Lippincott, 2005; Westrienen and Lynch, 2005).

Scholarly incentives for open access to data

Publication of data, per se, is recognized as a scholarly contribution in only a few fields. Yet scholars are being encouraged, and sometimes required by funding agencies, to share their research data. Their options for doing so depend on whether their research field has established data repositories, whether their university libraries or other campus entities are accepting responsibility for curating data, or whether they or their research partners have established community repositories. If none of these options exist, scholars can post datasets on their personal websites for downloading, or can release them upon request, on a case-by-case basis. In some cases, journals will post datasets online as appendices to articles.

Deterrents to open access to data

The immature infrastructure for publishing data is not the only barrier to data sharing. Reasons for not sharing or not contributing data to repositories can be grouped into four categories (Borgman, 2007). First is that scholars are rewarded for publication, not for data management. Second is the effort required to document data. Describing and tracking data for one's own use and that of current collaborators is far simpler than documenting them for use by unknown others. For data to be released openly, richer explanations are required of the methods by which the data were collected, cleaned, analysed, recorded and interpreted. Public repositories may additionally require that data be organized in compliance with community standards for metadata and ontologies.

Third is the concern for competition and priority of claims. Scholars collaborate, but they also compete to be the first to publish a finding or a new interpretation. Scholars typically will not release data until their results are published, or until they have finished mining the data, which may take yet longer. Fourth are concerns about intellectual property. Researchers rarely own their data in the legal sense, but they usually can control them. Data that result from grants funded by governments may fall into the public domain, for example. In other cases, scholars may be analysing data obtained from public or private sources. Regardless of the legal realities, scholars may be reluctant to release their data out of concerns for misuse, misinterpretation or 'free riders' – exploitation by those who did not invest the effort in data production such as obtaining grants and supervising the research.

Variances in data sources and types, and in research questions across the disciplines, influence scholarly practices. Data about living people require anonymization, for example. Priority for discovery, whether for a new planet, particle or program, usually is handled by placing embargoes on data until publication of findings. Release of data from collaborative projects can be hampered by lack of agreement about who has the authority to release them or by conflicting requirements of collaborators' institutions or legal jurisdictions. Investigators who acquire data from third parties, whether public or private, may not have the authority to release those data due to contracts that specify their application and use. Humanists, who rely most heavily on data from third parties, may find that permissions are not available, transferable or affordable.

Emerging roles for libraries in a scholarly infrastructure for data

Libraries are not alone in assessing their future role in the scholarly information infrastructure, of which data are but one component. A few issues are becoming clear for all concerned. One is that data resulting from publicly funded research, in all disciplines, is the highest priority for public access. These data are public goods, in the economic sense. Many other types of data have scholarly value, but the economic and policy issues are even more complex and beyond the scope of discussion here.

The long-term goal for e-research is to achieve critical mass in the amount of research data publicly available for reuse. Whether repositories are established by research fields or by universities, libraries or other public entities is less an issue than whether their content is readily discoverable and usable – data need to be described consistently and curated to standards acceptable to the scholarly communities they serve. Data curation is expensive for the same reasons that publishing is expensive: peer review, editorial processes, technical support and maintenance. Arguably, data curation is more expensive because of the special expertise in the subject domain that is required.

Components of the data infrastructure

The scholarly infrastructure for data has a number of component parts, which are in varying stages of development. The most progress is being made on the policy and technology components. Government research policy for open access to publicly funded data is being addressed at national and international levels, through individual governments and multinational agencies such as CODATA (Esanu and Uhlir, 2004; Long-Lived Digital Data Collections, 2005; Lyon, 2007; Uhlir, 2006). Mechanisms are being established, for instance, to assist research partners in making agreements on the ownership, access, use and reuse of data, and on conditions for release of data to others. Intellectual property agreements are being created that will promote sharing of data while retaining some degree of control by the data originators (David and Spence, 2003; Science Commons, 2006).

Technology now exists to discover data automatically and to establish links between related objects to form the value chain of scholarly content. Standards and tools mentioned above, including the Open Archives Initiative, OpenURL, CrossRef and Digital Object Identifiers, underpin the scholarly infrastructure for digital publications and can be extended to data. Digital Object Identifiers are already being used for data (Paskin, 2005), and the Object Reuse and Exchange project builds upon established mechanisms to create compound objects.

While the scholarly reward system remains publication-based, it is likely to adapt as computing- and data-intensive research environments become more endemic to all disciplines. More problematic is the need to establish sustainable institutional models for access to research data. Libraries and archives have institutional mandates for long-term curation and preservation, making them an obvious home for research data. However, libraries and archives often lack either the funding or the expertise to curate research data. Repositories within disciplines tend to have the requisite expertise, but often are supported by fixed-term research contracts. The challenge lies in combining institutional models, funding sources and expertise most effectively (Long-Lived Digital Data Collections, 2005; Lord and Macdonald, 2003; Lyon, 2007).

Toward a scalable and sustainable scholarly infrastructure

The overarching challenge is not only to combine these components of a scholarly information infrastructure into a coherent whole that will create large, public repositories of research data that can be mined and combined, used to ask new questions in new ways, and to replicate and verify prior research, but to do so in ways that are scalable and sustainable.

In the absence of comprehensive solutions, local solutions are emerging that threaten to fragment the scholarly record. Partial solutions include posting datasets on investigator websites or including them as supplemental materials in publisher databases. Neither of these approaches is scalable. Individual invest-igators are unlikely to document their data in ways that make those data easily discoverable or interpretable. Nor are individual investigators likely to take long-term responsibility for migrating those data to new software and hardware platforms or to new metadata and ontology structures of their fields. Without these investments, the data will decay, perhaps quickly. Including data as supplements to a journal article at least makes those data discoverable in association with that article. Such datasets are scarcely more likely to be in standard formats or to be upgraded as technology and standards evolve, however. In neither case are data stored in these ways necessarily discoverable by search engines. Data that are embedded in fixed formats such as PDF are especially problematic, as their structure is stripped away (Murray-Rust et al., 2004).

Creating publicly accessible repositories, with links to and from related resources (whether in public sources or in proprietary publisher databases), is the optimal solution. Piecemeal approaches to augmenting individual publications do not scale and do not form value chains, as the relationship between data and publications is rarely one-to-one. Proprietary databases of public research data are not feasible from either a policy or a market perspective.

Library roles and responsibilities

Among the few principles on which the many policy reports on data infrastructure agree are (1) data from publicly funded research should be preserved and made accessible for reuse, (2) open access to research data is essential, and (3) clear lines of responsibility among the many stakeholders need to be defined (CODATA-CENDI Forum on the National Science Board Report on Long-Lived Digital Data Collections, 2005; Cyberinfrastructure Vision for 21st Century Discovery, 2007; Long-Lived Digital Data Collections, 2005; Lord and Macdonald, 2003; Lyon, 2007). These reports do not agree on whether the research library, or any other specific entity, is the appropriate institution to take responsibility for research data.

Thus librarians are in a quandary about their roles with respect to data. Some are stepping into the leadership gap to claim responsibility for curating data, and are seeking new funds to pay for what may otherwise be an 'unfunded mandate'. Library leadership in data management is not being greeted with universal acclaim, however. Many scholars and policy-makers question whether librarians possess the disciplinary knowledge or the data-specific expertise to take on these roles. Where disciplinary data repositories exist, scholars may prefer to entrust their data to their colleagues rather than to their university libraries. The physical location of the data should not be a central concern; much more important is an assurance of its long-term curation and of the maintenance of stable links between objects in distributed environments. Maintaining access to data that have no home is the larger public policy challenge. It may be necessary for universities and countries to maintain public repositories for data deemed worth preserving.

A single solution to creating a scholarly infrastructure for data is unlikely. More likely are multiple solutions, perhaps divided by research field, type of data, and country. In the best-case scenario, technical and policy mechanisms will combine to support the value chain. In the worst case, those desiring access to research data will have to navigate labyrinthine networks, impenetrable technologies and intellectual property agreements, and conflicting metadata and ontologies, where they exist at all. If that happens, the ability to leverage our massive investments in research data will be lost, along with opportunities to ask new questions of these data.

For librarians to participate fully in the development of the next-generation scholarly information infrastructure, they must be fully informed about the policy and technology developments in this arena. Conversations about scholarly publishing, research data, repositories, open access and other aspects of scholarly communication are all too often confined to separate discussions within the library, publishing and research communities. A broader and more integrative conversation is needed. The library community can help by convening stakeholders from these and other groups. They can educate university faculty and academic staff about issues in data access, both their own data and that of others. Librarians need more expertise about research data, which is partly the duty of information schools. Curricula must be updated to reflect the ascendancy of research data in the scholarly information infrastructure.

Some of the frontiers of data infrastructure may appear to be 'old wine in new bottles', revisiting debates about access versus assets, current versus permanent access, consortia and distributed partnerships, and criteria for selection, preservation and curation. Yet data present a new set of concerns for the scholarly record. They are much harder to define than are books and journal articles. They are even more malleable, mutable and mobile than other forms of digital content. They are often embedded in tacit knowledge that is difficult, if not impossible, to document. Some data have untold future value and can never be replicated; other data may have minimal value and can be reproduced when needed (Borgman, 2007; Bowker, 2005). Determining how to distinguish these classes of data, and to anticipate which data have the greatest potential for reuse, is among the most interesting intellectual and professional challenges for librarians, archivists, data scientists and cybrarians, or whatever these future experts will be called.

References

Arts and Humanities Data Service (2006) www.ahds.ac.uk/ [accessed 28 September 2006].

Beazley Archive, University of Oxford, www.beazley.ox.ac.uk/BeazleyAdmin/Script2/ TheArchive.htm [accessed 31 March 2006].

Berman, F. and Brady, H. (2005) *Final Report: NSF SBE-CIZE Workshop on Cyber-infrastructure and the Social Sciences*, National Science Foundation, http://vis.sdsc.edu/sbe/ reports/SBE-CIZE-FINAL.pdf [accessed 30 April 2006].

Borgman, C. L. (2007) *Scholarship in the Digital Age: information, infrastructure, and the internet*, Cambridge, MA, MIT Press.

Borgman, C. L. (in review). Data, Disciplines, and Scholarly Publishing, *Learned Publishing*.

Borgman, C. L. et al. (2007) Drowning in Data: digital library architecture to support scientists' use of embedded sensor networks, *JCDL '07: Proceedings of the 7th ACM/IEEE-*

CS Joint Conference on Digital Libraries, Vancouver, BC, Association for Computing Machinery, 269–77.

Bowker, G. C. (2005) *Memory Practices in the Sciences*, Cambridge, MA, MIT Press.

Buckland, M. K. (1991) Information as Thing, *Journal of the American Society for Information Science*, **42** (5), 351–60.

CODATA-CENDI Forum on the National Science Board Report on Long-Lived Digital Data Collections (2005) *U.S. National Committee on CODATA, National Research Council*, www7.nationalacademies.org/usnc-codata/Forum_on_NSB_Report.pdf [accessed 29 September 2006].

Cox, J. and Cox, L. (2003) *Scholarly Publishing Practice: the ALPSP report on academic journal publishers' policies and practices in online publishing*, Association of Learned and Professional Society Publishers.

Crow, R. (2002) *The Case for Institutional Repositories: a SPARC position paper*, The Scholarly Publishing and Academic Resources Coalition, www.arl.org/sparc/bm~doc/ir_final_release_102.pdf [accessed 6 March 2008].

Cyberinfrastructure Vision for 21st Century Discovery (2007) National Science Foundation, www.nsf.gov/pubs/2007/nsf0728/ [accessed 17 July 2007].

David, P. A. and Spence, M. (2003) *Towards Institutional Infrastructures for E-Science: the scope of the challenge*, Oxford Internet Institute Research Reports, University of Oxford, http://129.3.20.41/eps/get/papers/0502/0502028.pdf [accessed 6 March 2008].

Directory of Open Access Repositories (2007) University of Nottingham and University of Lund, www.opendoar.org [accessed 25 July 2007].

Esanu, J. M. and Uhlir, P. F. (eds) (2004) *Open Access and the Public Domain in Digital Data and Information for Science: proceedings of an international symposium*, Washington, DC, The National Academies Press, http://books.nap.edu/catalog/11030.html [accessed 30 September 2006].

Harnad, S. and Brody, T. (2004) Comparing the Impact of Open Access (OA) vs. Non-OA Articles in the Same Journals, *D-Lib Magazine*, **10** (6), www.dlib.org/dlib/june04/harnad/06harnad.html [accessed 30 September 2006].

Hellman, E. (2003) OpenURL: making the link to libraries, *Learned Publishing*, **16** (3), 177–81.

Hey, A. J. G. and Trefethen, A. (2003) The Data Deluge: an e-science perspective. In Berman, F., Fox, G. and Hey, A. J. G. (eds), *Grid Computing: making the global infrastructure a reality*, Chichester, Wiley.

Hey, T. and Trefethen, A. (2005) Cyberinfrastructure and E-science, *Science*, **308**, 818–21.

Incorporated Research Institutions for Seismology (2006), www.iris.edu [accessed 30 September 2006].

Kurtz, M. J. et al. (2005) The Effect of Use and Access on Citations, *Information Processing & Management*, **41** (6), 1395–402.

Long-Lived Digital Data Collections (2005) National Science Board, www.nsf.gov/nsb/documents/2005/LLDDC_report.pdf [accessed 1 October 2006].

Lord, P. and Macdonald, A. (2003) *E-Science Curation Report – Data Curation for E-science in the UK: an audit to establish requirements for future curation and provision*, JISC Committee for the Support of Research, www.jisc.ac.uk/media/documents/programmes/preservation/e-sciencereportfinal.pdf [accessed 15 November 2007].

Lynch, C. A. (2003) *Institutional Repositories: essential infrastructure for scholarship in the digital age*, ARL Bimonthly Report, 1–7, www.arl.org/newsltr/226/ir.html [accessed 1 October 2006].

Lynch, C. A. and Lippincott, J. K. (2005) Institutional Repository Deployment in the United States as of Early 2005, *D-Lib Magazine*, **11** (9), www.dlib.org/dlib/september05/lynch/09lynch.html [accessed 1 October 2006].

Lyon, L. (2007) *Dealing with Data: roles, rights, responsibilities, and relationships*, UKOLN, www.jisc.ac.uk/media/documents/programmes/digitalrepositories/dealing_with_data_report-final.pdf [accessed 15 November 2007].

Mahoney, A. (2002) Finding Texts in Perseus, *New England Classical Journal*, **29** (1), 32–4.

Mass Digitization: implications for information policy (2006) Report from *Scholarship and Libraries in Transition: a dialogue about the impacts of mass digitization projects*, Symposium held on 10–11March 2006, University of Michigan, National Commission on Libraries and Information Science, www.nclis.gov/digitization/MassDigitizationSymposiumReport.pdf [accessed 29 July 2006].

Meadows, A. J. (1998) *Communicating Research*, San Diego, Academic Press.

Murray-Rust, P. et al. (2004) Representation and Use of Chemistry in the Global Electronic Age, *Organic and Biomolecular Chemistry*, **2** (22), 3192–203.

Object Reuse and Exchange (2006) www.openarchives.org/ore/ [accessed 15 November 2006].

OpenURL and CrossRef (2006) www.crossref.org/02publishers/16openurl.html [accessed 30 October 2006].

Paskin, N. (2005) Digital Object Identifiers for Scientific Data, *Data Science Journal*, **4** (1), 1–9.

Perseus Digital Library (2006) Tufts University, www.perseus.tufts.edu/ [accessed 22 April 2006].

Protein Data Bank (2006) www.rcsb.org/pdb/ [accessed 4 October 2006].

Reference Model for an Open Archival Information System (2002) *Recommendation for Space Data System Standards*, Consultative Committee for Space Data Systems Secretariat, Program Integration Division (Code M-3), National Aeronautics and Space Administration, http://public.ccsds.org/publications/archive/650x0b1.pdf [accessed 4 October 2006].

Science Commons (2006) A Project of Creative Commons, http://sciencecommons.org/about/index.html [accessed 6 October 2006].

Scopus in Detail (2006) Elsevier, www.info.scopus.com/detail/what/ [accessed 31 March 2006].

Sloan Digital Sky Survey (2006) www.sdss.org/ [accessed 15 August 2006].

Survey Research Center, Institute for Social Research (2006) University of Michigan, www.isr.umich.edu/src/ [accessed 4 October 2006].

Tenopir, C. and King, D. W. (2000) *Towards Electronic Journals: realities for scientists, librarians, and publishers*, Washington, DC, Special Libraries Association.

The Digital Object Identifier System (2006) International DOI Foundation, www.doi.org [accessed 5 October 2006].

Uhlir, P. F. (2006) The Emerging Role of Open Repositories as a Fundamental Component of the Public Research Infrastructure. In G. Sica (ed.), *Open Access: open problems*, Monza, Italy, Polimetrica.

UK Data Archive, www.data-archive.ac.uk/about/about.asp [accessed 5 October 2006].

Unsworth, J. et al. (2006) *Our Cultural Commonwealth: the report of the American Council of Learned Societies Commission on Cyberinfrastructure for Humanities and Social Sciences*, American Council of Learned Societies, www.acls.org/uploaded files/publications/programs/our_cultural_commonwealth.pdf [accessed 5 March 2008].

Van de Sompel, H. and Lagoze, C. (in press) Interoperability for the Discovery, Use, and Re-Use of Units of Scholarly Communication, *CT Watch Quarterly*, **3** (3), www.ctwatch.org/quarterly/print.php?p=84 [accessed 5 March 2008].

Van de Sompel, H. et al. (2004) Resource Harvesting within the OAI-PMH Framework, *D-Lib Magazine*, **10** (12), www.dlib.org/dlib/december04/vandesompel/12vandesompel.html [accessed 5 October 2006].

Westrienen, G. v. and Lynch, C. (2005) Academic Institutional Repositories: deployment status in 13 nations as of mid 2005, *D-Lib Magazine*, **11** (9), www.dlib.org/dlib/september05/westrienen/09westrienen.html [accessed 5 October 2006].

3

Denmark's Electronic Research Library: implementation of user-friendly integrated search systems in Denmark

Bo Öhrström

Introduction

In 2003 Denmark's Electronic Research Library (DEFF in Danish) became a permanent activity on the Danish budget after a five-year project period. The Ministry of Culture, the Ministry of Education and the Ministry of Science, Technology and Innovation continued to finance DEFF annually through the national budget with 17 million DKK (2.3 million euros). 1 January 2007 marked the beginning of a new planning period with a new steering committee, a changed organization and additional activities.

DEFF is a co-operative organization for Danish research libraries. All participants in DEFF have slowly learned to seek co-operation in most areas in order to avoid duplicating work and to increase the value of individual efforts. The main target group for DEFF is still researchers, lecturers and students at institutions of higher or further education and research institutions within the public sector, who are primarily serviced directly through the institutions that participate in DEFF. The overall objective is to ensure an optimal exploitation of the institutions' research-based information resources. The implementation of user-friendly integrated search systems in Denmark is in this respect an obvious activity within the framework of the DEFF strategy. Parts of the systems can be shared, and the systems support the overall objective of DEFF.

Challenges for a research library

DEFF has identified three important activity areas for research libraries in Denmark, which are the results of the changing roles of libraries in the digital environment (DEFF, 2006). These areas pose major challenges for the libraries, and therefore become targets for DEFF's manpower and funding efforts:

1   In the e-publishing area libraries are defining new tasks for themselves, and DEFF is among other things supporting institutional repositories and migration of journals to Open Access. Furthermore, research registration and a common research database are in focus. DEFF has been the political advocate for Open Access in Denmark and has provided support for it through an EU petition in February 2007 made by the Knowledge Exchange partnership. DEFF's partners in Knowledge Exchange are the German Research Foundation (DFG) in Germany, the Joint Information Systems Committee (JISC) in the UK and the SURF Foundation (SURF) in the Netherlands. In the near future DEFF will be launching pilot projects with publications' underlying datasets in line with the development of e-science and e-research.

2   In the e-learning area libraries are looking for their place in an increasingly blended learning environment, where learning takes place in both the electronic and the physical environment with use of both virtual and physical resources. Librarians are to some extent developing the relevant new competencies to co-operate with teaching staff in facilitating learning. The projects supported by DEFF in this area have to a large extent sought to develop information provision in relation to e-learning. This includes integration of library services with the institution's virtual learning environments, and the provision of information resources for particular courses. Another important area has been finding new ways to develop the student's information literacy.

3   In the area of information provision the efforts of DEFF and the libraries can be divided into three sub-areas: efficient delivery of traditional print content, more Danish digital content and mediation of foreign language digital content. The first is in response to the continued high user demand for printed material not yet digitized. The second is a clear result of Denmark having its own, minor language. Finally mediation of foreign digital content is crucial, since large amounts of research and study are based on the extensive licensed foreign digital content.

Provision of foreign language digital content

The acquisition of licensed foreign-language digital content has been a major co-ordination activity throughout the existence of DEFF, and it has proved to be very successful. The basic idea is that there should be efficient sharing of work and funding, where the research libraries decide which products to fund with their own money and the DEFF Secretariat handles the repetitive administrative work. This means that the DEFF Secretariat acts as head of all major consortia agreements in Denmark, handling all contact with vendors, negotiation, administration, financial transactions, intellectual property administration and mediation about content of licences. As one basic solution all journals are offered through a journal manager system from TDNet called DEFFnet. The development of access to electronic content has been explosive over the past eight years, and today the licence co-operation means that:

- 178 libraries participate
- More than an additional 200 institutions have access to licensed resources
- 130 products are licensed
- 20,000 journals in full text, 40,000 e-books and 200 reference books are covered
- 106 libraries use DEFFnet as their journal access point
- 54 libraries use DEFFnet as their administrative journal manager and access point.

The total invoicing through the Secretariat is expected to be in excess of 120 million DKK in 2007.

The use of electronic resources has also grown steadily. By 2005 more than two-thirds of the total number of loans for 17 larger research libraries were digital (downloads) compared with less than one-third traditional physical loans. The most used publisher is Elsevier, with more than 1.5 million articles downloaded by the Danish consortium in 2006.

Danish studies on user behaviour and use

Despite the fact that the number of downloads of digital articles is growing steadily, a series of analyses show that the knowledge of foreign digital content is surprisingly low, and users' access to this content through libraries is not very efficient, nor is it complete. In other words a higher use can be expected with the introduction of better tools in the library environment.

The studies can be divided into three categories:

- usability studies
- user surveys
- ethnographic studies.

A usability study (Gardner and Sandberg Madsen, 2004) concluded that the libraries' websites were not good enough and pointed to three challenges for digital research libraries:

1   Research libraries are not the only providers of information. Google is a

significant competitor to the digital libraries, and the simple user interface sets a standard for information retrieval.

2   Electronic resources are not exploited efficiently. Users want to search at article level, but if bibliographic databases have unclear content and different search interfaces it confuses the user.

3   The users do not know that their search results are not exhaustive. Most of the users are satisfied, as long as they just receive results.

A user survey (Pors, 2005) documents the finding that commercial search engines are preferred also in library-related searches. The survey states that as far as students are concerned, Google totally dominates among search engines, and nearly all of the libraries' relevant electronic services have a much lower degree of use.

Finally, an ethnographic study (Akselbo et al., 2006) shows that libraries are perceived to have no role in the user's selection of digital content. Many users select their material themselves through, for example, Google, Amazon, recommendations from colleagues and references in journals, and will only use the library system for ordering material or the journal manager system to access full text. One main conclusion is that to increase the knowledge of relevant foreign digital resources and stimulate use the library must take note of the user's wishes: to search like Google and view like Amazon. One way to approach this is the implementation of user-friendly integrated search systems, which has become one of DEFF's focus areas in 2007.

Integrated search systems

An integrated search system is the newest attempt to fulfil the wish of easy search and delivery of relevant information. It is one of the steps in the search development chain, where focus is increased on user interfaces with a single search field:

- library catalogue
- federated search
- integrated search.

The library catalogue has always been the very backbone of library work, and the demand for a single search field makes it necessary to create a catalogue record for each resource. The drawbacks of this are that the catalogue is not designed for huge amounts of data, the search system is often poor, intelligent presentation is not easy, the cataloguing process is very labour-intensive and the integration of electronic resources is difficult. The advantages are that the work and technology are familiar.

Federated search (also called metasearch) is based on just-in-time processing (Sadeh, 2006). The user submits a query to a number of information resources simultaneously and exploits the fact that each resource has its own search engine. The results of the query are returned to the federated search system, which converts the results to a unified format, de-duplicates the results and presents them to the user. The resources can be located anywhere and their data stored in different formats. The just-in-time processing refers to the fact that the federated search system will only process data when a query is launched – the system does not store any data from the connected information resources. The federated search system will display results when the individual search systems answer, and the search is only finalized when all answers have arrived, or a fixed time-out has been reached.

The demand for a single search field is fulfilled by the use of parallel searching and presenting the results afterwards. The disadvantages are that good results are dependent on common standards for the individual databases, there are limited possibilities for intelligent presentation and it is difficult to secure a user-friendly presentation from many different sources. The advantages are that the individual system's functionality is exploited, it is easy to use, linking is easy and the results are up to date.

Integrated search is based on just-in-case processing (Sadeh, 2006). The user submits a query to a single repository, which stores extra information already processed, based on a number of information resources' data and possibly the data itself. The extra, new information can be ranking information, which allows relevance ordering of the search results when the results are presented to the user. The original resources can be located anywhere, and their data stored in different formats, but the processed index is placed in one big repository, possibly together with the original data. The just-in-case processing refers to the integrated search system already having used huge processing power before the searches in order to make the search results better for the user. The integrated search system will display results instantly after the query has been submitted, owing to the availability of pre-processed data in the single repository.

The demand for a single search field is fulfilled by the collection of data and pre-processed indexes on top of these data. The disadvantages are that it is difficult to get access to all relevant data, the technology is hardware-intensive and demands significant IT skills, and finally document delivery and access control are not trivial considerations. The advantage is that the technology delivers the functionality that the users expect from Google and Amazon.

National architecture

The Danish focus on user-friendly integrated search systems is not only a commitment to exploit integrated search technology, but can also be seen as an implementation of a national infrastructure. The systems are complex to develop and operate and the amount of basic data has to be extensive to make the searches valuable to the user. One example of the national infrastructure element is that a large university library might only have 5% of the relevant information resources for a user in its own holdings. The user wants to search in all relevant quality research information, meaning that all information resources should be presented independently of which institution provides them. To support this user behaviour the library needs among other things a larger amount of data, more seamless document delivery systems and new technology for access control systems. This can only be obtained in co-operation with other libraries, where a community is established to provide data, document delivery and services, thus enriching the display of search results.

To support optimal search conditions for the Danish researcher and student, the architecture illustrated in Figure 3.1 is under implementation.

Figure 3.1 displays in a simplified way the different components in the complete architecture. Starting from the bottom the small rectangular boxes illustrate the data layer. Each box holds relevant research data grouped by type, for example electronic article data marked 'Global articles'. The biggest ellipse aggregates selected collections of data and allows the integrated search systems (three darker boxes) to import and index all or parts of the aggregated data. These systems perform searches for the users, and the searches can be enriched by the use of behaviour data (smaller ellipse), for example 'Others who borrowed this also borrowed . . .'. If the search results in material which is not accessible online, the material can be ordered (the rectangular box at the top right).

The same figure also shows in which areas this joint infrastructure invites co-operation:

- aggregation of data in specific areas (small rectangular boxes)
- provision of repository with aggregated data (large ellipse)
- web services for enrichment of search results
- joint document delivery (rectangular boxes on the right)
- access management (not depicted)
- user data/data mining (small ellipse).

The consequences for the libraries include:

- increased co-operation in many areas
- library service and information provision based on user preferences
- increased consolidation of library IT systems as complexity increases
- increased focus on document delivery and access management

- new roles for local libraries – closer co-operation with the parent institution and more value-adding activities in supporting research and learning.

Common data pool

The aggregation of data in specific areas (small rectangular boxes in Figure 3.1) has its own special challenges for each area. The important access to licensed electronic resources is dependent on sufficient data delivery from all relevant publishers. This includes all metadata, but also as much full text as possible, since the full text will improve the search results. The DEFF Secretariat will secure the necessary contract extensions according to a prioritized publishers' list, and already a lot of basic work has been done by the staff operating an existing search engine for the STM subject areas.

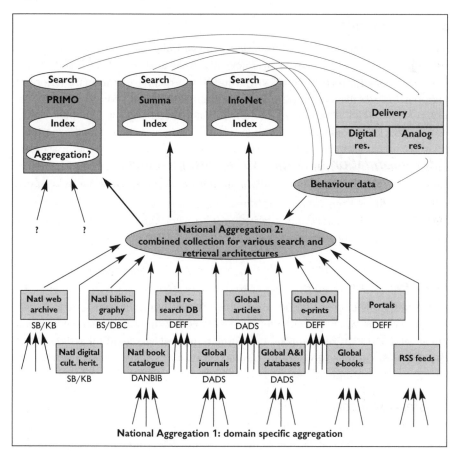

Figure 3.1 *Danish integrated search architecture*

The Danish integrated search systems

Figure 3.1 shows three integrated search systems, two of which are being focused on by DEFF. These are:

- Summa, an open source project developed and operated by the State and University Library and backed by a number of public libraries (Christensen-Dalsgaard (2006) and Lund, Lauridsen and Hansen (2007)).
- Primo, developed by Ex Libris and under implementation in the Royal Library, the Technical Knowledge Center of Denmark, Aalborg University Library and the Administrative Library (Madsen, 2006).

Examples of features in an integrated search system are considered below:

Sort by relevance

The system searches all the different data sources and presents results for the user in a single search result sorted by relevance. Relevance could be based on the degree to which a record matches the query, the quality of the material or the material's match to a user's need. Relevance could also be based on the resource's age.

Extra information that adds value and meaning

Information from other websites is integrated into the user interface. It could be editorial reviews from Amazon, information from special Danish websites with author portraits and recommendations, CD covers and music samples or the function 'Others who borrowed this also borrowed . . .'.

Pictures

In many cases the users identify a resource visually and an obvious possibility for enrichment is to show, for example, the cover of books from Amazon.com or covers of Danish CDs. Pictures and contact information of relevant staff for assisting with the search can also be presented.

Clusters or facets

Much of what the user would specify in an advanced search interface without quite being able to predict the outcome is presented within the search results as automatically generated clusters or facets of interesting information, just by using a single search field. Clusters can be used in searches where the user is trying to find something specific, or in searches where the user doesn't exactly know what the goal is. Clustering helps the user and presents relevant suggestions during the search process, instead of imposing the burden of refining the search criteria on the user at the beginning of the search process.

Two systems, not one

In a world where management strives for lower IT complexity and costs, it can seem strange that two similar systems are under consideration, not one. This apparent paradox is partly a result of an evaluation ordered by the DEFF Steering Committee and carried out by consultants (Gartner Group, 2006). The consultants examined the use of both systems, and a few of the main conclusions are:

1 The front-end solutions Summa and Primo are extremely relevant for the research libraries' aim of offering optimal search tools to students, researchers and other stakeholders.
2 Both systems have a number of very similar functionalities.
3 The two front ends can be exchanged relatively flexibly with other comparable components.

When considering the dissemination of one or the other system, it is important to remember that they have been developed on the basis of different strategic approaches. Instead the efforts should be focused on agreeing common standards, which include ensuring that the database is open and the data model is flexible enough to be able to handle future changes. In other words, the future will elect the winner between these two systems or point to an entirely different system.

Use of Google Scholar

Discussion of scholarly search systems cannot omit Google Scholar. Google Scholar is indeed an existing integrated search system, where the user submits a query to an enormous single repository, which stores information already processed with ranking information. The ranking algorithm 'takes into account the full text of each article as well as the article's author, the publication in which the article appeared and how often it has been cited in scholarly literature' (Google, 2006).

Like Google, the general Google Scholar system provides the user with a single search field, which has greatly inspired the users' wish for this simple interface in all systems. A vision of indexing all scholarly information and in reality a very large number of data sources forms the solid base for the searches.

The drawbacks are several. It is not possible to ensure that all Danish resources are available, since the data are not systematically found and indexed by Google Scholar. Google Scholar is a closed, complete system, which does not allow full integration within a virtual library environment. Additionally, the libraries lose relationships with their users, who will turn to self-service in situations where the libraries' services could provide better results. Finally, it is not clear which coverage and which precise ranking Google Scholar offers. This can lead to wrong or incomplete results, if Google Scholar is the only search system used.

The advantages are obvious. The system is available, extremely fast and easy to use. It is not complicated to set up, and operations are simple for a library.

Summary

New demands from users inspired by their successful use of Amazon and Google, in addition to insufficient use of expensive foreign digital resources, strongly encourage the introduction of integrated search systems in Denmark. These systems represent a new kind of service, with promising results for the users, and they are expected in the foreseeable future to strengthen the library's role in the world of commercial players. Evaluation shows that Google Scholar cannot be the single solution to all users' searching today. It is believed that the Danish solutions described will deliver a better service for the user, at least in the foreseeable future. User evaluation shows positive results, but the evaluation needs to be done on a larger scale during 2007.

References

Akselbo, J. L. et al. (2006) The Hybrid Library: from the users' perspective, www. statsbiblioteket.dk/publ/fieldstudies.pdf.

Christensen-Dalsgaard, B. (2006) Summa – et bud på fremtidens søgesystem, *DF Revy*, **8**, (December), 6–11.

DEFF (2006) DEFF Strategy Discussion Paper, www.deff.dk/content.aspx?itemguid= {C017EFBD-93EC-4815-9777-E3B79B8CDFA2}.

Gardner, J. and Sandberg Madsen, J. (2004) Det Brugervenlige Digitale Forskningsbibliotek: best practice rapport baseret på usability test of 11 store forskningsbibliotekers websteder, www.deff.dk/content.aspx?itemguid={82D05DC8-469A-44EB-96F1-04934A6A1903}.

Gartner Group (2006) Danmarks Elektroniske Fag- og Forskningsbibliotek (DEFF) Komparativ Vurdering af Summa & Primo, www.deff.dk/content.aspx?itemguid= {DC5246C6-05C6-4E42-91C0-1D681866E740}.

Google (2006) Google Press Center: product descriptions (2006), www.google.dk/press/descriptions.html.

Lund, H., Lauridsen, H. and Hansen, J. H. (2007) Summa – integrated search, www. statsbiblioteket.dk/publ/summaenglish.pdf.

Madsen, J. (2006) Fra Søg Til Find – Primo i Danmark, *DF Revy*, **1**, (January), 4–7.

Pors, N. O. (2005) Studerende, Google og Biblioteket: en undersøgelse af 1694 studerendes brug af biblioteket og informationsressourcer, www.bs.dk/publikationer/andre/studerende/index.htm.

Sadeh, T. (2006) Google Scholar Versus Metasearch Systems, http://library.cern.ch/HEPLW/12/papers/1/.

4

An African experience in providing a digital library service: the African Virtual University (AVU) example

Pauline Ngimwa

Introduction

This paper discusses the African Virtual University (AVU)'s experience in delivering digital learning resources to students and academics in its partner institutions across sub-Saharan Africa. Although digital resources are perceived as perfect supplementary resources to the deprived traditional libraries, the AVU has had first-hand experience in the successes and challenges of exploiting these resources in an African context. The fundamental lesson learnt is that the relatively poor technology status in Africa, including limited bandwidth and inadequate ICT infrastructure critical to successful exploitation of these digital resources, tend to reduce their benefits for African higher education. This is supported by a number of studies that have been carried out in the recent past by the AVU. The studies further show the negative impact that these low bandwidth levels have had on the overall access, utilization and usefulness of the educational digital resources to the learners and academics in African universities. In addition, this has directly impacted on the level of basic information literacy in a modern electronic environment that most of the African students encounter for the first time when they join tertiary education.

The paper presents examples of the nature of the digital resources that are used by the AVU, ranging from library resources to open educational resources (OERs). The AVU, recognizing the negative impact this technological situation has had on education, has in the past three years invested in exploring alternative creative solutions. Some of these initiatives have successfully evolved to become continent-wide projects, as will be discussed later in this paper. This includes a project to expand bandwidth through VSAT (very small aperture terminal) technology deployment in the AVU's partner institutions at an affordable cost by aggregating bandwidth demand. Other examples include the use of hard disks and local servers to store and make available digital content that would otherwise require huge bandwidth if they were to be made available online, thus making it possible to easily access targeted sets of resources in ways that are both pedagogically effective and cost-effective.

The African Virtual University is a pan-African educational network established in 1997 as a World Bank project to serve the countries of sub-Saharan Africa. Since 2002, after a successful pilot phase, the AVU has become an independent inter-governmental organization based in Nairobi, Kenya, with a regional office in Dakar, Senegal. It is an innovative educational organization established to serve the higher educational needs of African countries, and has become a leader in open, distance and e-learning (ODeL) initiatives in Africa. The AVU currently operates in 27 countries and is physically located in 57 learning centres within the African partner institutions which constitute its network.

Examples of learning resources employed at the AVU

The digital library

The digital library is a vital academic support tool for AVU students. The remote locations from which our students operate was the prime motivation for the creation of the library. It was necessary that an academic resource that cuts across boundaries should be employed to support all the students uniformly and so the digital library was developed to meet this need.

AVU students are varied and have unique characteristics which distinguish them from conventional library users. Being distant learners, the majority of them are part-time students who are engaged in other activities during the daytime. They come together at an agreed time to meet their facilitators and are only able to use library facilities during their free time. With the digital library, it is easy to provide these students with quality, current and relevant information resources uniformly. They have access to the world's scholarly publications that are available electronically. Because this resource is shared across all our learning centres, it is not necessary to provide similar resources physically in each of the individual centres. This cuts down on costs of material acquisitions and administration.

It should also be noted that the cost of printed textbooks is too high for the majority of African students to afford. For instance, one of the degree programmes offered requires access to textbooks costing an average of US$200 per student. The provision of e-book databases helps to reduce the burden of the high costs of the textbooks on individual students.

Besides providing access to AVU students, the library is heavily used by the African universities' researchers and thus supplements the existing libraries, most of which have a serious scarcity of current research information such as journal articles. In so doing, AVU makes a contribution towards improving the standards of learning and research in Africa. In order to make this possible, the library has taken advantage of the presence of now widely available open-content resources and integrated this with a few proprietary resources from leading publishers. This enables non-AVU members to access the majority of the resources without necessarily requiring log-on details. Currently, the library holds over 4000 full-text journals and 8000 e-books in English and French. Development of this collection has been achieved in partnership with development agencies that already exist to provide affordable research resources in the form of electronic books and journals.

Open educational resources (OERs)

Alongside the development of digital libraries there has been a proliferation of other digital education content, such as OERs. The development of OERs presents part of a solution to a challenge that has for so long plagued learning, scholarship and research in developing countries – the need for increased access to a wider range of educational resources. In recognition of the potential this development has for the transformation of learning and teaching in Africa, particularly in the area of ODeL, the AVU has invested a lot of effort in setting the stage for the development and implementation of OERs in Africa. The AVU has conceptualized a framework that looks at the evolutionary process of OERs. The framework considers fundamental elements of this process, which include the OERs' creation, organization, dissemination and utilization, all held together by supporting elements or pillars that include technology, policy, capacity enhancement, sensitization, collaboration and research. Key among these pillars and of relevance to this paper is the technology. These resources are intended to be open and free but this is only a reality to those who are able to access a basic technological infrastructure, i.e. computers with appropriate software and good internet connections. The current state of technology in Africa is an impediment to this possibility.

As part of the implementation strategy, and in an attempt to overcome some of these potential challenges, the AVU adopted a collaborative approach by bringing development agencies, as well as African institutions, within its network. Already there is a project under implementation which has brought together academics from ten countries to develop an e-learning program whose modules could in future become OERs. This process has enabled African academics to appreciate the OER movement. They have also being undergoing a capacity enhancement process on how to create and recreate OERs.

The AVU learning architecture and access to learning resources

To achieve effectiveness in the use of the above resources, the African Virtual University has adopted a learning architecture that establishes the framework for the programme development model, instructional design model, pedagogical model, delivery model and technology model. Within this framework, the learner is considered as an independent learner who takes control of the learning process while the lecturer takes the role of a facilitator. To achieve this high level of autonomy, the learner should have all necessary learning support at his/her disposal and, in particular, access to information resources. The role of the library support and learning resources thus takes a central place in the learning process. Johnson, Trabelsi and Tin (2004) present a new model of a library for distance learners, who in most cases are remote library users. In this library model, the library serves as a facilitator by offering continuous support to the learners, thus enabling them to interact and communicate among themselves and with information providers and to participate collaboratively to make available rich collections of online scholarly information resources.

Furthermore, the learning architecture is premised on the principle of 'just in time' learning. This recognizes the various learning opportunities from different sources available to learners whenever they need them, wherever they may be and however they are able to access them effectively. Modern technology enables access to electronic educational/information resources anytime, anywhere, as affirmed by Johnson, Trabelsi and Tin (2004): 'virtual library permits e-learners to access library and networked resources and services anytime and anywhere that an internet connection and computing equipment are available'.

At the same time, learning architecture considers the varying technological levels the African students find themselves in, ranging from those students situated in areas with minimal or no technology to those who have ready and fast internet access and appropriate ICT equipment. This then calls for a blended approach to the formats of the information resources.

The learning architecture therefore advocates appropriateness and flexibility in the way technology is used to support these programmes, taking into consideration the diverse technological contexts across the African continent.

The challenge

Some facts

The AVU has in the past carried out two surveys that have revealed certain crucial facts about the digital library in relation to access, awareness and use. The *Gap*

Analysis Report (African Virtual University, 2005a), which covered the status of distance learning activities in all of our African participating institutions, revealed that low bandwidth contributed to the limited use of the electronic resources in all these universities. According to this survey, it is not uncommon to have a journal article fail to load at all, as the time required to download a resource depends on the time of the day and the day of the week. In general, this survey established the fact that poor internet connectivity affects the general awareness of the existence of the digital resources at the participating institutions, leading to a very low rate of use.

We also carried out a similar survey (African Virtual University, 2005b) that was more targeted to the utilization of the AVU digital library in selected AVU learning centres, where there has been some effort to increase bandwidth. The findings were not very different from those of the GAP analysis survey. Out of the students interviewed, only 8% of them said they had very good accessibility. 22% had adequate accessibility, while 32% had very poor accessibility.

These two surveys clearly demonstrate that there is a relationship between library access, awareness and use. The fact that the internet connection affects use means that it has not been easy to create an awareness of the available resources. Similarly, it has not been easy to train users on basic access methods, let alone deliver an information literacy programme. To illustrate just how bad this can be, simple online demonstrations on the use of the digital library in some of the partner institutions often hang before the students are able to understand the basics, because of the absence of adequate bandwidth to support live downloads. These trickle-down effects have a negative impact on the general status of the development of digital librarianship on the continent. Very few librarians have embraced this development and even those who understand it are, sadly, not always privileged to have good and enabling technology at their disposal. Fortunately the AVU has taken an active role in creating awareness among library professionals, for instance by sharing experiences during librarians' meetings.

How bad is the connectivity problem in the African institutions?

The African Tertiary Institutions Connectivity Survey (ATICS), conducted in 2004 by the AVU on the existence of the bandwidth in higher education institutions in Africa, concluded that the internet connectivity in these institutions is 'too little, too expensive and poorly managed' (African Virtual University, 2004). To put this characterization into context, the survey went further to explain that 'an average African university has bandwidth capacity equivalent to a broadband residential connection in Europe, pays 50 times more for their bandwidth than their educational counterparts in the rest of the world and fails to monitor, let alone manage, the existing bandwidth . . .'. What this survey also revealed was a significant lack of knowledge about bandwidth quality and management. Most of the institutions surveyed (66%) did not have a committed information rate (CIR) for their connectivity or did not even know what CIR is. They ended up paying more for their bandwidth. The same goes for bandwidth management. Luckily some organizations, such as the International Network for the Availability of Scientific Publications (INASP), have addressed this challenge by conducting bandwidth management and optimization workshops in partnership with African institutions.

Towards overcoming the challenge

In order to overcome the challenges described above, the AVU over the past three years has been exploring a range of innovative solutions, some of which have now been expanded to include other African institutions, as discussed below.

The AVU VSAT solution

In 2003, the AVU commissioned a study to investigate the feasibility of using VSAT technologies to provide low-cost connectivity to African institutions. The report of this study recommended the use of C band over KU band and a consolidated approach in purchasing as key in achieving lower costs for bandwidth. In line with the recommendations of the report, the AVU took the lead in consolidating bandwidth requirements in the participating institutions through the formation of a bandwidth consortium. Aggregating the bandwidth demand in most of the participating institutions meant that it would be easy to negotiate for lower bandwidth costs and thus improve connectivity.

Through the consortium, the AVU was able to provide connectivity to 16 of its partner institutions in Africa at significantly reduced cost. In addition, the AVU also facilitated the installation of the VSAT equipment in all the member institutions in a package that included installation, configuration, commissioning and activation of the network; necessary training to handle the VSAT network; and technical support to the sites. As an incentive, the AVU also provided free equipment to all institutions undertaking the AVU degree or diploma programmes with financial support from the World Bank and CIDA. A typical equipment set (2.4m dish system) costs US$28,000.

Negotiations for VSAT licences in some countries have not been very easy and the AVU once again has been very useful in these negotiations through making the necessary introductions with the respective government ministries in each of the countries concerned. This initiative has ensured access to adequate bandwidth across the participating institutions and hence improved access to the digital resources. In addition, through training, there is now better understanding of bandwidth management across these institutions.

The Partnership for Higher Education in Africa bandwidth consolidation project

Based on the expertise that the AVU has gained on bandwidth consolidation and VSAT technology in the African higher education scene, the AVU collaborated with the Partnership for Higher Education to manage the initial part of its Africa-wide Bandwidth Consolidation Project, which comes to an end in 2007 (Partnership for Higher Education in Africa, 2007). This partnership has benefited from the financial support from four major US foundations, which pooled their resources to support a number of African universities gain cheaper and more reliable internet access. With support from these foundations, and in collaboration with the AVU, a coalition of 11 African universities and two higher education organizations arrived at an agreement with the satellite service provider Intelsat to bring vastly expanded internet bandwidth capacity and capability, at approximately one-third the cost, to academic institutions on the continent.

During this period, the AVU has been the host institution for the Bandwidth Consortium. On behalf of the consortium, the AVU negotiated with Intelsat, the satellite service provider, and managed to bring down the cost of bandwidth by one-third. The contract with Intelsat provides access to 93,000 Kilobits per second (Kbps) of bandwidth each month compared with 12,000 Kbps, which is what was available to these institutions about two years ago. The cost per Kbps to the African universities has dropped from an average of $7.30 per month to $2.33.

'Storewidth' approach in addition to bandwidth

A very cost-effective and reliable approach that is increasingly gaining popularity in large institutions such as universities is to make as many internet-based resources as possible available at a low cost by using a large local information store on their local area networks. Bandwidth in these networks is free since the institutions own the equipment. Massive storage devices containing digital content can then be plugged into these networks and shared simultaneously at high speeds. The AVU carried out a pilot initiative called the e-Granary Library that uses this methodology and found it to be a viable option. In the meantime, a digital library project for the AVU's Francophone students is focusing on the use of the CD-ROMs to store e-books, as this seems to be a more viable way of accessing the e-books than using online e-books with erratic internet access.

Use of mirror servers: MIT OpenCourseWare (OCW)

The now widely published MIT OCW offers a free and open website of high-quality teaching and learning materials that have been organized as courses. These have been created by the MIT faculty for their own classroom teaching and then offered freely for worldwide publication on the OCW. Each of the modules contains the course's subject matter and pedagogy and the complete set of materials used in the course. Anyone in the world can use these courses to teach or learn. However, these resources contain heavy content that requires adequate bandwidth for effective use, which, as already highlighted above, implies that the rich and openly available educational content is not effectively accessed by those who have poor internet connections, mainly the sub-Saharan African universities, as reflected in Table 4.1.

Table 4.1 *Use data – MIT OCW site access by region (MIT, 2005)*

Rank	Region	Est. daily visitors	% of MIT OCW traffic by region	% of total internet users by region
1	North America	5,352	45.4	29.6
2	Western Europe	2,234	19.0	26.1
3	East Asia	2,153	18.3	28.3
4	Latin America	694	5.9	5.0
5	Eastern Europe	465	3.9	2.0
6	South Asia	301	2.5	2.6
7	Middle East and North Africa	187	1.6	2.1
8	Central Asia	165	1.4	1.2
9	Pacific	163	1.4	1.9
10	Sub-Saharan Africa	53	0.4	0.9
11	Caribbean	19	0.2	0.2

In 2005, the AVU partnered MIT to provide access to the OCW for its African partner institutions through mirror servers that provide a copy of the entire OCW content. This was successfully piloted at Addis Ababa University in Ethiopia and the University of Nairobi, Kenya, with overwhelmingly positive feedback. Staff and students who participated in this pilot project reported increased awareness of the importance of the OCW in their teaching and learning activities.

Conclusion

In conclusion, it is important to note that the bandwidth issue in Africa will improve drastically when all regions have been linked via high-speed undersea fibre networks. Before this has happened, satellite bandwidth is the most efficient means of obtaining connectivity for our institutions. It is our hope that most of our institutions will join existing bandwidth consortia so that they can benefit from cheaper connectivity. Other innovative solutions like those discussed in this paper must be considered. If more of the OERs and other information resources can be made available in the institutions' local networks, the chances of them being more useful and consequently having greater impact on the learning process will be enhanced, even though this approach denies the distant learner the possibility of remote access. However, such an arrangement is better than having nothing at all.

References

African Virtual University (2004) *The ACTIS Report*, AVU.

African Virtual University (2005a) *Gap Analysis Report*, AVU.

African Virtual University (2005b) *The AVU Digital Library Usage Survey*, AVU.

Diallo, B. (2006) The African Virtual University: a decade of elearning experience in Africa, *eStrategies Africa*, **1** (2), 78–9.

INASP (2003) Optimizing Internet Bandwidth in Developing Country Higher Education, *INASP Infobrief*, **1**, www.inasp.info/uploaded/documents/infobrief1-bandwidth-english. pdf.

Johnson, K., Trabelsi, H. & Tin, T. (2004) Library Support for Online Learners: e-resources, e-services and the human factors. In Terry, A. and Fathi, E. (eds), *Theory and Practice of Online Learning*, Athabasca University.

Massachusetts Institute of Technology (2005) *MIT Courseware. Evaluation: access findings: geographic distribution of users*, www.ocw.cn/NR/rdonlyres/FA49E066-B838-4985-B548-F85C40B538B8/0/05_Prog_Eval_Report_Final.pdf.

Partnership for Higher Education in Africa (2007) *The Bandwidth Consortium: opening the power of the internet to African universities*, www.foundation-partnership.org/pubs/press/ bandwidth.php.

5

Project StORe: expectations, a solution and some predicted impact from opening up the research data portfolio

Graham Pryor

It has long been recognized that a fundamental role of the university library is the provision of safe custody and the assurance of measured access to the wealth of published scholarship. Traditionally, the library has been synonymous with a collection of books, although an effective 21st-century library service is more likely to be defined by the extent to which it enables access to information in non-print formats, particularly that which is accessible by electronic means. Yet, while the utility of the university library has extended conspicuously to the provision, and interpretation, of digital resources, including most recently the installation of repositories for the preservation and dissemination of research papers, its principal focus has remained upon items or objects that one may consider in some way to have been published, whether in printed or electronic form.

The persistence of such a limited account of library business is perhaps surprising, given the importance vested by universities in their conduct of research and the kudos they perceive it to bestow upon them, since the research output that is visible from published scholarly and scientific articles represents only a fraction of any institution's research undertakings. It is important to ask, therefore, whether libraries might be expected to display a natural interest in the stewardship of all or any of the larger set of 'unpublished' research data that is produced.

While research publications are, for the moment at least, the commodity upon which research performance is assessed, they each serve a resolutely narrow purpose: to present a case and persuade the reader to a particular point of view. As such, they will generally comprise a finely tuned orchestration of theses, arguments and opinions, developed from a tiny sub-set of data that has been carefully selected and filtered from the much larger accumulation generated.

Paradoxically, this larger and predominantly digital collection of research data, from which scholarly articles are eventually derived, constitutes an indisputably valuable asset in its own right, not simply because it is the product of considerable financial and intellectual investment, but for the reason that it has within it the potential for accruing value from further manipulation, analysis and re-use. As with any valuable asset, it deserves a proper mechanism for custodianship and curation that, in tandem with an appropriate level of managed access, will improve the options for maximizing the return on investment. When seeking to fulfil this important role, it seems reasonable to postulate that given their several centuries of experience in delivering stewardship for published information, librarians might be called upon to apply their particular portfolio of expertise in sustaining the key intellectual asset that is research data.

If they are waiting for a call to arms they need wait no longer. Currently, the UK's research councils annually invest almost £3 billion of public money in research, covering the full spectrum of academic disciplines, and increasingly they are concerned that data generated from that research should be managed in ways that better reflect their value. Only this year, the Biotechnology and Biological Sciences Research Council (BBSRC) and the Medical Research Council (MRC) have issued new data policies, both based on principles adopted from the OECD report *Promoting Access to Public Research Data for Scientific, Economic and Social Development* (OECD, 2003), which recognize that publicly funded research data are a public good, produced in the public interest, and should be openly available to the maximum extent possible. Recognizing issues of ownership and intellectual rights, both Councils would allow a limited period of exclusive use, but they require that new research data must be properly curated throughout the information lifecycle and, when released, should include high-quality contextual information, or metadata.

Project StORe (Source-to-Output Repositories) has been sponsored by the Joint Information Systems Committee (JISC), which provides support to UK education and research by promoting innovation in new technologies and through the central support of ICT services, and by the Consortium of Research Libraries in the British Isles (CURL). The project was conceived by members of the UK's research library community as an initiative that would apply digital library technologies to create new value for published research. Ostensibly a technical project, its primary objective has been the design of middleware to enable bi-directional links between source repositories containing research data and output repositories containing research publications, with the aim of producing direct electronic links between research papers and their source data (see Figure 5.1).

Hence, researchers would be able to navigate directly from within an electronic article to the source or synthesized data from which that article was derived. Conversely, direct access would also be provided from source data to the

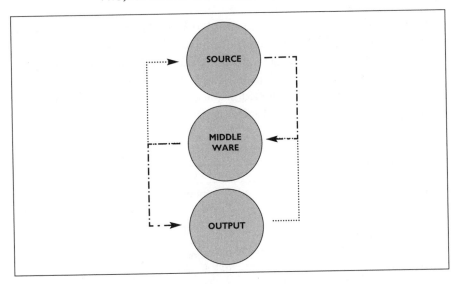

Figure 5.1 *Bi-directional links between source repositories containing research data and output repositories containing research publications*

publications associated with those data. The technical challenge of developing this functional middleware was compounded by the diversity of the research data environment, where the StORe project identified 64 scientific data types actively being deposited in *source* repositories. Whereas these included images, plots, instrument data, spectra, telemetry, sequences and databases, to name but a small selection, *output* repositories would contain published articles or other texts, usually comprising publications at a pre- or post-refereeing stage, working papers and PhD theses. Output repositories are also frequently referred to as institutional repositories, since they are commonly developed first as an institutional resource, frequently on the basis of a university library initiative. It is also correct to refer to publisher repositories as belonging to the genre. Hence, a suite of online periodicals may be considered to be hosted within an output repository.

The relevance of traditional library skills and experience to the design of middleware for bridging this heterogeneous environment should be apparent. Librarians comfortable with the digital age have already articulated generic tools for use in other equally diverse contexts: metasearch interfaces to publisher and local databases, metadata harvesters and link resolvers, all based upon recent digital library protocols and standards such as OAI-PMH and qualified Dublin Core, with which they have proved themselves adept in providing the kind of high quality contextual information that is now being demanded by the research councils.

To develop a suite of middleware features that would reflect actual needs and aspirations, the project's initial task was to survey researcher behaviours and the processes employed in the generation, organization and sharing of research data. This survey of seven scientific domains, employing an online questionnaire and one-to-one interviews, was conducted in the spring of 2006 by a team based at institutions in the UK and USA (Table 5.1).

Table 5.1 *Survey of seven scientific domains*

Surveying university library	Subject
Edinburgh (lead) / Johns Hopkins	Astronomy
Birmingham	Physics
Imperial College	Chemistry
London School of Economics	Social sciences
Manchester	Biosciences
University College London	Biochemistry
York (for the White Rose Partnership)	Archaeology

The team's individual survey reports together provided a comparative topography of the current and potential use of source and output repositories and, after detailed analysis by the project's systems implementers, it proved possible to develop a generic technical specification for the creation of bi-directional links that would directly reflect user requirements. Consequently, a suite of pilot middleware was built and successfully tested in the social sciences domain by staff at the UK Data Archive between November 2006 and June 2007. Yet, despite this technical accomplishment, and while we were not diverted from our main objective, we found that the survey had opened up a far broader territory than was originally envisaged.

During the survey, researchers had reacted favourably to the opportunities predicted from the putative StORe middleware, with 85% of those who responded declaring that a facility to transfer directly from within an electronic publication to the data upon which its findings are based, or to link instantly to all the publications that have resulted from a particular research dataset, should prove advantageous. This result encouraged us to proceed to the development phase. At the same time, while our plans for enhancing the functionality of repositories had originally been laid to improve opportunities for information discovery and data curation, specifically by promising to open a new access route to scientific research data, it quickly became evident that we were also challenging the familiar concept of the academic library, not to mention the very nature of academic publishing.

Traditionally, the publication of research has been understood as the delivery of scholarly output in the form of a printed or electronic document, the process representing a synthesis of large volumes of original and processed data. Most importantly, published papers will have been subject to critical and informed peer review. Subsequently, these papers have been preserved and made available in academic libraries or through electronic portals supported by them. Now, by directly linking these papers to the data from which they were originally derived, the opportunity to explore the basis of a published scholarly argument is at once enlarged and the more detailed background to the testimony of a hypothesis, which previously it was impossible to include in a journal article, is made accessible. Furthermore, the authority of claims made in an article will be more critically assessed when the option to examine the underlying data enables other researchers to compare their own research, data and results.

Of course, making public (or *publishing*) data that has not been through a rigorous process of peer review carries a number of obvious risks. Not least is the potential for invalidating any published paper that follows, if making the data available in advance is judged to have pre-empted the paper as an original piece of work. This may at first seem like a strong rebuttal of the argument for making data public, but achievable measures for managing such risks do exist, ranging from embargoes and other time constraints on data release to the implementation of robust mechanisms for governing online data upload. More significantly, I would contend that the actual process of making the data public provides its own means of protecting the value of a published paper, since the visibility of its underlying data will serve to improve the quality of the published arguments made within it. In a context where members of the research community at large can access and 'peer review' a paper's source data, few would dare to publish without first being satisfied that awkward questions pertaining to the robustness of conclusions reached might not be raised and pursued!

Nonetheless, the cultural change suggested by this new option to 'publish' research data may be harder to achieve than is implied by such an analysis, and the StORe survey uncovered a realm of attitudes and activities amongst the research community that are not normally exposed to the librarian or information systems provider. Curiously, the strongest messages received were apparently unrelated: a serious necessity to improve upon basic data management practices and the importance of resolving compelling and negative issues of data ownership.

Both the StORe online questionnaire and the series of one-to-one interviews produced evidence of a need for expert assistance with information discovery and organization, whether this amounted to familiarization with resources and equipment, in the application of techniques for data organization and deposit, or with the particular challenge of selecting and assigning metadata. Yet we encountered a general lack of awareness, even resistance, when it came to the availability and use of professional support, which was evident across the seven domains. Notwithstanding the adverse experiences described by researchers, who admitted that metadata assignment was especially demanding in terms of the intellectual effort required and the burden of time it placed upon them, the development and administration of research data and repositories was not immediately associated with the activities and skills of specialized information intermediaries, albeit their perceived role in data preservation was remarked upon by respondents to the astronomy survey. Neither could it be established that declared self-reliance led to the practice of good data management. Consistently emphatic in their understanding that the correct assignment of metadata is crucial, and acknowledging a need for assistance from specialists in developing and administering metadata, researchers in all disciplines identified a clear link between the condition of metadata used and the level of support provided by information specialists; but when asked to consider who is responsible for the assignment of metadata to their research output, by far the largest number (212 of the total 377 respondents) claimed that they personally decide which terms to use. Supporting comments indicated that although in a number of cases reference was being made to standard thesauri or schema, this was by no means the norm.

A pervasive culture of self-sufficiency amongst academic researchers goes some way to explaining this general indifference to the role of library or data specialists. Respondents to the StORe survey referred to professional library support having been offered and rejected, expressing a view that it is for researchers themselves to sort out their data problems, and reliance upon documentary or online machine support was consistently preferred to human intervention. As Table 5.2, taken from the questionnaire, illustrates, a majority was found not to seek help when using output repositories (often the province of library professionals) because they perceive that there is no assistance available. More disconcerting were the supplementary comments to the table, in which researchers expressed little confidence in what support is provided while claiming sufficient comfort with technology to believe themselves equipped to use most IT-enabled services.

Table 5.2 *Question 24*

Do you receive support and/or guidance in your use of output repositories? (This need not take the form of personal support from someone else but could be online prompts, links and advice from within the repositories themselves.)		
Documentary support	17.6%	66
Personal support provided by an intermediary	7.7%	29
Repository-enabled support	22.1%	83
No support is provided	28.2%	106
Unknown	20.7%	78
Other	3.7%	14

This notorious reluctance to welcome central services to the heart of the research demesne is a barrier that is familiar to many support staff, and the establishment of trust has to be at the core of any attempt to found a productive relationship.

Results from the StORe survey also suggest that false assumptions about the notion of *e-research* and, more specifically for StORe, the underlying principles of *e-science*, may have reinforced this barrier. The number of researchers today who do not use information technology will be insignificant, but while many may assume some proficiency it does not make them all accomplished *e-researchers*. The components of this new landscape are twofold: the ubiquitous and 'always on' high-speed networks, shared infrastructures, cross-community middleware and data standards that together provide a working platform are, for the most part, invisible. Like the power supply to our homes it is there to be switched on, and may be utilized inexpertly and almost at will. But these new technologies and resources will prove advantageous only if they provide researchers with the means of significantly enhancing and improving upon their established research processes and priorities; and in most cases this requires the engagement of information or data professionals with the expertise to bring *e-research* within the reach of more than a handful of enthusiasts and early adopters.

So who is failing to effect this engagement?

The use of output repositories is one area that has been subject to numerous advocacy campaigns by members of the academic library community, often supported by the availability of training. Yet an attitude commonly encountered during the StORe survey was summed up by one repository user who remarked with some pride that his university had even 'assigned a librarian to our department to help with searches, but I have not used her services'.

The source of this reluctance to engage with professional support is not necessarily trivial and may be found deep in the research tradition. Information technology enables collaboration and the StORe middleware would add to this a new level of openness, but in many areas of the research community the prevailing culture remains one of individual research endeavour. This was underlined when we sought opinion on the methods used for enabling data access and sharing. Most researchers subscribed to the principle of sharing data but there were significant levels of concern about making data available for public access, principally on account of the risks that might contribute to an individual's research profile being usurped (Table 5.3).

It was no surprise, therefore, when we invited comments on the principle of open access that opinions were ambivalent, being determined by the researcher's role as either producer or consumer of the data in question.

In practical terms, methods for data sharing were found to reflect the predominantly private nature of research, with more than 50% relying upon printed or electronic mail to support their efforts toward collaboration, supplemented by the personal exchange of portable media (e.g. CD-ROMs or USB drives). This seemed to indicate that the application of technology remains subservient to the more traditional and informal understanding of *networking*. The use of open network

Table 5.3 *Question 16*

What factors would discourage you from sharing your research data?	
The threat of loss of ownership	202
Risks to an established research niche	104
Risk of premature broadcast of research findings	235
Subversion of intellectual property rights, including copyright	163
Ethical constraints relating to my research	58
Consideration of data protection and other confidentiality issues	115
The time/effort required to enable sharing	193
Risk of diversion from principal objectives through the generation of additional work	144
Risk to commercialization opportunities	59
Increased competition for funding	77

drives, published URLs and repositories was limited by comparison.

When introducing this discussion of cultural change I referred to two messages received during the StORe survey. Concerns over data ownership have already been discussed, but it might now be appropriate to retract my assertion that certain data management practices found wanting were unrelated. We were of course concerned to discover a very high volume of original and valuable research output being kept on laptops, PC hard drives, CD-ROMs and other non-networked and inadequately protected storage, and whatever the reason for such practice, some assistance in improving data curation techniques is long overdue. However, when we asked what measures were normally used by researchers to control access to their data, almost one-third referred to storage on standalone computers, which may offer some kind of rationale for this unsafe course of action.

Watching developments in 'Big Science' repositories like the Wellcome Trust's UK PubMed Central it seems reasonable to suggest that the joint deposit of articles and data is a natural next step in the evolution of publishing. The UK's JISC is already funding several projects in its Digital Repositories programme to explore options for the citation of data, and there are many aspects of research today where knowledge is represented as data rather than solely in the form of scholarly publications. The human genome project is a prime example. So can this shift in publishing be managed and informed information access be assured, without the dynamics of technological evolution being subdued by the processes that typify publishing?

By enabling bi-directional links between data and publications, Project StORe may be perceived as contributing to the change in scholarly communication practice; but such technological innovations also require the continued presence of knowledge management expertise to ensure that any opportunities they spawn are effectively optimized throughout the information lifecycle. This will not be easy, given the barriers already discussed in this paper. StORe's solution, to adopt a Web 2.0 approach already familiar to a cohort of e-researchers, enabled us to incorporate both their aspiration to collaborate and their anxiety to protect. It replicates the environment in which the modern researcher interacts both socially and at work, having a structure similar to services like MySpace or Flickr and, most critically, it allows them to remain in control. Using the StORe middleware, researchers decide which of their data items are to be made public or private, they define their collaborations with colleagues or 'friends', and it is for them to choose which items are to be deposited in a repository and made available for publication. Libraries and librarians too must find some means of melding with the research traditions of individual disciplines, in order to provide assistance without usurping the sense of responsibility that researchers have for their research and the data they generate from it. The stewardship of scholarly output may once have seemed naturally to belong with the library, but more recent advances in technology dictate that it now needs to be regained.

Note

Source repositories often function as national data centres, such as the UK Data Archive (for social sciences) at the University of Essex or the Archaeology Data Service at York. Examples of output repositories include the London School of Economics' Research Articles Online and the Edinburgh Research Archive at the University of Edinburgh

References

CURL, The Consortium of Research Libraries in the British Isles, www.curl.ac.uk/.

Dublin Core metadata element set, www.ukoln.ac.uk/metadata/resources/dc.

JISC, The Joint Information Systems Committee, www.jisc.ac.uk/ .

OECD (2003) *Promoting Access to Public Research Data for Scientific, Electronic and Social Development*, http://dataaccess.ucsd.edu/Final_Report_2003.pdf.

Open Archives Initiative and the OAI Protocol for Metadata Harvesting, www.ukoln.ac.uk/distributed-systems/jisc-ie/arch/faq/oai.

Project StORe, http://jiscstore.jot.com/WikiHome.

UK Data Archive (www.data-archive.ac.uk) is located at the University of Essex.

6

Publishing, policy and people: overcoming challenges facing institutional repository development

Margaret Markland, Jayne Burgess, Sarah Taylor and Helen Standish

Much has been written in recent years about the development of open access institutional repositories, and how an institution such as a university can stock them with its research outputs, particularly refereed articles published in scholarly journals, thereby making the findings of its researchers freely available to the wider community. It is an idea which has attracted generous project funding in the UK and elsewhere, and which has triggered debate between supporters and sceptics alike. Since the first Budapest Open Access Initiative in 2002 (www.soros.org/openaccess/read.shtml), the number of universities with institutional repositories in the UK and indeed worldwide has certainly grown, yet the number plentifully stocked with the 'full text of these articles' as envisaged by the Initiative continues to be quite small.

A key finding of an important enquiry by Swan and Brown (2005) into the attitudes of authors towards institutional repositories is also often reported. It is that 81% of authors would willingly comply with a requirement by their employer or research funder to deposit copies of their articles in an open archive (Swan and Brown, 2005, 63). And yet the number actually doing so remains far fewer.

This paper brings together data from an evaluation of the SHERPA project (www.sherpa.ac.uk/), funded by the UK Joint Information Systems Committee (JISC) and carried out by the Centre for Research in Library and Information Management (CERLIM) during 2005, and insights (illustrated by quotations) from the more recent experiences of a team of library staff at Manchester Metropolitan University (MMU) as they continue to create, manage and develop their institution's repository, e-space at MMU (www.e-space.mmu.ac.uk/e-space/).

The SHERPA project aimed to investigate a new model of scholarly communication by creating institutional repositories in 13 UK research-led university libraries. These repositories were to be managed by library staff, populated with freely available full-text copies of articles published in scholarly journals and written by researchers at these universities. The project therefore was concerned to see how this new model of depositing copies of publications in a repository would sit alongside traditional journal publishing. Authors would be encouraged to self-archive their publications, rather than using librarians as intermediaries.

It was clear from the SHERPA evaluation work that three main factors were hampering repository development:

1   Publishing: the publishing habits of authors.
2   Policy: institutional policy and support for the repository.
3   People: very particular reservations about deposit held by individuals.

Much work has been done by the international library and research communities since 2005 to promote and bring about the development of institutional repositories, so some of these earlier findings were re-examined in 2007 to see how much had changed, and whether the kinds of repositories which had emerged over the previous two years were different from original expectations.

Publishing

'I feel no urgent need to deposit articles already published'.

Authors' 'publishing' habits

In order for any research findings to have value to the community, they must be shared in some way with other researchers. Yet despite the fact that internet services have pervaded so much of our educational, social and personal information space, when it comes to publishing research results, on its own 'the web' simply will not do. Neglected web pages, changing URLs, and 'file not found' searches are only a few of the irritants which all too often hamper the retrieval of online documents. Unless we are eminent in our field, placing a document on our personal website does not guarantee that anyone will come to see what we have put there. It is a risky promotional strategy. Yet it is one which seems to be supported and approved by the publishing industry.

At the time of the SHERPA study it was easy to find publishers' journal policies which permitted an author to make available the PDF of the paper via the personal website of the author, or the intranet of the organization where the author worked, or to post a pre-print on their personal or departmental website, and their contribution as published on their own or their departmental home page, but not in an institutional repository. Project officers reported that they felt sure that the reason for this was that publishers perceived repositories as a greater threat than personal web pages, because the latter were 'less organized' and 'probably less visible than institutional repositories'. Academics, however, were comfortable with this type of dissemination of their work, and equated some of their well-established online activities with 'publishing'. When asked where else they publish their work (other than in scholarly journals), their responses included 'on Departmental websites', 'on my personal website' and 'on a website for my research group'. Having done so, they were reluctant to duplicate their effort by depositing in an institutional repository, saying 'I already make my publications available on my personal website, why should I place them in a repository too?'

Two years later, these attitudes were also reported by the MMU e-space managers; it still seems to be a common perception among academics that a list of citations on a website equates to 'publishing'. However, e-space managers turned these 'rather handy pots of content' to their advantage. They used them early in their advocacy campaign as a way of discovering individuals whom they might target as potential depositors in the fledgling repository. Trawling the university website established the names of around 700 such authors, all of whom were contacted on an individual basis. The response rate was less than 10%, but those who did respond were for the most part reasonably prolific authors. This enabled the early deposit of a substantial visible body of research output, with the result that other potential depositors could see how these were displayed, how easy they were to find, and, perhaps most importantly, that their peers in other parts of the university considered it worthwhile to use the new service. The upshot of this early advocacy strategy, using personal websites as a source of potential repository content, was that the repository grew from five items in January 2006 to 850 by August 2007.

Traditional scholarly publishing

The repository is not, of course, a replacement for traditional scholarly publishing, though the aims of both are to record research findings in a sustainable way for the longer term. Running through many conversations with SHERPA repository managers was the complexity of the relationship between themselves and the scholarly publishing industry. Central to this was the contentious legal issue of copyright, particularly as these managers were aiming to deposit the full text of their institution's research outputs. When asked whether publishers' copyright restrictions had proved to be a barrier to the population of their repositories, two-thirds of SHERPA repository managers said unequivocally 'yes'. They reported that the potential for straightforward full text deposit was limited. As one put it, 'Despite Stevan Harnad's e-mails about 90% of publishers being "green", most of the papers I receive don't comply with publishers' copyright agreements'. The devil, it seems, is in the detail, and clarifying detail is time-consuming. For example, there was concern that even when copyright clearance was granted, 'one still usually ends up searching through the publisher's website to find the precise form of words they require for acknowledgement'. Then there were the discrepancies between copyright policy as presented on a publisher's website, and the copyright agreements which authors had been asked to sign. There was uncertainty that a valid action now may not be permitted in the future; 'permissions are driven by publishers' perceived commercial pressures. Therefore a change of policy by publishers could make this a problem once again, and the issue of authorial rights cannot be ignored or the underlying issues left as a potential problem in the future.' The phrase 'I am not a lawyer but. . .' became a familiar sentence opener!

This resulted in much time-consuming liaison between project staff and publishers, to clarify unhelpful mixed messages. For example, 'I have had a [publisher's] manager in my office stating categorically that the company acknowledges its green status and supports open archiving' while at the same time another employee of the same publisher tells the same repository manager that he 'is concerned about the distribution of published articles within such databases' and 'feels that restrictions are currently necessary for the well-being of the journal subscription base'. Where project officers erred on the side of caution, and meticulously sought permission from the publisher to deposit every article of interest, their letters and e-mails often went unanswered, or the publisher claimed not to have the capacity to deal with many tens of requests for permission to upload individual articles.

For the MMU e-space managers the situation is a little different. Depositing the full text of journal articles is desirable, but not essential. The article citation is always deposited as quickly as possible. Finding out whether full-text deposit is then permissible has become easier thanks to one legacy of the SHERPA project, namely the RoMEO database of publisher copyright and self-archiving policies (www.sherpa.ac.uk/romeo.php), which they use as key tool. 'First and foremost, I check the SHERPA RoMEO database . . .. I can be assured that the information presented there is current.' However, contacting publishers who are not included in the database still remains a time-consuming and difficult task. E-space managers report that it may still take weeks or even months to get a response from a publisher, but interestingly that smaller publishers are often more willing to grant permission to archive full text than the larger publishing houses.

Policy

Mandatory and voluntary deposit

The mandatory deposit into a repository of a full-text copy of every research output immediately upon publication, if not before, remains the nirvana of the open access movement. SHERPA project managers agreed that a policy of mandatory deposit would be the only sure trigger to fill their repositories with such materials. However, they were constrained by the intrinsic impermanent status of their project funding. As one project officer said, 'We secured a cautious endorsement of the repository – but only on the understanding that it is being endorsed as part of an experimental project rather than necessarily having any implications for institutional policy or practice.' She continued 'I think that any endorsement is welcome and may help to populate the repository – though it falls far short of the type of institution-wide policy that is likely to be needed to encourage (or mandate) widespread self-archiving by authors.'

Over the past few years, few UK universities have gone down the road towards mandatory deposit. What has changed is that some funding providers are beginning to mandate deposit (though not always immediate deposit) into an institutional or subject repository as a condition of their research grants. Supporters of mandatory deposit are clear in their belief in its efficacy. Harnad says that 'Research has shown that if employers or research funders require self-archiving then 95 per cent of researchers will do it and 81 per cent will do it willingly' (Harnad, undated). Others emphasize that without a mandatory institutional policy, the repository manager's task will be difficult. Sale, for example says 'expending money on author support policies without a mandate is like pushing a large rock up a hill. It does not work and is demonstrated not to work . . ... If you've got the repository before the mandate, make it crystal clear to everyone (especially in higher management) that a mandate is in your sights and you are not going to let go of it until you get what you want and the forces of reaction are defeated. Use the word "Luddite" if you have to.' (Sale, 2006).

The MMU e-space repository does not operate with the support of an institutional mandate, and with present staffing levels this would be impractical. The growth of its content is due to the concerted efforts of a small group of repository managers to collect as much material as possible either by assisted deposit or by promoting self-archiving. Its aim 'to collect and preserve all of the research output of MMU and make it freely accessible via the World Wide Web' is being achieved by a range of advocacy strategies which are labour-intensive and tailored to be sensitive to scholarly communities in different subject areas. Rather than adopt the sometimes suggested strategy of targeting one or two departments with particularly prolific research output and trying to get everything from them, the approach taken was to show that the repository was not just biased towards certain departments. Every faculty in the University is represented in the repository, and most departments display at least a few papers. Thus authors can look at e-space, see where their research would fit in, and take steps to deposit their publications alongside those of their peers.

Assisted and self-archiving

SHERPA repository managers found that a policy of offering assisted deposit was the most successful way of ensuring that they captured research outputs. However easy self-archiving could be made, they said that 'providing a good mediated deposit service' was essential. Academics said that it was not the actual deposit process – the 'six clicks' – which they found difficult, but the preparatory stage beforehand. They complained about having to collect the detailed information required for the deposit process. 'The questions were detailed – in particular, it was a nuisance to find the actual volume to look up the ISBN / ISSN number.'

A facility to self-archive has recently been added to the MMU e-space repository and though the numbers of researchers doing so is small, contrary to received wisdom they have proved to be very capable of providing accurate and full metadata. Despite this, self-archiving is not proving to be a time-saver for repository managers, who check every entry to ensure consistency of presentation and copyright compliance, and have had to refuse the full-text deposit of one self-archived article which would have contravened copyright.

Hosting the repository

Whereas the SHERPA project repositories were all developed in-house, the MMU repository was a pioneer of the hosted repository model. It is one of only five UK universities currently hosted by Open Repository (www.openrepository.com/), a service provided by BioMed Central, which uses DSpace software. The decision to go down this route was taken because of a lack of appropriate technical support within the library, and the availability of customer service and support has been beneficial. Repository managers have been encouraged to contribute ideas for the development of and improvements to the software. Despite this, software changes have sometimes been slow to happen, and not always quite what was hoped for: 'Their development obviously hinges on commercial factors, whereas an in-house development would be more centred on direct user needs.'

People

The final factor which impedes the filling of a repository with content is the perceptions and sometimes misconceptions of individuals within the institution. Academics interviewed in the SHERPA project institutions offered many further reasons why they were reluctant to deposit.

Others have not done so

The 'after you, no after you' scenario was common. Academics were 'waiting to see what happens' before committing themselves to making deposit in the repositories part of their normal work practice.

The repository is not driven by the needs of academics

Some academics suggested that repository development was being driven by library priorities rather than the needs of themselves and their peers. None were swayed by the 'journals crisis' argument or knew the cost to their institution of the journals in which they published. The Open Access movement was hardly seen as relevant to them, being 'largely political, not driven by academics or the needs of academics'. Humanities authors in particular seemed to find the concept not applicable to themselves, but 'a "science" issue and not really relevant to all disciplines'.

Self-deposit takes too much time and effort

It was clear that depositing their publications in an institutional repository was just not a high-priority activity for academics. Some cited 'lack of time' or that they were 'too busy to deal with detailed questions' which were a 'nuisance', and many felt quite strongly that 'someone else, perhaps a librarian' should do this for them.

Sorting out copyright is too difficult

Academics rarely seemed to understand copyright matters and had no wish to learn about them. It simply was not their job to do this but 'should be the duty of the repository, not the depositor'. 'We have a copyright person here who, e.g. clears copyright for study packs, and I'm sure he knows far more than I do how to get clearance without any bother.' Any extra complexities, such as the need to obtain third-party copyright permissions, were prohibitive. 'In my case', said one academic 'getting copyright in the first place [for the book] meant writing to obscure bodies in Japan and in some cases paying large sums (£150 or more) for use of the image in just one academic book edition.'

Citation and versioning are not sufficiently clear

Some academics want only the final version of their papers to be cited. They were 'not willing to make anything other than the final publisher version available in the repository', and were 'not keen to have their post-print in the same archive as "non-peer reviewed" materials'. There was a fear across all subject areas that mandatory deposit in a repository would lead to a lack of rigour in bibliographic referencing. The effect of this upon the individual author was explained by one clinical medicine academic. He said, 'I don't want people to cite a published paper by giving the institutional repository address rather than the published reference in *The Lancet*! This would damage my citations for the paper . . .. When I read someone else's paper I want to know that I am reading the published version and can quote from it without fear that it has been changed.'

The e-space repository managers do not report these types of problem. They are, of course, not working under the same pressure to fill their repository with full-text content, and so have taken the more pragmatic approach of accurate citation with links to full text where possible. They aim to provide a service of benefit to both individual depositors and to the university, which can realistically be managed within their resource constraints.

Conclusion

The SHERPA evaluation illustrates a number of difficult and detailed issues which faced SHERPA repository developers, and how they dealt with these. Their focus was upon the feasibility of filling repositories with openly available full-text research papers in line with very specific aims and objectives, but this proved difficult for many reasons. They did provide a variety of repository models for others in the community to copy and also a still expanding knowledge base, which they continue to share willingly with other repository developers. Their efforts have done much to inform and further the expansion of institutional repositories in the UK and beyond.

The MMU e-space repository was designed from the outset to be a high-quality institutional asset with a strong user focus, and has developed in a pragmatic way to fit the needs of the institution. It is an example of what can be achieved by a small team of repository managers working within clearly defined parameters. Having started by targeting text-based scholarly publications, the repository may in future widen its scope by encouraging the deposit of different types of resources in non-text file formats, so as to reflect the outputs of a university which teaches a wide and varied range of scholarly subjects. At the same time, it has provided a testbed for its hosting service, which is now attracting more universities and other types of institution to follow this model.

Most of the major research-led universities in the UK now have an institutional repository, and many teaching-focused universities have adopted them also. Few mandate full-text deposit but research funding providers are beginning to do so, and this may give impetus to fulfilling the original vision of the SHERPA project. As well as displaying citations of research publications, with full text copies where possible, repositories also provide space where the intellectual output of the university, such as theses, reports, grey literature, learning objects, image and sound resources and, increasingly, research data, can be captured, preserved and curated for scholars of the future.

References

Harnad (undated) *Open Access: self archiving should be mandatory*, http://users.ecs.soton.ac.uk/harnad/Temp/shcorrex.html.

Sale, A. (2006) *Re: Ian Gibson on Open Access*, *American Scientist* open access forum discussion list dated 2 May 2006, http://users.ecs.soton.ac.uk/harnad/Hypermail/Amsci/5334.html [accessed 12 November 2007].

Swan, A. and Brown, S. (2005) *Open Access Self-archiving: an author study*, Key Perspectives Limited, www.jisc.ac.uk/uploaded_documents/Open%20Access%20Self%20Archiving-an%20author%20study.pdf.

7

Libraries as a social space: enhancing the experience of distance learners using social software

Jane Secker and Gwyneth Price

Introduction

LASSIE (Libraries and Social Software in Education) is funded by the Centre for Distance Education, University of London, UK, and runs from March to December 2007. Led by the London School of Economics and Political Science (LSE) and the Institute of Education, its project partners also include the London School of Hygiene and Tropical Medicine, the University of London Research Library Services and the Open University Library. Colleagues at LSE represent the Library, the Centre for Learning Technology and LSE Archives.

LASSIE is exploring how 'social software' (or 'Web 2.0', see below) might enhance the use of library services by distance learners. The project addresses two concerns. First, University of London External Programme students do not make full use of electronic library resources; the reasons for this are varied, including a low awareness of how to access library resources and information literacy issues. Second, LASSIE provides an opportunity to explore how social software is affecting libraries and their services. The project will gather empirical evidence about which technologies enhance the experience of students, specifically distance learners, and those which are less valuable. The project also provides advice for the wider library community.

Another important element in the project is to examine the role of libraries as a social space. LASSIE recognizes that physical libraries have changed considerably over the last ten years, to reflect changes in the nature of education. The importance of collaboration, group work and communication in teaching and learning are widely recognized and libraries are being built as key learning spaces to reflect this shift. LASSIE is therefore interested in how virtual libraries might become more social. This paper is largely based on the literature review completed in July 2007.

Project overview

The research for LASSIE to date has primarily been gathered through a review of the literature, focusing on three key areas:

1 Libraries and social software: definitions and key developments.
2 What are the current issues in supporting distance learners and how might social software address these?
3 How are libraries developing as a physical and virtual social space?

The full report is published on the LASSIE website (Secker, 2007). [However, because of the fast pace of change in this field, it was updated in late 2007 (Secker, 2008). (Eds)] The literature review was published at a time when many UK libraries were either actively exploring social software or considering their next step and therefore its value goes beyond LASSIE. The review enabled the project team to identify key initiatives to date, and informed the second phase of the project, the case studies. These are scheduled to run from July until November 2007, and are a series of small scale pilots. Selected social software will be used to support a library service and feedback will be collected from librarians, students, course tutors and administrators about the potential value. The case studies are briefly reported in this paper.

The Web 2.0 literature review

The process of undertaking a literature review was itself a valuable research exercise, demonstrating the challenges faced when doing research in the Web 2.0 world. Gilster (2007) highlighted these challenges. As a result, tools such as news readers (e.g. Google Reader) and internet search engines were used to supplement the references found in traditional bibliographic databases. In undertaking this literature review on social software, we developed new research skills and tried out new tools, using social software wherever possible to facilitate our research. However, it remained a challenge to stay abreast of developments in this fast-moving field.

The literature review

From the literature review it was clear that many libraries in the UK are currently grappling with the concept of social software or Web 2.0 and are exploring definitions of 'Library 2.0'. A lot of experimentation is being undertaken, much of it as a sideline rather than officially funded research. Developments in the USA appear to be around 18 months ahead of other countries. In the UK, librarians clearly feel they should be doing something to address the development of social software, although many are uncertain what exactly it is, and what might be effective or useful. The LASSIE literature review therefore usefully provides some valuable definitions of social software and of Library 2.0, as well as an overview of the key technologies that libraries might consider using. Feedback to date has suggested that this section of the review was particularly useful for librarians wanting an overview of this topic.

Definitions

The project decided to use the term 'social software' rather than the more abstract and controversial phrase 'Web 2.0', although we recognized that these terms have broadly the same meaning. Providing a clear and simple definition was challenging. However, it is clear that the internet has changed recently. Adding content to the web has become easier, communication and collaboration have become increasingly important and more software is now hosted remotely and accessed via the internet, rather than installed on a desktop PC. Some overall characteristics of social software were identified as:

- the development of social networks
- content created by users rather than created by an organization
- the development of user profiles
- the use of 'folksonomies' or tagging to attach keywords, created by users, to items to aid retrieval.

Key technologies

The ideas and concepts associated with social software are best understood by considering some of the tools and technologies that fall into the definition. To many people, social software simply means blogs and wikis but adopting this narrow definition leaves many librarians struggling to see how these tools might be used in their organization. Ironically, some of the most valuable social software tools, such as utilizing RSS to provide information and social bookmarking, are less well known. Librarians are also less clear about how social networking could be used to support learning, although many are clearly dabbling out of curiosity.

The literature review therefore provided an overview of the key technologies which included:

- RSS feeds/syndication/atom
- blogs
- wikis
- social bookmarking and resource sharing

- social networking sites: (MySpace, Facebook, Elgg, LinkedIn, Ning)
- media sharing
- virtual worlds
- other social software.

Details about social software tools are available in the literature review (Secker, 2007) and constraints on space mean these are not included in this paper. Nevertheless, it is worth briefly mentioning a few tools, such as RSS. This is not in fact social software, but a way of communicating information in an XML format that newsreader software can understand. RSS has become an important way of using social software effectively. Most blogs have RSS feeds, which users can subscribe to, to ensure content is pushed to them, rather than having to visit the blog. Bradley (2007) argues that RSS is fundamental to Web 2.0 technologies. While people don't need to understand it technically, RSS underpins most social software and hence is paramount. Blogs, meanwhile, are probably the most popular type of social software and establishing a blog was one of the first activities the LASSIE team undertook. Social bookmarking tools allow users to store their bookmarks or internet favourites remotely on a site so they can be accessed from any computer connected to the internet, rather than being stored within a browser. Sites such as del.icio.us (http://del.icio.us) were particularly useful for storing and sharing any relevant websites for the purposes of the project. LASSIE set up an account which is available at http://del.icio.us/lse_lassie/.

Social software in libraries and Library 2.0

'Library 2.0', the application of social software to enhance libraries, was a phrase coined by Michael Casey in 2005. Casey sees Library 2.0 as being about 'user-centred change' (Casey and Savastinuk, 2006). The term encapsulates the idea that we can enhance library provision using social software. Library 2.0 is a somewhat controversial term: Crawford (2006) found 62 different views and seven distinct definitions. He argues that librarians focus on the phenomena made possible by social software, meaning participation and the facilitation of conversations, rather than the technology. Miller (2005) argues, meanwhile: 'Leveraging the approaches typified by Web 2.0's principles and technology offers libraries many opportunities to serve their existing audiences better, and to reach out beyond the walls and websites of the institution.'

A useful diagram (Figure 7.1) by Michael Habib, available from Flickr, encapsulates his view of Library 2.0.

Libraries using social software

LASSIE found many examples of libraries which are experimenting with social

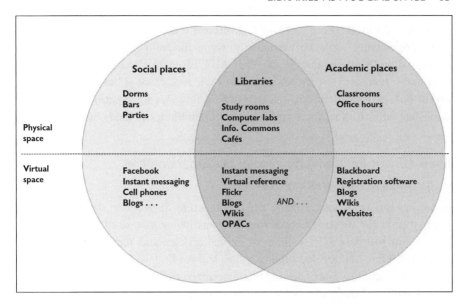

Figure 7.1 *Library 2.0 (reproduced from Michael Habib's Flickr site: www.flickr.com/photo_zoom.gne?id=222296001&size=o. licensed under Creative Commons)*

software to enhance their services. Libraries in the USA began exploring social software somewhat earlier than others and lessons can be learnt from their experimentation. Librarians in other countries are also starting to explore using social software, an example being O'Connell (2007), who works in school libraries in Australia. A few useful monographs have been published very recently, notably by Farkas (2007), who also developed an online course called 'Five weeks to a Social Library'. Bradley (2007) provides a valuable overview of Web 2.0 technologies and how they can be used by librarians, both personally and to enhance library services. Other notable books on the subject include Casey and Savastinuk (2007) and Sauers (2006), the latter looking specifically at blogs and RSS.

Examples of libraries using social software

Further details of these examples are available in the literature review (Secker, 2007).

MIT Libraries: RSS feeds (http://libraries.mit.edu/help/rss/barton/)

MIT Libraries are using RSS feeds to highlight new books in the library catalogue.

If a feed is selected according to subject interest it can be added to any web page. This functionality could be particularly useful for adding feeds to subject web pages or directly into courses in the VLE. MIT Libraries also have a Library News feed and a feed for new theses added to their repository. They also maintain a useful link of RSS feeds for research, which includes information about which publishers offer RSS feeds: http://libraries.mit.edu/help/rss/feeds.html.

University of Pennsylvania: social bookmarking tool (http://tags.library.upenn.edu/)

PennTags is a social bookmarking tool developed by librarians at the University of Pennsylvania for locating, organizing and sharing online resources. Users can collect and maintain URLs, links to journal articles and records in the library catalogue. They can develop bibliographies and reading lists, which can be shared with the community. Users download a specialized toolbar or use something called a 'bookmarklet', which allows content to be added to PennTags.

University of Huddersfield: user-generated content in the catalogue (http://webcat.hud.ac.uk/)

Increasing numbers of libraries are experimenting with allowing user content to be added to the library catalogue, including users' book reviews or other comments. The University of Huddersfield has used social software to enhance its catalogue, adding functions such as user reviews, ratings and pulling content from Amazon into the catalogue. They have also added features such as making recommendations based on borrower records, providing users with a link saying 'people who borrowed this book also borrowed . . .', and so on.

Librarian and library blogs

Librarians seem to like writing personal blogs. Examples on social software and libraries include:

- Information Wants to be Free, http://meredith.wolfwater.com/wordpress/index.php
- The Shifted Librarian, www.theshiftedlibrarian.com/
- Phil Bradley's Web 2.0 blog, http://philbradley.typepad.com/i_want_to/
- Are you 2.0 Yet?, http://briangray.alablog.org/blog
- Library Crunch, www.librarycrunch.com/.

Many libraries in the USA are using organizational blogs for posting library news. Examples include:

- Madison-Jefferson County Public library, http://mjcpl.org/
- Ohio University Library Business Blog, www.library.ohiou.edu/subjects/ businessblog/
- Kansas State University library blogs, http://ksulib.typepad.com/.

A best-practice tool, which was created to be a one-stop shop for ideas and information for all types of librarians, has been developed by Meredith Farkas, who is the Distance Learning Librarian at Vermont. This is the Library Success Wiki at www.libsuccess.org/index.php?title=Main_Page.

Libraries and social networking

Talis, the library management supplier, has funded Cybrary, its headquarters in Second Life, and anecdotal evidence suggests that several libraries are experimenting with offering services in Second Life. A valuable report on Second Life developments in the UK further and higher education sector was published in July 2007 (Kirriemuir, 2007).

Some libraries have also set up MySpace accounts, although social networking sites have had varying attitudes towards allowing this use. An example is Brooklyn College Library, which has over 3000 'friends' and is using MySpace to publicize library activities (www.myspace.com/brooklyncollegelibrary).

Groups for librarians are flourishing in several social networking sites. Facebook has several groups for librarians, such as the Library 2.0 Interest Group, which also maintains a website, and the group 'Librarians and Facebook', which has over 1000 members. Facebook also has a number of library-related applications that can be added to a personal profile to allow users to share reading lists, social bookmarks and other resources they are interested in. The social networking site Ning also has a useful Library 2.0 group (see http://library20.ning.com/).

Libraries supporting distance learners

The literature review also provided an overview of current issues for libraries supporting distance learners. One notable finding is that library services for distance learners are less well earmarked in the UK than in, for example, Canada, Australia and the USA. The Open University is the clear exception in the UK and is leading the way with developments to support its students. However, CILIP, the Chartered Institute of Library and Information Professionals, which is the UK's professional body for librarians, does not have a distance learning librarians' group.

Despite the growth in distance education in the UK, very few academic institutions have a distance learning librarian post, whereas in the USA and Canada this is fairly common. One explanation may be that UK library support for distance learners is often tied up with support for e-learning and off-campus users. UK distance learners in higher education have certainly benefited from the provision of off-campus access to library resources. Similarly, librarians in many UK institutions are increasingly making resources available from the virtual learning environment and not expecting their on-campus students to visit the library as frequently.

It is clear that in the USA and Canada, where support for distance learners is most developed, information literacy and providing training and support for users is a key issue. The literature review provided a useful overview of the University of London's External Programme which, while long established, has historically provided little library support for students. Library provision still varies depending on the course, but increasingly services are being centralized through the University of London Research Library Services. The Library is, however, still grappling with ensuring that distance learners know about the resources available and can get access to them at a more basic level. Nevertheless, research suggests that social software that improves access to library resources, focuses on developing information literacy skills and allows students to interact with each other to motivate them in their studies could be of enormous benefit to improving learning.

Libraries as a social space

The third section of the literature review highlighted how physical libraries increasingly play an important role as a social space, reflecting the changing nature of teaching, where group work and social interaction is more important. The development of 'Information Commons' throughout the USA, Canada and Australasia is linked to this movement. Two related ideas about library space have also gained ground in library literature more recently: the library as place and the library as the 'third place'. The latter is a reference to the sociologist Oldenburg's book *The Great Good Place* (1999), in which he lamented the disappearance of good public places, arguing that society desperately needs third places that are neither home nor work. These spaces allow people from different parts of a community to come together and engage with one another. Many public libraries in the USA and more recently in the UK are recognizing that they play an important role as a 'third place'. The funding to put in place the IT infrastructure in UK public libraries (The People's Network) means that all public libraries provide internet access. Many are also extending their opening hours, providing drinking and eating facilities and trying to shake off their image of being simply places of books.

Libraries also form a social space by bringing together learners from different parts of an institution. Indeed, LASSIE was partly inspired by a personal observation at the enquiry desk. A student having problems with library passwords was waiting at the desk one day and encountered another student carrying a stack of books. Noticing the books were on a similar topic to her own interests, they struck up a conversation and left the enquiry desk together realizing that, while on different courses, they were interested in broadly the same topic. As anyone who has used LibraryThing (www.librarything.com) can testify, social software allows these connections to be made far more easily. However, whether students want to visit a virtual library for social interactions is unclear. For example, evidence suggests that students want virtual social spaces to be purely social, rather than having input from faculty or library staff. Recent media reports in the UK suggested students were alarmed to find academic staff on Facebook. Some librarians also find 'mashing up' (to use a social software term) personal details one might reveal to friends with details one might share with work colleagues uncomfortable. The jury is therefore still out on whether libraries can and should replicate a social space.

The case studies

LASSIE is undertaking a number of small case studies, allowing the team to experiment with using different types of social software and to gain feedback on their value to distance learners. Case studies were chosen to explore particular tools and the issues they present not just to students, but to librarians, tutors and administrators.

The project as case study

The LASSIE team have used various tools since March 2007 to share resources and information. So, for example, a project blog was established in March 2007 and this is used by the principal researcher to keep the team and the wider community informed of developments. It is also a valuable way of documenting progress since the entries are dated, feedback is received from blog readers (through comments) and writing provides an opportunity for reflection. The team is also using social bookmarking to share resources (as mentioned previously), which is a valuable way of collecting internet resources and allows team members to be alerted to relevant resources that others find. Social networking sites have provided useful contacts for LASSIE, especially Ning, which has a Library 2.0 group, but also Facebook and LinkedIn. Finally, a newsreader to monitor blogs and news sources by subscribing to RSS feeds has been invaluable. Many of the new tools and publications have been picked up through subscriptions to blogs, rather than having to search the web. Google Alerts was also used with limited success to trawl the web for recent information on distance learning and Web 2.0.

Social software and reading lists

The first case study involving distance learners considers how social software could be used to present reading lists to students, as an alternative to more traditional paper based or online reading lists. The researcher has some experience of using an online reading list management system, so a comparison can be made. LASSIE has set up reading lists using a reference management tool called CiteULike (www.citeulike.org). The tool is intended as a personal reference manager but lists can be shared with other users. A reading list for LSE external programme students was selected for inclusion, being constructed by pulling references from Amazon onto the list. It generally seemed easier to manage journal references than book references with CiteULike, as it was sometimes problematic finding the correct edition. Ideally a librarian might also prefer to pull book records from a library catalogue rather than from Amazon. One of the main drawbacks was that the entire list could not be annotated (although individual items on the list could be). It also did not seem possible to put items on the list in a particular order. For an example, see the course reading list at www.citeulike.org/user/seckerj/tag/60introinfsys.

LASSIE is testing other social software tools such as H20 Playlists (http://h2obeta.law.harvard.edu/), which was developed by Harvard Law School for managing reading lists. Initial impressions were that this tool is less easy to use than CiteULike, in terms of adding books or articles. Items needed to be added manually, since there is no facility to pull records from Amazon or other catalogues. This slows down the process of creating a reading list. However, the software has features such as the ability to add annotations and notes for students. It is also possible to add headings to the list and re-order the list. As part of this case study both systems will be piloted with distance learners in autumn 2007 and feedback will be gathered.

Social bookmarking / resource sharing

A second case study has been exploring social bookmarking as a way of creating a subject guide of internet resources for students. Experiments are currently under way to create a list of resources for distance learners on the TRIUM course at LSE. These students are based around the world, visiting LSE briefly but then having remote access to library resources. In the past a traditional library guide has been made available from the virtual learning environment as a Word document. An online list of resources has been created using the social bookmarking site del.icio.us and students will be given access to this. Feedback will be gathered from students where possible. However one of the main challenges was adding library resources to this type of list. Many library systems, such as LSE's Electronic

Library, do not allow deep linking to resources, and so the key databases could not be added to del.icio.us. Access to library databases is often set up so that students enter the site from the link in the Electronic Library and as a result the number of resources that could be added to the list was limited.

Information literacy and social software

The literature review revealed that information literacy, and students' familiarity with library resources and how to use them effectively and ethically, is one of the key challenges for distance learning librarians. In the USA, many libraries have developed online information literacy tutorials to tackle this issue. Social software through technologies such as podcasting offers a new way of developing training materials. LSE Library teaches classes to full-time students on a range of topics. However, an experiment to create an online 'screencast', which included PowerPoint and audio, was developed as part of the LASSIE project and made available to students from the library website. Feedback from students is currently being gathered to establish how this type of tutorial might complement or, in the case of a distance learner, replace a face-to-face training session.

The citing and referencing podcast has attracted considerable interest from other libraries and is available from www.lse.ac.uk/library/insktr/citing_referencing.htm.

Further research

Other case studies will be written up as part of LASSIE, including documenting the use of the blog by LSE Archives and the associated challenges and issues. Another case study examines how a team of librarians at the Institute of Education use a wiki to share information and to develop library guides. The case studies alongside the literature review should provide valuable evidence for libraries that are considering social software initiatives.

Conclusion

Social software has the potential to change the provision of library services. Our research suggests that libraries should experiment with technology, incorporating blogs or RSS feeds into their websites where appropriate. Some social software such as podcasting and resource sharing can also be used in information literacy initiatives. The adventures of LASSIE will continue until December 2007, and further evidence will be gathered from the case studies. LASSIE will make recommendations about the types of social software that are usefully employed by libraries, including those which provide valuable support for distance learners and those that help all learners. As physical libraries become increasingly social spaces, so social software may provide valuable support to those users who never or rarely visit us.

References

Bradley, P. (2007) *How to Use Web 2.0 in your Library*, Facet Publishing.

Casey, M. E. and Savastinuk, L. C. (2006) Library 2.0: service for the next-generation library, *Library Journal*, 1 September, www.libraryjournal.com/article/CA6365200.html.

Casey, M. E. and Savastinuk, L. C. (2007) *Library 2.0: a guide to participatory library service*, Information Today, Inc.

Crawford, W. (2006) Library 2.0 and 'Library 2.0', *Cites & Insights*, **6** (2), http://citesandinsights.info/civ6i2.pdf.

Farkas, M. (2007) *Social Software in Libraries: building collaboration, communication, and community online*, Information Today Inc.

Gilster, P. (2007) Digital Fusion: defining the intersection of content and communications. In Martin, A. and Madigan, D. (eds), *Digital Literacies for Learning*, Facet Publishing.

Kirriemuir, J. (2007) *A 'Snapshot' of UK HE and FE Developments in Second Life*, Eduserv Foundation, www.eduserv.org.uk/foundation/sl/uksnapshot072007.

Miller, P. (2005) Web 2.0: building the new library, *Ariadne*, **45**, www.ariadne.ac.uk/issue45/miller/intro.html.

O'Connell, J. (2007) *Hey Jude Blog*, http://heyjude.wordpress.com/.

Oldenburg, R. (1999) *The Great Good Place: cafés, coffee shops, bookstores, bars, hair salons, and other hangouts at the heart of a community*, Marlowe & Company.

Sauers, M. P. (2006) *Blogging and RSS: a librarian's guide*, Information Today.

Secker, J. (2007) *Libraries, Social Software and Distance Larners: draft literature review*, http://clt.lse.ac.uk/Projects/LASSIE_lit_review_draft.pdf.

Secker, J. (2008) *Social Software, Libraries and Distance Learners*, Final version, http://clt.lse.ac.uk/Projects/LASSIE_lit_review_final.pdf.

8

The rise of recommendation and review: a place in online library environments?

Kara Jones and Kate Robinson

Introduction

Online collaboration and interaction, self-publishing, personalized categorization and sharing of content: these are all hallmarks of our internet exchanges today. More websites and online services are building on these activities and encouraging their users to add their own content or highlight useful or quality resources.

This paper is an exploration into the issues surrounding the rise of recommendation and review services and whether they're of benefit to library users in online academic environments. Should we be taking advantage of this opportunity to build communities and conversations, or should this remain the domain of online trade and commerce? Does user-generated content add value to our resources, or does it weaken its integrity? We take a look at the review and recommendation services currently available in academic library online environments, and explore the issues involved in adding user-generated content to our resources, using research undertaken for our own pilot project entitled 'Around the world in 80+ books'.

Why investigate user-generated content?

Reviews, recommendations and personalized categorization are all types of user-generated content. This content is produced by the end-user or consumer, rather than the traditional sources such as copywriters, publishers and commercial content creators. A personalized perspective or review of a book is one form of user-generated content, as is writing an online journal or weblog; another is uploading music or photographs to file-sharing websites. In the wider picture this is part of the Web 2.0 architecture of participation (O'Reilly, 2005). These days almost half of adult internet users interact or read Web 2.0 sites online, from publishing blogs, posting ratings and reviews, using RSS, tagging web pages, using social networking sites, listening to podcasts and so on (Li, 2007). The development of internet technology has widened our interaction and content creation activities. As Coyle (2007, 290) notes, 'users have become accustomed to creating content on the Web . . . [they] have an expectation that they will find a community at their electronic destination. They also expect to interact with their information resources, not to consume them passively.'

The expectations of our users, along with technical developments such as application programming interfaces (APIs) to import data into our resources, suggest that now is the time actively to investigate adding user-generated content to our online environments.

Why do people use reviews and recommendations?

Getting advice or opinions from others is an important part of any selection or purchase decision. We ask for referees for job candidates, we read customer reviews on Amazon before buying the latest bestseller, and we check TripAdvisor before booking our holiday hotel. Often our decisions to buy, read or visit something are formed by information provided by our peers, colleagues, neighbours or fellow consumers. We've always used recommendation, reputation and reviews to make our decisions, and with the explosion of information brought by the internet it seems a logical progression for these two concepts to meet.

In terms of information management, user-generated content is one of three ways in which we select or evaluate information. Clearly the best method for evaluating information is to build personal expertise and subject knowledge. Senior academics, for example, are aware of key authors and texts in their field of research. They have an established set of trusted sources they might use. Secondly, we use an information literacy approach to evaluating information, basing our decisions on evidence present in the resource. A website, for example, might be evaluated on the basis of the authority or credibility of the author, a particular bias of the site, the currency of the information, whether it's from an academic, government or commercial website, and so on. This is a skill we develop to select information from previously unknown sources. Finally, we use the wisdom of others to make decisions such as reviews, recommendations and ratings from other people who have used this information. This method works best when we can identify with the author, or use a system based on reputation to establish trust. This last method for information selection, along with the familiarity of library users with online communities, is the reason we're investigating reviews and recommendation in our online library environments.

What's currently happening?

There is a definite move towards integrating user-generated comment within online library environments around the globe. Libraries and library system vendors are actively investigating and adding mechanisms for engaging library users and building communities around our resources. In an academic environment, we've often used virtual learning environments and forums to engage our students with learning and teaching activities. Evolving technologies means these communities can be built directly into the resource itself. The following examples show how reviews, recommendations and similar services are being used.

The library catalogue

The library catalogue seems an obvious place to engage with library communities and, thanks to sites like Amazon and LibraryThing, our library users are often familiar with reviews, comments, ratings and suggestions for resources.

Dave Pattern, Library Systems Manager at the University of Huddersfield, UK, recently surveyed librarians around the world to gather thoughts on potential features for library catalogues. His research included the following features for user-generated content (Pattern, 2007):

- *Also borrowed*: 'people who borrowed this also borrowed . . .' suggestions based on circulation data
- *User tagging*: allowing the user to apply their own keywords (tags) to items in the OPAC
- *User comments*: allowing the user to add their own reviews and comments to items in the OPAC
- *User learning*: an 'intelligent' OPAC that makes personalized suggestions based on what the user does
- *User ratings*: allowing the user to add their own ratings or scores to items in the OPAC.

These features generated interest amongst the 700-plus librarians who responded to the survey. Huddersfield have implemented unmoderated ratings and moderated comments in their catalogue, with use by students and academic staff. Examples of potential uses for comments in a catalogue record include lecturers highlighting particular chapters, distance learning students sharing evaluations of resources that might normally be done face to face in a tutorial, or a librarian placing a comment on a heavily used out-of-print textbook, suggesting alternative texts.

Tagging of resources

Tagging is best described as personalized cataloguing of resources for sharing. This feature is part of a larger movement called social bookmarking. Tagging is a tool which has been deployed already in both university catalogues and abstracting and indexing databases. Tags are often displayed as a 'tag cloud', where the most popular words are shown larger, indicating hot topics.

Two examples of tags used to add personal subject headings to information resources include PennTags and Engineering Village. PennTags, from the University of Pennsylvania, is a social bookmarking tool for locating, organizing and sharing online resources. PennTags are promoted as a portable 'favourites' or 'bookmarks' tool, and as a social discovery system to see what others are posting and what tags they are using (University of Pennsylvania, 2007). Engineering Village is an abstracting and indexing database which has also enhanced its descriptors and keywords by adding tagging features for resource discovery and sharing.

Literature awareness services

The arrival of BioMed Central's 'Faculty of 1000 Biology' is another strong indication of the value of recommendation to information users. Its strength lies in a key feature to successful communities – reputation. Faculty of 1000 Biology is a literature awareness tool that highlights and reviews the most interesting papers published in the biological sciences, based on the recommendations of a faculty of well over 2300 selected leading researchers ('Faculty Members').

At the University of Bath we subscribed to Faculty of 1000 Biology in March 2007, which after a trial proved wildly successful with the Biology and Biochemistry Department. The openness and transparency of the credentials of reviewers was key to convincing busy researchers that this tool would help filter professional reading down to manageable levels.

Case study: Around the World in 80+ Books

Doubtless there is a move towards adding user-generated content to our information resources, but it brings with it risks and issues we have navigated away from in the past. It is sensible to consider the issues involved, such as moderation, ownership, and responsibility to help make informed decisions. At the University of Bath, we investigated these issues as part of a pilot project to build a community of library users around a particular collection of material, books personally recommended by international students and staff as a 'taster' of their home countries and cultures.

The University of Bath prides itself on the diversity of its student body. As a reflection of this we began a project in 2006/7 with our international staff and students to exploit and enrich the library's collections. We asked for personal recommendations of international libraries which participants had used or studied in and literature they had read which they felt would give readers a flavour of their home countries. Copies of each of the listed texts were added to library stock and wherever possible the collection included both the original and English-language versions. The books were then compiled into web-based and hard-copy reading lists arranged by country, with direct links into, or references to (depending on format), our library catalogue. Pictures of the recommended libraries with a short quote explaining why participants had chosen the library and their experience of it were brought together in an exhibition on the main service floor of the University Library, with images included on the web. This is a living project and further recommendations are still being received. Some examples of suggestions include those in Table 8.1.

Table 8.1 *Selections from reading lists*

England	Malawi
Austen, J. *Emma*	Chimombo, S. *The Wrath of Napolo*
Collins, W. *The Woman in White*	Chimombo, S. *The Bird Boy's Song*
Grahame, K. *The Wind in the Willows*	Mapanje, J. *The Last of the Sweet Bananas*
Mitford, N. *The Pursuit of Love*	White, L. *Magomero: Portrait of an African*
Le Carré, J. *Tinker Tailor Soldier Spy*	*Village*
Sweden	**Pakistan**
Lindgren, A. *Pippi Longstocking*	Faiz, A. *O City of Lights: Selected Poetry* and
Moberg, V. *The Emigrants*	*Biographical Notes*
Söderberg, H. *Doctor Glas*	Hamid, M. *Moth Smoke*
Strindberg, A. *Miss Julie*	Sidwha, B. *The Crow Eaters*

Issues to be addressed in the project

Whose reading list is it?

The decision as to where to experiment with this technology was carefully made. This booklist is a collaborative venture already, based on personal recommendation and supporting leisure reading rather than any academic course of study. We felt that to begin with an academic's reading list would raise ethical concerns, most obviously the undermining of academics' ownership of their own reading lists. Traditionally academics have been able to recommend any book which they feel supports their course without any suggestion that this book might not be fit for purpose. With review these lists are opened up to criticism. It could be something which confident academics would welcome, but there are questions also about who is able to make such judgements as to what is appropriate for particular course reading: is it the students, or is it the academic? What if the book is one written by the same academic? We felt these concerns could be better addressed by initially providing an example in a safe environment such as the 80+ booklist.

Risk management

With all projects it is wise to give some consideration to risk factors. Of most interest to us was considering the impact of doing this or not doing this. To go ahead would, we felt, encourage wider reading, build communities and add value to our resources. In this context it would encourage participation and also allow people to understand what it was about a particular book that they wished to recommend and share with others. Asking for recommendations which give a flavour of a person's country brought some interesting stories in the process of the project and these would be good to share with the community. The choice of a particular book may also be contentious or lead to further thoughts or recommendations from others. This environment might well encourage participation in the project, lead to the discovery of material within the library, or enhance library stock if resulting purchases were made. Without attempting to build such a community there is a risk that the project will not continue to grow.

Authority of the library catalogue

Where should the reviews be? Should they be in the catalogue or should we be focusing more on moving the catalogue to the conversations, instead of trying to draw the conversations in by, for example, putting the catalogue in Facebook, or on Moodle (our university's virtual learning environment)? Is this about enhancing our catalogue or about building up a conversation and community around our holdings? Over recent years many library catalogues have, by technical necessity, become split between a catalogue dealing with mainly hard copy material and supplementary lists of web-based resources (databases, e-journals lists, etc.) with robust links which are not yet supported effectively by many library management systems. There is often a split between the breadth of information available on the catalogue depending on where it is hosted, i.e. in the library on dedicated library terminals or on the web. Library catalogue terminals are often locked down to ensure availability, restricting access to linking to web-based resources. The ideal of the catalogue as a one-stop shop for all library users has already been lost, so does it matter where these conversations take place? Would hosting them in the traditional library catalogue undermine the integrity and quality of the catalogue where traditionally only librarians add data, or does this really matter? If we do not move forward and extend some ownership of the catalogue to others, are we hastening its demise?

We agreed to pilot two approaches and then review based on our experience and our users' preferences. The first was to attach a wiki to each of the 80+ books library catalogue records for use by our university community. The second was to link to another review site, in this case LibraryThing, so our users could read comments posted there and add their own to them if they choose to do so.

Moderation?

For social technologies to function effectively we felt it was important to have as open and unfettered system as possible. We want people to participate, so shouldn't we try to make it as straightforward and as instantaneous as possible? We should begin with a concept of initial trust. While this may be the ideal approach it does raise some concerns which we felt could be addressed in the following ways. A sign-in system could discourage inappropriate comments. We have an in-house authentication system which would allow us to see who had posted comments to the wiki. By not anonymizing the comments people are able to associate with the authors. It adds openness, transparency and a level of accountability when details are visible. It could also be used to show some data about reviewers which might well have relevance to their review. If we did move to using this technology for academic's reading lists participants would be able to see if the reviewer was on their course and consequently reviewing the book from the same perspective. We would need to take data protection requirements into account.

It would be up to the users to alert us to any unacceptable reviews or automated spam and for us to take action at that point. All that would be required is an initial disclaimer for contributors to click to agree that we would take this action if required. This raises the question of ownership of the comments where we are encouraging users to populate discrete areas of our library catalogue. Our view was that our disclaimer would also reserve the right to remove anything at any time, to change and introduce moderation, etc. downstream and to change the policy itself if needs be, thereby giving us flexibility from the start to make changes when we need to.

For our second approach, using LibraryThing, we agreed to link out to reviews rather than import them into the library catalogue, making it clear to users that they were leaving the university's area and interacting in a different space. Our view is that LibraryThing, although out of our control, holds reasonable comments.

Seeding

How then do we get people to add their reviews? What is the incentive? In some respects the initial use of LibraryThing alongside the wiki is to begin to populate the catalogue with 'ready-made' reviews which may encourage others to add theirs. There would need to be marketing or promotional activity to encourage community engagement and we could use our usual library channels for this. However, by using special collections or grouping related resources to encourage a community such as the Around the World in 80+ Books, reading lists, etc. we may be able to encourage more engagement than if we initially attached wikis to every book on the library catalogue. This approach might instil a sense of community and ownership of the reviews. It may also be an area lecturers choose to engage with for teaching their students, as use of this technology could form part of an assessment.

Other possibilities could be through the use of the library management system itself. We could join up people's requests for items (reservations) and use the automatic notification e-mail to ask the requestor to leave a comment on or rating of the item. We could also use the Expedia model, which e-mails you after your holiday to suggest you rank or rate the hotel you stayed in. Again using links to the library management system we could generate an automatic e-mail to the borrower once they have returned a book with a link to the review section asking if they would like to participate.

Technical issues

The technical issues involved with adding user-generated content to library environments are reducing. The advent of the application programming interface, (API) has extended opportunities for content from one database or website to plug into another, allowing systems to interact, and this service can be used to bring content from Amazon, for example, into the library catalogue.

There are decisions to be made on how to display ratings or reviews on the library catalogue. The system on trial at Bath for adding comments is based on a wiki, with each entry dynamically created as necessary. Authentication is another issue, particularly if it's decided that reviewers must log in to a system to encourage transparency. In a community such as a university, computing services departments may need to authorize authentication with a Lightweight Directory Access Protocol (LDAP) or similar authentication server.

Conclusion

Integrating user-generated content into library environments is becoming technically more feasible, and our library customers are generally more comfortable using and adding to these communities. Discussions at the University of Bath Library have highlighted a number of issues that need consideration before adding reviews, recommendations and ratings into the library catalogue. Deciding the level of risk involved and how to manage this risk is key. Prioritizing this service development in relation to other library initiatives is likely to be another key consideration, as it's a value-adding rather than core service. On the other hand, our library users are coming to expect a community at their online destination, and are comfortable interacting with resources.

As the Around the World in 80+ Books project develops, we will be able to use the experience gained to inform decisions on rolling out this service on a larger scale. These reflections will also be helpful for decision-making should options for adding user-generated content be added to upgrades or new versions of our library management system.

References

Amazon, www.amazon.co.uk.

Coyle, K. (2007) Managing Technology: the library catalogue in a 2.0 world, *Journal of Academic Librarianship*, **33** (2), 289–91.

Li, C. (2007) *Forrester's New Social Technographics Report*, Groundswell: Winning in a World Transformed by Social Technologies, http://blogs.forrester.com/charleneli/2007/04/forresters_new_.html.

LibraryThing, www.librarything.org.

O'Reilly, T. (2005) *What Is Web 2.0: design patterns and business models for the next generation of software*, O'Reilly.com, www.oreillynet.com/pub/a/oreilly/tim/news/2005/09/30/what-is-web-20.html?page=1.

Pattern, D. (2007) *OPAC Survey Results – part 3: self-plagiarism is style*, www.daveyp.com/blog/index.php/page/2/.

TripAdvisor, www.tripadvisor.com.

University of Pennsylvania (2007) *What is PennTags?* http://tags.library.upenn.edu/help/.

9

Re-usable learning objects for information literacy: are they practical?

Nancy Graham

Introduction

This paper will explore the emerging themes from the Eduserv-funded Birmingham Re-Usable Materials (BRUM) project. Particular elements of the project stand out as needing further exploration, including the technology used in the project and design attributes of the re-usable learning objects (RLOs), liaison with academics and students and issues for the future, including use of Web 2.0 to deliver information skills training. The paper will look at how practical it is to create electronic RLOs for information skills training and the key issues to consider.

Background

The BRUM project ran from June 2006 to February 2007 at the University of Birmingham (UK). The project aimed to create electronic RLOs to support students in developing information skills. The project team (consisting of two librarians) worked with a group of four academics to deliver the learning objects within curricula and to gather qualitative feedback from students using questionnaires and a focus group. The findings of the project were published in a project report available from www.is2.bham.ac.uk/blasst/brum.htm.

Fifteen new RLOs were created and hosted on a web page. The RLOs were used in lectures and an institutional virtual learning environment (VLE) (WebCT) and different software was used to create such RLOs as a quiz on referencing and an online demonstration on literature searching. In the focus group students were asked to evaluate the RLOs and to discuss information skills training in general.

Technology and attributes of RLOs

There is a plethora of software to create RLOs and the project team took this as an opportunity to try out different software and evaluate the results. Different software was used to create RLOs on the same topics to appeal to different learning styles. The project team were also aware that the RLOs should reflect the need to support independent learning and so created learning objects that had specific attributes designed to do this.

Use of new and different software

The project team utilized everyday software, including Microsoft PowerPoint, and bought in new software for the creation of some RLOs, including Macromedia Captivate, Camtasia and Turning Technologies' Turning Point.

PowerPoint

Microsoft PowerPoint was used to create a 'choose your own adventure' style learning object which colleagues had seen used to good effect elsewhere. Even though this piece of software is easy to use and well known, when used to create this sort of RLO the planning stage proved complicated and confusing. As a 'choose your own RLO' allows the user to choose from three options on almost every page there have to be several possible pathways to follow. Users also found this to be fairly confusing and difficult to navigate. This type of RLO could be used to good effect for a short, simple task but the thorough preparation needed may put many colleagues off.

Captivate

The team created several automated demonstrations using Captivate and even though the software was new it was fairly easy to use. This software records on-screen actions and allows the creator to add text boxes with explanations and has a limited interactive element. The learning objects made with Captivate proved very popular with the students, as they are visual and include explanations of actions. It is also possible to slow down a demonstration or repeat sections. Students felt that they were able to take charge of their learning in their own time with the Captivate demos and that they were an attractive and fun way to learn.

Camtasia

This software works in the same way as Captivate but has a more sophisticated audio recording system allowing the team to appeal to aural learners and those with visual impairments. Using Camtasia the project team captured soundbites about using the library service from students, meaning that users of these RLOs would be learning from their peers.

Turning Point

This personal response system software proved to be very popular with the students, for several reasons. It is completely interactive, so students are not passive learners but are having to think and respond to questions. Also, owing to the anonymous nature of the handset, students do not need to feel embarrassed at not knowing the right answer. The anonymity and immediate feedback from the system means that lecturers can gauge what their class is thinking straightaway, allowing for further discussion of the topic.

Institutional readiness

The use of any technology to support learning and teaching should have the backing of academics in order to make it successful. It is therefore important that academics themselves become familiar with existing and emerging technologies that support evolving pedagogies and that they work alongside colleagues, including librarians and IT technicians, to develop appropriate resources for their students.

This collaborative working should ideally be supported by a university-led agenda to promote innovation in learning and teaching, including independent learning. Although the bottom-up approach is often successful in winning over individual academics to use new technologies, a top-down, institutional approach ensures that there is consistent and sustainable support for innovation. Claire McGuinness explores these issues and supports the view that a university-led top-down approach is often more successful in encouraging academics to accept new ways of working and that we are beginning to see a 'teaching and learning environment that is growing more receptive to the idea of IL' (McGuinness, 2007).

Key attributes of RLOs

As the project team began the design and planning process of each RLO the key attributes of each one were taken into account. Any new learning objects should reflect the way in which our students like to learn and how they like to interact with technology. Using the findings from the SPIRE project (White, 2007) the attributes of the RLOs can be linked to the attributes associated with the well used technologies of 18–24 year olds.

Flexibility

It was felt that the RLOs should be as flexible as possible, so that students can access them wherever they have internet access and whenever they want to learn. Statistics from the SPIRE project (White, 2007) show that students are happy to access learning resources out of hours, so this approach was appropriate. The BRUM RLOs were designed to be able to be used within face-to-face lectures, VLEs and web pages, thus appealing to different ways of learning.

Small, self-contained

The project RLOs were also designed to be small and self-contained and do not necessarily have to be used in conjunction with each other to be effective. The team designed the learning objects so that they could be embedded in a learning context on their own and still be useful. This element of the RLO design is mirrored in the objects that students themselves are used to using, such as video clips, music, text and web links in their online social spaces. The team felt it important to evaluate small learning units with students as they would be used to using technology in this way.

Self-paced, interactive

It was crucial for the RLOs to be self-paced and, where possible, interactive. These elements are ubiquitous in many technologies, especially web technologies, where self-made web content is becoming the norm. In order to encourage independent learning, learning tools must be self-paced, as learners will feel comfortable at being able to approach new tasks in their own time and repeat them if necessary. Many students now have moved on from being passive observers or receivers of education and, in many cases, leisure pursuits. Music, films and television programmes are now available on demand so that consumers are in complete control of when, where and how they interact with them.

Re-usable and re-purposable

The RLOs also had to be capable of being re-used and re-purposed. The software used to create the RLOs is accessible and affordable, meaning that anyone wishing to adapt the learning objects can do. Sites such as YouTube show that students, among others, are happy to re-use and re-purpose recorded material created by someone else.

Aggregated

In some ways contrary to the element of being small and self-contained, the team also consider it important to create the RLOs in such a way that they could be used together to create a learning package. A range of RLOs could be put into a WebCT section for students embarking on their first extended assignment, including RLOs on literature searching and referencing, supporting the entire research process.

Liaison with academics and student engagement

Liaison with academics

As part of the planning stage in the provision of any new resource to support learning there must be a thorough consultation with academic colleagues. In the case of this project it was crucial to involve the academics at every stage, including the selection of appropriate learning objects and choosing when and where to use them. If using RLOs for information skills is to be practical and efficient, then time spent liaising with academics has to be taken into account.

As the overall aim of the project was to have a suite of RLOs for academics to use as they saw fit, it was also important for them to be accessible and easy to use. The project team decided to host the learning object files on an open web page rather than on an institutional VLE, to encourage access and use. It is also crucial to work with academics in a timely way and support their students at times that suit them. The team were keen to deliver the RLOs within curricula, whether this was using a TurningPoint quiz at the end of a lecture or putting a referencing demo in a relevant WebCT section. Good liaison skills are crucial in determining the most appropriate use of new resources with academics.

In discussions with academic colleagues at the beginning of the project it became clear that while they were happy to pick relevant learning objects and give some brief feedback, they were more comfortable with the project team uploading the RLOs and supporting their use in lectures. If our goal is to encourage academic colleagues to use these learning objects without our help, then more work needs to be done in making them easy to use and relevant. Notably, the academics who persisted with the project throughout its duration did not find involvement onerous and claimed that the project had saved them time in the long run, as their students used the RLOs to gain much-needed skills in research.

Student engagement

Perhaps the most important element of the project was to gather feedback from the student participants. It was important to evaluate how accessible and user-friendly the RLOs were and if they were effective in improving the students' information skills. Assessing an improvement in skills is difficult without testing the skill itself so a diagnostic questionnaire was designed to ascertain the level of confidence in each student with regards to a specific task including referencing or conducting a literature search. The questionnaire was divided into two sections to be answered before and after using the learning object.

While this type of evaluation is not ideal it did elicit some useful immediate feedback. More detailed feedback was gathered in a focus group of 12 students taken from classes involved in the project. Students were divided into pairs and asked to evaluate a particular type of RLO (audio recording, quiz, demo). This provided the team with detailed evaluation of the RLOs and the much-needed student perspective. Students suggested that without proper promotion they would not have known about these RLOs and would not have thought to ask for them. This viewpoint is important if we are to reach out to the students on their terms. The students also argued that use of the RLOs would be low unless using them could be explicitly linked to an improvement in academic performance or helping to pass exams.

Since 2005, final-year university students across the UK have been requested to fill out the National Student Survey (HEFCE, 2007) to find out how they rate a range of services and facilities. Results from this survey can determine improvements and changes to a library service. However, the survey does not take into account student expectations and so the feedback on quality of services and facilities can be difficult to translate into actual evaluation. Arranging student focus groups to gather detailed qualitative feedback on information resources is time-consuming and needs thorough preparation but the results from these sessions can be invaluable, as we can explore themes in greater depth than a survey can and thus respond and develop services more appropriately.

Focus groups and questionnaires are just one way to reach out and engage with our users but perhaps more innovative networking could be employed. Inviting academic and student colleagues on to our new technologies group could be one way to involve them to a greater degree. Conducting more market research and using students for testing new technologies and evaluating this could be another form of fruitful engagement.

Issues for the future and Web 2.0 developments

Issues for the future

The BRUM project is now complete but further areas of exploration have emerged. These include the need to keep up with new technologies and explore their uses in supporting learning in higher education (HE). The recently published Joint Information Systems Committee (JISC) report on Web 2.0 in HE (Franklin and van Harmelen, 2007) focuses on just this issue and gives many useful recommendations.

There is a small group of interested information professionals at the University of Birmingham that meets regularly to explore new technologies and their possible uses for supporting information skills in HE. This is just one example of how librarians can keep up with new developments and experiment with new ways of working. However, it is also important to keep up with how students and colleagues are using new technologies to support their learning and research. The BRUM project achieved this on a small scale with the student focus group but interaction with our users (students and academics) should be on a regular basis and in greater depth.

Web 2.0 developments

The JISC funded SPIRE project published results of its online tool use survey (White, 2007) in March 2007 and the findings highlight the use of Web 2.0 tools such as MSN Messenger amongst 18–24 year olds to be higher than their use of others such as Bloglines (to organize RSS feeds) and del.icio.us to organize articles and links using tags. The most popular Web 2.0 applications for this age group include instant messaging, blogs for reading and social networking sites such as MySpace and Facebook. These findings can help us to understand the behaviour behind the use of technology for learning, too. According to Hartman, Moskal and Dziuban (2005), 'Blended learning provides a unique opportunity to bridge generations, providing the face-to-face contact requested by Baby Boomers, the independence preferred by Gen-Xers, and the interaction and sense of community desired by Net Geners.' In order to support learning in an appropriate way it is important for librarians to be prepared to engage with students who are about to enter higher education. This means embracing Web 2.0 technologies, experimenting with new ways of using technology to support learning and understanding how students like to learn.

Two of the BRUM RLOs (an audiovisual recording about using the university's proxy server and one on referencing) were uploaded on to YouTube, the video sharing website. To date, the proxy server RLO has had 1259 hits (University of Birmingham, 2006). Owing to the way the videos are searched for and viewed the project team have no way of knowing who is watching them or if YouTube users are finding them by mistake. However, it does illustrate the wide reach of a site such as YouTube and that as a resource discovery tool it can be very powerful. More exploration and experimentation should be done utilizing sites such as YouTube to bring RLOs to a greater audience of students.

The JISC also recently published a report into use of Web 2.0 for creating content in HE (Franklin and van Harmelen, 2007). The report highlights the need for further JISC-funded research into Web 2.0 applications and their uses and a need for UK higher education institutions (HEIs) to create flexible guidelines regarding use of Web 2.0, as many of these applications and technologies are still in their infancy and are going through a period of flux. Many HEIs have already embraced Web 2.0 ways of working and some even have Web 2.0 strategies in place.

It is clear that this new way of working and pursuing leisure interests is changing all the time and that students are comfortable with using new technology for their learning. It is our challenge to explore ways to use Web 2.0 to enhance information skills training and to explore further the expectations and demands of our students now and those that will be coming in to HE in the next few years.

National collaboration

As well as having dialogue with our users we must engage with the larger community of practice; discussion with librarians and academics in the UK and further afield on information literacy and skills training can help to formulate and plan our own services and resource provision.

During the BRUM project the team was in contact with colleagues running similar projects in the UK, including those in London (Birkbeck College, 2007), Cardiff (Cardiff University, 2007) and Huddersfield (University of Huddersfield, 2007). This informal dialogue is essential in understanding how a small-scale project such as BRUM fits in with other patterns of use and projects nationally. Further engagement with librarian colleagues is essential to make best use of the findings of the BRUM project and to explore the issues in a systematic way.

Possibilities of further projects with others in the UK include a symposium on the use of RLOs for supporting information skills; an online forum/repository for information skills learning objects; further use and evaluation of national repositories such as the Jorum; and the re-use and re-purposing of existing RLOs and evaluation of this process. The momentum of the project will be carried forward through these forums.

Conclusion

The BRUM project focused on using electronic learning objects to support students in developing their information skills. Librarians and academics worked together to provide contextualized learning and the project team gathered qualitative feedback. Feedback from academics and students provided further issues for exploration, including student engagement and different uses of technology to support learning. In order to respond appropriately to the changing information skills needs of users (academics and students) the dialogue with students and academics and information colleagues in the UK will continue. Furthermore, engagement with the community of practice should ensure that emerging themes from BRUM are explored in a systematic way to help shape future developments in using RLOs for information skills at the University of Birmingham.

Reference list

Birkbeck College (2007) *Project LibLOIL*, www.bbk.ac.uk/lib/life/skills/.

Cardiff University (2007) *Information Literacy Resource Bank,* http://ilrb.cardiff.ac.uk.

Franklin, T. and van Harmelen, M. (2007) *Web 2.0 for Content for Learning and Teaching in Higher Education,* Joint Information Systems Committee (JISC), www.jisc.ac.uk/media/documents/programmes/digitalrepositories/web2-content-learning-and-teaching.pdf.

Hartman, J., Moskal, P. and Dziuban, C. (2005) Preparing the Academy of Today for the Learner of Tomorrow. In Oblinger, D. and Oblinger, J., *Educating the Net Generation,* Educause, www.educause.edu/EducatingtheNetGeneration/5989.

Higher Education Funding Council for England (2007) *The National Student Survey,* www.thestudentsurvey.com.

McGuinness, C. (2007) Exploring Strategies for Integrated Information Literacy: from 'academic champions' to institution wide change, *Communications in Information Literacy,* **1** (1), www.comminfolit.org/index.php/cil/article/view/Spring2007AR3/14.

University of Birmingham (2006) *How to use the proxy server,* www.youtube.com/watch?v=7moRvkgLLC0 [accessed 30 July 2007].

University of Huddersfield (2007) *Information Literacy: a guide to research techniques and strategies,* www.hud.ac.uk/cls/infolit/.

White, D. (2007) *Results of the 'Online Tool Use Survey' Undertaken by the JISC-funded SPIRE Project,* http://tallblog.conted.ox.ac.uk/wp-content/uploads/2007/03/survey-summary.pdf.

10

An introduction to the LearnHigher Centre for Teaching & Learning (CETL), with particular reference to the information literacy learning area and its work on information literacy audits at Manchester Metropolitan University

Bob Glass and Jillian R. Griffiths

Introduction

In 2003 the UK Higher Education Funding Council (HEFC) created 74 Centres for Excellence in Teaching & Learning (CETLs) through a detailed and competitive bid process. The successful CETL bids covered a wide range of educational activities throughout higher education in the UK.

Most CETLs are solo projects, though 19 are collaborative in nature. The largest of these is LearnHigher. The LearnHigher CETL is a collaborative project involving some 16 higher education institutions (HEIs), covering 19 learning areas in learning development in higher education (HE). It was originally conceived as a 'one-stop shop' for resources of excellence for practitioners and students involved with learner development in UK HE. The LearnHigher website (www.learnhigher.ac.uk) further defines its context and purpose (Glass, 2007a).

As the country's biggest collaborative HEFCE-funded Centre for Excellence in Teaching and Learning, LearnHigher is a partnership of 16 universities and the Higher Education Academy. The CETL is committed to improving student learning through practice-led enquiry, building a research base to inform the effective use of learning development resources. LearnHigher is a network of expertise seeking to enhance professional practice and student learning, and build capacity both within the network and across the wider sector.

The LearnHigher partnership has a large and diverse amount of expertise. Each of the 16 partner institutions is engaged in enquiry-led practice which aims to build a sound evidence base in learning development across a broad spectrum of learning areas that underpin activity across all academic subjects.

Throughout the five-year programme LearnHigher will be undertaking a strategic approach to research, to build and disseminate a sound evidence base in learning development. Practitioners across the sector will be encouraged to share in, and contribute to current pedagogic understanding.

LearnHigher will also be a gateway to tried and tested resources in a broad range of learning areas. Each of our 16 partner institutions contributes research-driven, peer reviewed and evaluated resources in 20 learning areas. 'In conjunction with the Higher Education Academy, LearnHigher will create a portal service to provide resources and materials to the whole of the sector. Staff in both support roles and teaching roles will be able to use these resources in their course delivery and, in time, resources will be available for students to support their studies' (www.learnhigher.ac.uk/).

The learning areas

Clearly, identifying, labelling and agreeing on what the learning areas should address was an important issue at the outset of the project. Much debate took place regarding what the learning areas should be and who should address which area. It was always understood that the final selection would inevitably include some overlap and would always be, to an extent, contentious. In the end the areas shown in Table 10.1 were chosen in the light of relevance to the project aims and the expertise of the individuals and institutions taking part.

Institutions

This grouping provides a very effective mix of 'traditional' and 'new' universities for the project and strengthens the effectiveness of its peer-reviewed resources and research outputs. As well as this, personnel working in the learning areas come from varied backgrounds, including learning support, teaching, research and administration. Commonality is expressed in the shared commitment to enhancing learning development in HE.

Aims and objectives

One of the strengths of the LearnHigher bid, aside from the relevance of the purpose and collaborative nature, was the detail and robustness of its aims and objectives. These were clearly stated from the outset of the projects and the group, as a collective and as individual learning areas, have tried very hard to stick to them.

The aims and objectives of LearnHigher are clearly defined on the CETLs website at www.learnhigher.ac.uk (Glass, 2007a).

Table 10.1 *Learning areas*

Learning area	HEI
Learning for all (inclusivity)	University of Worcester
Referencing and plagiarism Group work	University of Bradford
Personal development planning	Bournemouth University
Oral communication Maths, numeracy and statistics	Brunel University
Mobile learning Problem solving and creative thinking	Liverpool Hope University
Assessment	University of Kent
Listening and interpersonal skills	University of Leeds
Understanding organizations	The University of Liverpool
Independent learning and self-directed study	The University of Manchester
Academic writing	Nottingham Trent University
Report writing Time management	University of Reading
Information literacy	Manchester Metropolitan University
Critical thinking and reflection	University of Plymouth
Research methods	University of Lincoln
Reading and note-making	London Metropolitan University
Visual analysis	University of Brighton

Aims

1 To build a research and evidence base across the LearnHigher network to inform the effective use of learning development resources.
2 To develop, identify, quality-assure and share electronic resources for higher education staff to integrate into their curriculum and for students to use in support of their own learning development.
3 To develop, identify, quality-assure and share electronic resources for students to use in support of their own learning development.
4 To share resources across the sector through the Higher Education Academy portal services.
5 To become a nationally and internationally recognized centre for excellence in learning development.

Objectives

LearnHigher CETL funds will be used to reward current excellence, develop and extend existing good practice consistent with institutional/partnership priorities to reach wider student and staff audiences through the following activities:

Building mechanisms for sharing excellent materials and resources

1 Working with the Higher Education Academy to create a LearnHigher portal (Connect) service that can be embedded in all HEI sites.
2 Building a technical framework and support to enable the distributed sharing of materials and resources to be effectively and reliably handled.
3 Sharing existing good materials, identifying or developing new learner development materials and resources for learners and staff.
4 Developing a more robust quality assurance process for materials and resources.

Building capacity in the LearnHigher Network

5 Strengthening the current network of practitioners.
6 Building practitioner capacity across the LearnHigher network in terms of broadening expertise and staff skills.

Creating institutional impact

7 Establishing a reward mechanism in each HEI.
8 Raising the profile of LearnHigher work across the HEI partners for greater institutional impact.
9 Having the opportunity to create further institutional embedding strategies.

Evaluation

10 Creating baseline data and developing effective monitoring strategies for use of the resources.
11 Enhancing current evaluation work.

Research

12 Building a research community and portfolio of evidence-based research that helps develop our understanding of effective strategies for supporting learners into new areas of higher education study.
13 Becoming an internationally recognized centre for excellence in learner development.

Dissemination

14 Providing an opportunity for all HEIs to access materials and resources.
15 Engaging others in LearnHigher sub-networks that are creating excellent materials, undertaking research or involved in embedding in their own institutions.

Steering group meetings and central and local learning area plans, together with workshops, have been used to ensure adherence and effective development of plans.

Management and communications

Given the collective size of LearnHigher, effective management and good internal communications within the group were seen as critical to the success of the project. A project director (Jill Armstrong), manager (Michelle Verity) and key administrative staff were appointed to work from the project lead institution, Liverpool Hope University. Group communications are facilitated by the standard e-mail, Jiscmail and a web-based Scandinavian virtual learning environment (VLE) called Fronter (www.fronter.com). Face-to-face communication is facilitated by three two-day steering group and development meetings at partner institutions across the UK per year. Individual learning areas elected learning area co-ordinators in their home institutions and hold similar local events. The group also appointed an external assessor to monitor and inform the overall direction of the CETL in line with the stated aims and objectives.

Generally, the measures adopted have proved successful. Both management and communications have been very effective. Two years into the project, LearnHigher has performed well, it has developed into an effective cohesive group and found a sense of collective identity. First- and second-year tasks have been completed as planned and the stated aims and objectives have been adhered to. There have been no major disagreements, or evidence of communication gaps, so far. We are now at the end of year two of the five-year life cycle of the CETL and the group has, on the whole, delivered all of its promised outcomes. Minor issues have surrounded the use of the selected VLE. This had been intended to provide a single interface solution for a range of electronic communication needs; however, it has not been as well received and exploited by the group as had been hoped. There may be a number of reasons for this: lack of engagement, yet another interface to use, training issues, time available to commit to using it, etc. Therefore we are currently reviewing this area of operation with a view to finding a more engaging solution.

The LearnHigher Suite at MMU

A capital funding grant from LearnHigher in 2006 provided a unique opportunity to create the new LearnHigher Suite at MMU (Glass, 2007b). This student-centred facility, planned and developed using the latest guidelines and advice on social and flexible learning areas from organizations such as the JISC (Smith, 2006), has considerably enhanced the quality of the learning environment available to staff and students. It also provides a high-profile home for the LearnHigher CETL in the institution.

The information literacy learning area

The information literacy learning area at MMU is administered through a team made up of academics, library practitioners, learning support advisers and research associates. Formal meetings take place once a term, though ad hoc collaboration takes place all the time. There are particularly close links with MMU library staff, as well as links with the MMU Learning and Teaching Unit, MMU Learning Support and CERLIM (The Centre for Research in Library and Information Management). A student member will be appointed in the coming year.

Activities and resources created

In 2005/6 the information literacy team at the Department of Information and Communications created five re-usable learning objects (Glass, 2007b):

- The Internet Detective (WebCT): in co-operation with Intute and the University of Bristol
- Info Skills (WebCT): in co-operation with MMU Libraries
- Information Literacy for HE Students (interactive website): Tallinn University
- The Citing Proficiency Tutorial (WebCT): MMU Information and Communications Dept
- Avoiding Plagiarism Tutorial (WebCT): MMU Philosophy Dept.

We also produced a baseline report on information literacy at the home institution, and a literature review and an information literacy mapping exercise based on selected (LearnHigher HEI member) institutions in the UK were published. We also presented poster sessions and gave seminars at a range of information literacy and information-related conferences in the UK and Europe. Conferences included LILAC (the Librarians' Information Literacy Conference), the Higher Education Academy Information & Computer Sciences conference, the BOBCATTS (LIS) conference, the LDHE (Learning Development in HE) symposium and the HEA Open Learning Spaces event at the University of Warwick.

There has been European co-operation with Universities in Estonia, the Czech Republic, Austria and Ireland. Two research and development visits to the USA have taken place, involving the following universities: Florida State, Syracuse, Illinois at Urbana-Champaign, Tennessee at Knoxville, James Madison, North Carolina Central and North Carolina at Chapel Hill. Each of the visits included interaction with the LIS department (or equivalent), the university library and the public library service.

The CETL has also provided funding to support library staff attending information literacy-related conferences (e.g. LILAC).

The period 2006/2007 will see the introduction of six further learning objects, a tutor-centred information literacy website (launched at the LILAC conference in March 2007), an extension to the peer review process and the trialling of a web-based information literacy audit for stage one HEI students.

Additionally, further capital funding from LearnHigher has been used for the refurbishment and development of a student-centred learning space, the LearnHigher suite of rooms in the Geoffrey Manton Building at MMU (October 2006).

Information literacy audits

There has been some interesting debate recently regarding the assessment of students' information literacy skills. A number of key questions have arisen, such as: What standards and criteria should we use to assess students? What are we actually trying to measure? What type of test is the most appropriate? What do the results mean? How do we measure improvements? and (on the effects of intervention) Is a 'one test fits all' solution practical?

A number of information literacy audits or tests exist in the USA and Australia, and in the UK Susie Andretta has created one at London Metropolitan University (Andretta, 2005). The SAILS test is fairly well know in the USA. However, one of the most widely trialled information literacy tests is the Adpatex software-based 'Online Information Literacy Test' from Steven Wise and his team at the Institute for Computer Based Assessment at James Madison University, Virginia, USA (Wise and Yang, 2003). This test comprises some 65 multiple choice questions assessing a range of information literacy competences. Question content was by Lynne Cameron, Instructional Services Librarian at James Madison, and a group of colleagues from other US university libraries (Wise et al., 2005).

Information literacy testing at MMU

As part of the research contribution to the Information Literacy Research Area of LearnHigher it was decided to run an information literacy audit for all stage one students in the Department of Information and Communications in late 2006. This project was supported by a small grant from the Learning and Teaching Group in the Humanities, Law and Social Sciences faculty at MMU, and the Department of Information and Communications. Additionally it was decided to include around 20 students from another department in the faculty in order to generate comparative data.

A number of international standards exist which define levels of information literacy competences. In the UK SCONUL (The Society for College, National and University Libraries) has defined the standards for higher education based on

'The Seven Pillar Model' (SCONUL, 1999), Similar models such as ACRL and ANZIL exist in the USA and Australasia respectively. The Online Information Literacy Test that we decided to use was ACRL, based on James Madison University's Online Information Literacy Test (ACRL, 2000). There were a number of reasons for this, including the nature of the test, the similarities in the standards and the availability of a 'product' that was ready to use. Most of the testing took place during December 2006 and February 2007. Seventy-five students in the common undergraduate programme of the Department of Information and Communications and 20 from the Economics Department in the same faculty were tested. The psychometric test (which is charged for on a per-student basis) is based on 65 multiple choice questions. Sixty of the questions are static, five are used as 'practice' questions for development purposes and are varied as required by the test developers. It takes between 60 and 75 minutes for students to complete the test, depending on the speed of the student taking the test. The test measures performance in four of the five information literacy competencies identified in US-formulated ACRL standards (ACRL, 2000); written abilities cannot really be addressed by this kind of test. Students receive their score immediately at the end of the test, and tutors are provided with an extensive range of statistics relating to the student performance, question scores and overall test results. The data file is provided in Access, Excel, SPSS or other formats. We undertook our analysis using SPSS, as this was the most convenient format to use at MMU.

Preliminary results in detail

Two performance level standards have been defined by the ACRL ILT creators, Proficient and Advanced. A score of 39–53 out of 60 (65–89%) is required for a student to be assessed as Proficient, and a score of 54+ out of 60 (90+%) for a student to be assessed as Advanced. A Proficient student will be able to:

- describe how libraries are organized
- define major library services
- choose appropriate types of reference source for a particular information need
- identify common types of citations
- employ basic database search strategies
- locate a variety of sources in a library or online
- discriminate between scholarly and popular publications
- use information legally and ethically.

An Advanced student is able to attain the criteria for Proficient and will also be able to:

- modify and improve database search strategies
- employ sophisticated database search strategies
- interpret information in a variety of sources
- evaluate information in terms of purpose, authority and reliability
- understand ethical, legal and socioeconomic issues relating to information access and use.

In total, 81 students participated with the ACRL ILT, 62 from the Department of Information and Communications (ICO) and 19 from the Department of Economics (ECON). The majority of students from both departments achieved good results (see Figure 10.1), thus:

- The majority of students scored between 50 and 59, well above the score required for Proficient.
- The mean score for ICO students was 59.6 (in the Advanced classification).
- The mean score for ECON was 60.8 (in the Advanced classification).
- 6.2% of students failed to reach the Proficient grade (four ICO students and one ECON).
- 28.4% of students were classed as Proficient.
- 65.4% were classed as Advanced.

Initially it was planned that the ILT would measure the five ACRL standards. However, it was deemed that one of the standards was incompatible with a multiple-choice item format and is assessed differently (Standard 4: student able

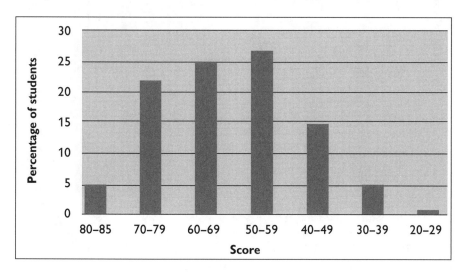

Figure 10.1 *Results for all students*

to use information effectively to accomplish a specific purpose). Therefore the four standards assessed via the ILT are:

- Standard 1: defines and articulates the nature and extent of the information needed
- Standard 2: accesses needed information effectively and efficiently
- Standard 3: evaluates information and its sources critically and incorporates selected information into his or her knowledge base and value system
- Standard 5: understands many of the ethical, legal and socio-economic issues surrounding information and information technology.

Results across these four standards (see Figure 10.2) show that the majority of students:

- were able to answer questions concerning defining and articulating the nature and extent of the information needed correctly: ACRL1 (69% correct)
- were not able to answer questions concerning accessing needed information effectively and efficiently correctly: ACRL2 (48% correct)

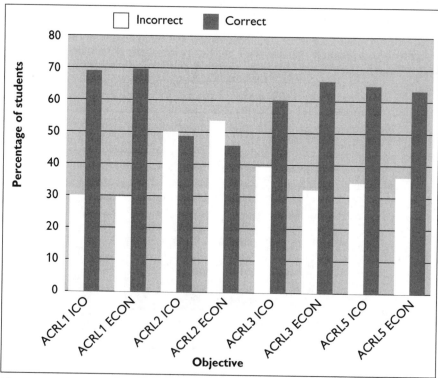

Figure 10.2 *Results for each objective by cohort*

- were able to answer questions concerning evaluating information and its sources critically and were able to incorporate selected information into their knowledge base and value system correctly: ACRL3 (63% correct)
- were able to answer questions concerning understanding many of the ethical, legal and socio-economic issues surrounding information and information technology correctly: ACRL5 (65% correct).

From these results it would seem that the majority of students have little or no difficulty identifying the information they need, are able to evaluate the information and sources, and incorporate the information into their knowledge and understand some of the legal and ethical issues surrounding use of information. Where they struggle is with how they go about accessing that information (see Figure 10.3) – skills which are core to our profession, critical in information literacy and an area where the library can, and does, provide excellent training; and this training can be further directed and targeted by understanding the results of this test.

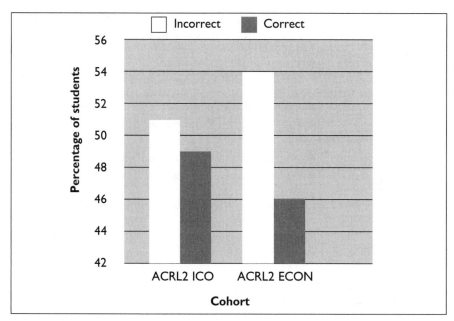

Figure 10.3 *ACRL2: accessing needed information effectively and efficiently*

Areas to target for training

Areas that students had difficulty with, and which therefore needed to be targeted for training, included the following:

Constructing and implementing effectively designed search strategies

Students:

- did not know how to expand searches or apply them to different databases, or how to identify additional relevant items from a citation which had already been retrieved.

Refining the search strategy if necessary

Students did not understand how:

- phrase searching works and what titles would be retrieved when presented with a specific example and possible results
- known item search (journal article) works; they could not identify which strategy would retrieve a specific journal article when presented with a number of different possibilities
- known item search (book chapter) works; they could not identify which strategy would retrieve a specific book chapter when presented with a number of different possibilities
- truncation works and what would be retrieved when presented with a specific example and possible results
- to narrow a search when presented with a number of different possibilities
- to refine a search to suppress irrelevant items when presented with a number of different possibilities
- Boolean operators work and what would be retrieved when presented with a specific example and a range of different possible strategies.

Extracting records and managing the information and its sources

Students could not recognize different item formats from bibliographic search results presented to them from databases. They could not:

- identify the source of an item from its citation description (journal)
- identify the source of an item from its citation description (book)
- identify the source of an item from its citation description (book chapter)
- identify the source of an item from its citation description (newspaper)
- locate the full text of an article from its citation which has a link to 'Full-Text/PDF'.

Following the completion of the tests each student filled in a questionnaire, created and administered as part of a final year ICO student's research project.

The data from these questionnaires will be analysed in due course and will contribute to the analysis of the test outcomes.

We considered issues such as the suitability of the interface, use of multiple-choice format, the time limit we used (we ran the tests during one-hour seminars, with the possibility to 'run over' time if needed), and the level and type of language used in the test. We did not conclude that the impact of any of these factors would contribute to differing performance levels in the test by UK students compared with those from the USA.

These results are our initial findings and further analysis is ongoing. The next round of data collection is expected to take place during autumn 2007, with a further set of tests a year later. This will provide three years of consecutive data sets from the same students as they progress through their undergraduate academic career. The final data collection is expected autumn 2008, with results, plus an overall review of the findings available the following summer.

References

Association of College and Research Libraries (2000) *Information Literacy Competency Standards for Higher Education*.

Andretta, S. (2005) *Information Literacy: a practitioner's guide*, Oxford, Chandos Publishing.

Glass, N. R. (2006) *LearnHigher CETL: information literacy, the LearnHigher Suite at MMU*, LearnHigher, www.learnhigher.mmu.ac.uk/learnhigher-suite/.

Glass, N. R. (2007a) *LearnHigher CETL: information literacy, the project*, LearnHigher, www.learnhigher.mmu.ac.uk/project/.

Glass, N. R. (2007b) *LearnHigher CETL: information literacy, resources*, LearnHigher, www.learnhigher.mmu.ac.uk/resources/.

LearnHigher: Centre for Excellence in Teaching & Learning, www.learnhigher.ac.uk/pages/aims.php.

SCONUL Advisory Committee on Information Literacy (1999) *Information Skills in Higher Education: a SCONUL position paper*.

Smith, R. (2006) *Designing Spaces for Effective Learning: a guide to 21st century learning space design*, JISC, www.jiscinfonet.ac.uk/infokits/learning-space-design.

Wise, S. L. and Yang, S. (2003) *The Adaptex Assessment System (Version 1.5)*, US Department of Education Fund for the Improvement of Postsecondary Education.

Wise, S. L., Cameron, L., Yang, S. and Davis, S. (2005) *Information Literacy Test: test development and administration manual*, Harrisonburg, Institute for Computer-Based Assessment; Center for Assessment & Research Studies, James Madison University.

11

Information skills through electronic environments: considerations, pitfalls and benefits

Maggie Smart and Cath Hunt

Introduction

The increasing availability of resources in electronic format has obvious benefits for distance learners in particular but in order to maximize those benefits library induction and ongoing support are essential. The use of virtual classroom sessions to provide library support to off-campus students is a relatively new concept; however, meeting students live online allows us to provide advice, guidance and training from induction through to completion of their studies. In this chapter, we describe our approach, discussing what has worked and what has been less successful, as well as outlining some of our plans for the future.

Background

Salford is situated in north-west England, less than two miles from Manchester city centre. The University of Salford as we know it today has come together through a complex history of mergers and separations spanning well over 100 years. Throughout this time, it has retained strong links with industry, and partnerships with business, industry and the public sector remain important to Salford's teaching and research activities.

The university has a student population of around 18,000 and a staff of over 2500. Part-time students account for approximately 23% of total student numbers overall but on postgraduate taught programmes part-time students outnumber full-time students.

The Information Services Division (ISD) is responsible for library and information technology services at the University of Salford. The schools (academic departments) at Salford are supported by dedicated ISD liaison teams, who work to ensure that the services ISD provides are appropriate. Liaison officers in these teams are subject or IT specialists who support distance learners alongside the campus-based students in their schools.

Over the past three years, we have worked with the School of the Built Environment to establish a new approach to library support for their internet-enabled MERIT research programme and we have recently extended this work to cover one of the School's taught postgraduate programmes, the MSc Real Estate and Property Management.

MERIT programme

In January 2004, the School of the Built Environment added an internet-enabled, non-residence PhD programme (the MERIT programme) to its portfolio. The programme has truly international reach, with students located in countries around the world, including Ireland, Canada, Saudi Arabia and UAE. At an initial meeting with the MERIT programme leader, before the first cohort of students registered, it was agreed that ISD would deliver two slots in the four-week induction. For this cohort we kept the structure of the ISD sessions exactly as agreed in that first meeting. Since then, as our relationship with the School has developed, we have taken the lead in organizing the sessions as we feel appropriate.

Our use of electronic environments

We deliver our sessions using Wimba Live Classroom in conjunction with Blackboard (Salford's virtual learning environment). e-Library forms an integral part of the library services we offer, providing access to the array of databases and other online information sources both on- and off-campus, and e-mail plays an important role as a supporting means of communication.

Wimba Live Classroom

The live virtual classroom, Wimba Live Classroom, supports audio, application sharing, text chat, polling and content display; with version 5, Live Classroom also offers a number of enhancements, including follow-the-speaker video and emoticons (icons such as smiley faces that act as emotional punctuation marks). Yet despite the array of features available, the requirements for taking part in a Live Classroom session are quite simple. Live Classroom talks about participants (students) and presenters (instructors) and the basic requirements currently specified by Wimba for participants and presenters are shown in Table 11.1.

Table 11.1 *Basic Live Classroom requirements*

Computer with Windows 2000+, Mac OS X 10.2+ or Linux*
* Mac OS9 and Linux have limited features and functionality
128 Mb RAM (256 Mb recommended)
Web browser: IE 5.0+, Netscape 7.0+, Mozilla 1.0+, Safari 1.1+ (browser must be
Java and JavaScript enabled)
Internet access at 56k or above

In addition, headphones or speakers are required to hear the audio and a microphone is required to take part in live conversation. Kirlew (2007), in his paper describing a pilot using Live Classroom at Virginia Commonwealth University Libraries, also discusses system requirements and the results of his evaluation.

Blackboard

Through Blackboard, students can download materials, interact with tutors and fellow students, submit work and check assessment results. All Salford modules have a presence on Blackboard and the modules that make up the MERIT programme are no exception. The extent to which Blackboard is exploited varies and the staff involved in the MERIT programme have worked hard to build a community spirit. As Grasman (2002) noted: 'Communication is the key to a successful internet-based course.' We are both enrolled as instructors on the modules and, alongside the academic staff, we are able to add any material we feel is appropriate. The material we provide on Blackboard complements what we do using Live Classroom and includes interactive tutorials covering information search strategies, Boolean and critical evaluation. We also provide links to user guides and other ISD services. In addition, there is a link to our dedicated e-mail address, which is monitored daily and which students use to contact us for advice and assistance.

e-Library

e-Library provides a single point of entry for accessing electronic (non-print) resources such as e-journals, e-books and databases. Users log in using their Salford network username and password. Useful features include the Multi-Search facility, which allows federated searching, and My Area, which allows users to customize e-Library to suit their particular requirements by saving database sets, searches and results, and to set up alerts. Because users are authenticated by logging in, they can check for any passwords they require to access specific resources.

Live Classroom in use

Drop-out rates in distance education tend to be higher than campus-based courses, possible causes being feelings of isolation and lack of personal attention (Rovai, 2002). The beauty of Live Classroom is that we can talk directly to the students – it allows us to replicate much of what we do with campus-based students who come in to the library for a group literature searching session or one-to-one. It helps to build relationships, to establish us as their point of contact for information support during their programme of study, and to promote use of ISD e-resources.

A typical Live Classroom session

The ISD element of the MERIT induction typically involves two Live Classroom sessions, which we run on separate days. The first session provides an introduction to ISD and e-Library; in the second session we look at selected resources in more detail. We look primarily at the practicalities of locating and accessing appropriate resources and how to get the most out of the search facilities of the various databases. To help us plan suitable content, the School sends us copies of the students' proposals, so that we are aware in advance of their broad areas of research. At the end of the first of the two sessions, we ask the students to log in to e-Library and access one of the databases before our second meeting, to check that their usernames and passwords are working correctly and that they know which password to use for what. Each session is scheduled for 90 minutes but, as with face-to-face sessions, the actual delivery time may vary, depending on the kinds of questions the students ask, how promptly they log in and whether any of them have technical problems.

One of the key aims of the Live Classroom sessions is to try to give the students the confidence to explore the resources at their disposal, in the knowledge that library support is available throughout their programme of study. We archive the sessions for students who were unable to log in, so that they can see and hear everything that was covered, although they cannot interact.

Factors influencing a session

We have found that many of the factors influencing a Live Classroom session are similar to those we would take into account in planning a face-to-face information skills session.

- Timing: MERIT students may be based anywhere around the world, in different time zones, so co-ordination and forward planning are important;

religious observances must also be taken into account. For UK-based students on the MSc Real Estate & Property Management programme, timing is equally important, as the majority of them work full-time, so evening sessions are essential.

- Location: it is important to have a room that is quiet (to avoid distracting background noise) and where sessions can be delivered without interruptions. We have also found it useful to have a telephone available, either to speak to the School's technical support officer or, on rare occasions, to contact a student directly.

- Content: the MERIT programme usually consists of small groups of students and, having previously seen their proposals, we can tailor the content of the sessions accordingly. With the MSc group, because of the potentially much larger numbers of students, the content has to be much more generic, with the emphasis on the range of sources available. We do, however, know that a law module forms part of the MSc programme, so we can include a demonstration of the Lawtel UK database for this group.

- The majority of students on the MERIT programme are based overseas, whereas the MSc students are UK based. This means that, with the MSc group, we can publicize and encourage them to use our document supply service and make them aware of additional facilities at their disposal such as the UK Libraries Plus scheme. The MERIT students all have a local adviser in addition to their Salford supervisor and this means they have access to advice about what might be accessible locally.

- Technical competence: students vary widely in levels of confidence and competence in using the Live Classroom system; for us, the School's technical support officer is generally on hand to resolve individual problems in the background as we continue to deliver a session. On occasion, if a student seemed to be having difficulty, we have found it useful to split a single 90-minute session into two shorter sessions.

Managing the technology

As with equipment in a lecture theatre, using Live Classroom in an effective way depends on becoming familiar and confident with the system. There is documentation available from Wimba, and the Wimba User Group is another source of support. Live Classroom provides a Setup Wizard which helps to identify many potential problems that might interfere with a session, and so it is important that both presenters and participants run this before logging in. At present we use only a subset of the features that are actually available in Live Classroom, focusing on the content frame to share PowerPoint slides, application sharing for the resource demonstrations, text chat and, of course, audio, so that we can converse with the students. The 'lock talk' feature ensures that our presenters' microphone is locked on, leaving our hands free to use the keyboard and mouse for the demonstrations.

On a practical level, one of the things we do when delivering a session is to have a laptop logged in via our wireless network to help us with timing. Screen refresh is not always instantaneous and this acts as an indicator of what the students might see on a slower connection – therefore helping us to pace each session appropriately. For the resource demonstrations, we open a new window rather than using the content frame in Live Classroom, so that as much of the screen as possible is visible without having to scroll up and down.

Teaching and learning styles and fostering interaction

We use a combination of demonstration and commentary, which should appeal to both auditory and visual learners, and we try, with varying degrees of success, to involve the students by asking them to suggest their own search terms and topics in addition to the ones we have prepared. We also encourage them to ask questions at regular intervals throughout the sessions, and these tend to vary between enquiries about database functionality to questions about their research topics. The fact that the questions are asked via Live Classroom rather than e-mail means that all the other participating students can benefit as well.

We have found that two presenters are far more effective than one, as the change of voice and pace helps to maintain interest. We also use a boundary microphone, which eliminates the need for individual microphones and helps to bring a conversational element to the session. Although these may seem very simple factors, they make a huge difference to the tone and quality of a session. As Ronayne and Rogenmoser (2002) found when using interactive television for library instruction: 'Just having both librarians up front together immediately raised the energy level and created a more dynamic classroom climate. Interaction with students increased . . . .'

Many students prefer to learn through practical experience, so we encourage them to try out at least one of the databases in their own time between sessions and we remind them to use the interactive tutorials on Blackboard. The archives of the sessions are useful not only for students who were unable to attend the live session, but as a 'refresher', particularly helpful for international students whose first language is not English.

Managing interpersonal issues

As with any kind of group instruction, it is possible that problems may arise if, for example, the input of a particularly dominant student starts to have a negative impact on the other participants. The groups we work with at present are generally small and comprise postgraduate students who are highly motivated and professional. So far we have not encountered major problems but the fact that we co-present the sessions means that one of us could deal with an issue individually while the other continued to deliver the session. In effect, the same strategies we use in a face-to-face session can be applied to the virtual classroom – first by trying to incorporate the comments or questions, then taking the individual student aside by using the text chat frame and, finally, dealing with matters outside the classroom if necessary.

Is the virtual classroom worth the effort?

Using Live Classroom has required investment from the School in hardware and technical support, and changes and challenges for the academic staff and for us in adapting to a new way of teaching and learning. Having worked with the system for over three years, we can now step back and begin to assess whether that investment has been worthwhile.

Distance learners, whether they are separated from the institution by time or distance, pay significant sums of money to undertake their studies. As they are studying to the same level and for the same qualifications as traditional campus-based students, they require and are entitled to equivalent library resources and support. The Live Classroom sessions go some way towards redressing the balance between what is offered to on-campus students (the full range of services and resources including group and one-to-one help from their liaison officer) and distance learners who are unable to visit the university in person.

Feedback and evaluation

Clayton (2004) highlights the importance of formal evaluation in order to collect and collate students' views on the usefulness of the training they received. When we first started delivering sessions on the MERIT programme we relied on feedback from the programme staff and, quite early on, had a formal review meeting with the programme director. After that meeting, we set about trying to carry out more formal evaluation, looking not just at immediate comments after the session but also trying to evaluate the longer term impact – have the students continued to use the e-resources and, if not, why not? We have tried several approaches, including short e-mail questionnaires and, more recently, an online evaluation form with a link from Blackboard, but without success. One reason for this may be the lack of time for reflection and the inbuilt reluctance that we feel ourselves in similar situations, but we are determined to persevere and our future plans include devising new approaches to evaluation.

On the other hand, spontaneous feedback from the students has been extremely positive and this has come to us directly and also via the School staff (both academic and technical). Partly as a result of the students' comments after our recent sessions for the MSc Real Estate & Property Management, ISD sessions will form an integrated part of that programme from the start of the new academic year.

In our experience the benefits of using Live Classroom far outweigh the limitations. As well as introducing the students to the resources they will need and building the relationships that mean they know where to come for assistance, the sessions have also helped to raise awareness of the wide range of library resources among staff in the School.

Future directions

We have a number of plans for the future, ranging from exploration of new features in Live Classroom to establishing our own dedicated space in the library for development work and delivering sessions.

- We would be interested to investigate closer integration of Live Classroom into Blackboard. Currently the two operate separately at Salford but are used to complement each other.
- We intend to evaluate some of the features that we have not yet used, including those that are new in Live Classroom 5: for example, follow-the-speaker video, which is voice-activated and automatically displays the image of the current speaker. This allows instructors and students alike to put faces to names and might help to provide a more direct indication of student engagement.
- We aim to follow up different approaches to evaluation. For example, students will be able to give feedback during live sessions using the emoticons – could we make use of this feature for evaluation purposes? We are also considering allowing time towards the end of sessions for students to complete the online evaluation, while bearing in mind the importance of time for reflection.
- Irrespective of whether you are delivering an online or face-to-face session, it can be easy to deter students by off-the-cuff searches that yield either no results or thousands of results that seem only vaguely relevant. Set against this are the benefits of spontaneous interaction and using that spontaneity as part of the learning process: not everything works first time and the answer lies in learning how to refine a search, rather than giving up. So one of our resolutions is to be bolder and turn the things that don't quite work into a learning experience.
- Since we embarked on Live Classroom, we have delivered our sessions from several different rooms in the library. We are now optimistic that we can justify investment in a dedicated room that will provide a fixed base for delivering

sessions and also a space where we can experiment and work with colleagues to develop new approaches – in particular finding new ways of making the sessions more interactive.

- We plan to offer more regular updates, keeping students informed about changes to the services we provide (e.g. new databases, new journals, changes to access methods). However, we are aware of the need to do this efficiently while taking into account the many other demands on our time.

For us, delivering live virtual classroom sessions has opened up new possibilities by extending the ways in which we can support Salford students, wherever they are located. We are confident that other groups of students could benefit and there is considerable enthusiasm amongst our colleagues to find out more about Live Classroom. We have learned a lot in the course of our work over the past three and a half years – and we are looking forward to doing and learning more.

References

Clayton, S. (2004) Your Class Meets Where? Library instruction for business and education graduate students at off-campus centers, *Reference Services Review*, **32** (4), 388–93.

Grasman, S. E. (2002) Teaching Engineering Economics via Distance Education. In *Proceedings of the 2002 American Society for Engineering Education Annual Conference & Exposition*, 5935–9.

Kirlew, P. (2007) *Enhancing Synchronous Online Library Instruction Services in Blackboard Using the Wimba Live Classroom System*. Special Libraries Association, www.sla.org/pdfs/sla2007/kirlewonlinelibinstrsvcs.pdf.

Ronayne, B. and Rogenmoser, D. (2002) Library Research Instruction for Distance Learners: an interactive, multimedia approach. In Brophy, P., Fisher, S. and Clarke, Z., *Libraries Without Walls 4: the delivery of library services to distant users: proceedings of an international conference held on 17–18 September 2001 by CERLIM*, Facet Publishing, 187–96.

Rovai, A. (2002) Building Sense of Community at a Distance, *International Review of Research in Open and Distance Learning*, **3** (1), 74–85.

12

Development of information-related competencies in European open and distance learning institutions: selected findings

Sirje Virkus

Introduction

While information-related competencies (IRCs) are generally perceived as an essential set of competencies of the knowledge society, understood in its broader sense, they have made little progress educationally (Correia and Teixeira, 2003). Several studies and reports have shown that many students lack IRCs and have highlighted the importance of and need to develop these competencies (e.g. Oberman, 1991; Ray and Day, 1998; Stern, 2003; UNESCO, 2006). Johnston and Webber (2003, 338) note that even in the USA, 'while much attention has been paid to information literacy by American policy-makers, librarians and academics, the results are still relatively narrow, giving a potentially superficial guide to the nature of a curriculum for information literacy in higher education'. Bruce and Lampson (2002) also argue that despite some progress over the past decade, library and information professionals still report that universal information literacy (IL) is a distant, if not a receding, goal.

This paper gives an overview and reports some of the selected findings of a research project on the development of IRCs within open and distance learning (ODL) universities in Europe. This research project grew out of the author's curiosity about why progress in developing IRCs has been so modest. It was believed that a better understanding of what academics, senior managers, librarians and students are thinking and doing would help better to engage them in effective development of IRCs. The paper is divided into four parts. The first provides a working definition of the concept of IRCs. The second describes the methodology of the study. The third presents the findings of the survey and the fourth reports findings of the case studies. Because of the space limits of this publication only selected findings are presented in this paper.

A working definition of information-related competencies

Focusing on her research on the higher education (HE) sector in Europe, the author prefers to use the term 'information-related competencies' instead of IL in this study. The reasons for using the former term is the conviction that the concept of IL is very elusive, its essence is hard to grasp, and its meaning is not always clear in a European HE environment. It was believed that the concept of competencies is more familiar and better understood among academic staff, students and senior managers in European HE settings. In addition, the concept of IRCs allows differentiation between several blocks of competencies related to information handling and use; for example, identifying, locating, gathering, selecting, storing, recording, retrieving and processing information from a variety of sources and media; developing successful information-seeking and retrieval strategies; mastering complex and multiple information systems; organizing, analysing, interpreting, evaluating, synthesizing, and using information; and presenting and communicating information clearly, logically, concisely and accurately. Thus, it might be easier to perceive how to integrate or embed different competencies or blocks of competencies into the learning process at different educational levels and thereby facilitate the development of these competencies (Virkus, 2003). IRCs in this study are defined as the skills, knowledge, attitudes, experience, attributes, and behaviour that an individual needs to find, evaluate and use information effectively (Virkus, 2006).

Methodology

The findings reported in this paper form a part of a doctoral study that aimed to investigate the ways in which IRCs are being developed within European higher ODL institutions. The general research strategy in this study was a mixed method research strategy, using both qualitative and quantitative methodologies, built into a two-stage research design. A survey provided a broad picture of a phenomenon, and case studies covered a more limited area of the same ground but in more depth. The first stage was a small-scale questionnaire survey carried out in 2003. The objectives of the questionnaire were to determine the extent and the ways to which IRCs were developed within European higher ODL institutions and to investigate the role of libraries within the development of IRCs. The results of the survey helped to identify institutions displaying good practice, issues and actors for the next stage of the study.

The second stage of the study involved a multiple case study in six European ODL institutions, where in-depth, semi-structured, tape-recorded interviews with 72 people were conducted. Site visits, documentary analysis and interviews were conducted during the period August 2003 to October 2004 in the six universities. In each institution, all of which had been identified as an examples of good practice, representatives from four groups of actors, namely 4–5 distance learning students, 3–5 faculty members, 2–5 librarians and 1–2 senior managers, were interviewed. All interviews were conducted in English, except one interview when the researcher had to switch to the local language, of which she had sufficient knowledge to conduct the interview.

Selected findings: survey

It was decided to focus only on the member institutions of the European Association of Distance Teaching Universities (EADTU). EADTU, established in 1988, has a long-standing reputation in the field of ODL and it is the important voice of the HE community for ODL in Europe. EADTU member institutions represent the most active and innovative actors in the field of ODL in Europe. It was believed that those institutions innovative in ODL are probably contributing actively towards IRC building as well and that there are cases of 'good practice' within EADTU member institutions from which the researcher would be able to learn most. Thus, all institutions offering ODL in Europe were the population and all member institutions of EADTU were the sample in the survey at the first stage of this study.

A questionnaire was designed on the basis of research questions and the literature review. The questionnaire consisted of six sections: policy, curriculum, research, higher degree supervision, academic development partnership and data about the institution. An e-mail questionnaire was distributed to all EADTU member institutions in Europe in March 2003 (156 conventional universities and 7 open universities). In total, 71 respondents from 16 countries submitted responses to the questionnaire. This gave the survey a total response rate of 43.6 %.

Institutional policy

Of the survey respondents, 38 (54%) declared that they have policy documents in their institutions that emphasize the need to focus on IRCs in curricula or in student learning; 23 (32%) indicated neither any form of institution-wide IRC strategy nor any initiative under development; 9 (13%) were not aware if there were such kinds of policy documents; and one respondent did not answer that question. It was noted that policy documents included such items as IL plans and lists of graduate attributes or 'qualities of graduates' and strategic plans in teaching and learning that emphasize the integration of problem-based learning and resource-based learning into the curriculum.

Additionally, 28 (39%) of the respondents answered that library staff belong to the educational committees that make decisions about curricula and learning; 35 (49%) indicated that existing procedures for review of curriculum design in their institution require the incorporation of ideas about IL development into the curriculum.

Integration of IRCs into the curriculum

Fifty (70%) respondents referred to collaboration between librarians and the faculties to integrate IL into the curriculum and 32 (45%) indicated that librarians were working closely with faculty on planning learning. In one institution librarians were always involved in developing courses. In three institutions they always provided online tutorial support, assessment and evaluation and in 15 institutions they always assisted students in the preparation of their literature reviews. In 10 institutions they always assisted students in the preparation of their assessed work and in two institutions librarians were always involved in product development, such as websites for courses and subjects. In five institutions they were always involved in the development of self-paced IL modules and in eight institutions they always developed web materials for students and staff. The extent of librarians' involvement in learning is detailed in Table 12.1.

Table 12.1 *Librarians' involvement in learning (%)*

	Always	Sometimes
Developing courses	1	68
Providing online tutorial support, assessment and evaluation	4	56
Assisting students in the preparation of their literature reviews	21	66
Assisting students in the preparation of their assessed work	14	68
Developing websites for courses/subjects	3	59
Self-paced 'IL' modules	7	51
Web-based learning materials that may be used by staff and students	11	63

The instruction or advice given to students on finding information to support their course work mainly included a brief tour of the library (38 institutions), handout and/or map (33), verbal instructions from tutors or staff (32), section in a student handbook (25), lecture or seminar especially devoted to these topics (17), course or series of lectures devoted to these topics (6), phased programme of detailed induction by staff (5) and several lectures/seminars on using the facilities (4). See Table 12.2.

In 14 institutions (20%) students earned credits for a unit or component on IL during their studies on a cross-disciplinary basis and in 34 institutions (48%) as part of a discipline-specific course. 18 institutions (25%) indicated that there were also other programmes that foster IL or a range of generic attributes including IL.

Table 12.2 *Integration of IRCs into the curriculum (%)*

	Always
A brief tour of the library	54
A handout and/or map	47
Verbal instructions from tutors or staff	45
A section in a student handbook	35
A lecture/seminar devoted to these topics	24
A course or series of lectures devoted to these topics	9
A phased programme of detailed induction by staff	7
Several lectures/seminars on using the facilities	6

Research

Thirty-two (45%) institutions were involved in IL research. However, in 21 (30%) the academic staff and in 17 (24%) librarians were involved in IL research. A partnership of librarians and academic staff in the area of IL research was mentioned in 4 (6%) institutions, but 34 (48%) indicated that such kinds of partnership can sometimes be found.

Higher degree supervision

Librarians and academic staff shared expertise and responsibility for helping students through the phases of higher degree research in 27 (38%) institutions. Librarians acted as co-supervisors ensuring that literature reviews were relevant in 15 (21%) institutions, kept supervisors and students up to date with information resources and services in 47 (66%) institutions and participated in the preparation of literature reviews and research proposals in 19 (27%) institutions.

Academic development partnership

In 36 (51%) institutions workshops and other activities were arranged to introduce academic staff to the idea of IL education. Additionally, 44 institutions (62%) indicated that there had been several workshops or other activities aiming to introduce faculty members to the idea of IL education during the previous 12 months.

Selected findings: case studies

The majority of questions in the case study interviews were aimed at gaining an understanding of respondents' views, attitudes, beliefs and behaviour related to the development of IRCs. The interviews covered the same thematic areas as the survey: policy, integration of IRCs into the curriculum, the role of the library in supervision, staff development and research. This section focuses only some of these themes, namely the respondents' views on the integration of IRCs into the curriculum, the existence of IRCs among students and staff, the concept of IL, the assessment of IRCs and the role of the library in IRC development.

Integration of information-related competencies into curriculum

It was quite obvious that the integration of IRCs into learning was in the early stages in all institutions where good practice had been identified in the period 2003/4. The main reasons for this were a lack of understanding or knowledge among teachers about how to integrate IRCs into learning, a lack of good and convincing examples of IRC development, a lack of human resources and time, high workload of academics and librarians, few enthusiastic leaders and a lack of a positive attitude toward IRC integration.

Some universities mentioned the modular nature of the programmes as a barrier to integrating IRCs. Another reason was that universities usually provide students with all the resources they require and therefore there was not always a need to find information independently. Pressure on students' and tutors' time and effort was also mentioned as a reason for not supporting independent information-seeking behaviour.

Lack of information-related competencies

The fact that many students do not possess IRCs and are not able to use and apply those skills when required was highlighted. A senior manager said: '. . . when they write essays, it's clear that the ability to make use of information services is not very well developed, it is not so [well] developed as we would expect.'

University managers also indicated the lack of IRCs among staff: 'I can't say that we would have a situation which is sufficiently good or we can be satisfied with the information literacy skills of our students or our staff members.'

A librarian said: 'We found out that a lot of teachers themselves don't have information competencies, they need this kind of information literacy them-selves . . . .'

The concept of 'information literacy'

The nature of the concept of IL was accepted and appreciated among students, academics, senior managers and librarians, but the term itself created confusion and was not sufficiently understandable. For example, a senior manager notes: 'It's [IL] too broad and at the same time it's not telling you very much when it wants to incorporate everything from getting or having an information problem to solving it and presenting the results to the outside world.'

An academic staff member indicates: 'Probably they don't talk and probably even don't think about it as information literacy. But they do see a range of skills – what we probably recognize as information literacy skills, important to learning . . . .'

A faculty member says: 'The first time I heard of it was four years ago, when two consultants from the library held a presentation. I remember I thought – hmmm, they do have a word for these things . . . .'

Neither was the term very familiar among students. A student notes: 'It is not an expression I would use in everyday language. When telling people about my course [recently taken IL course] I would just say it was learning to use the internet properly and search for information about a particular subject.'

Assessment of information-related competencies

Students' IRCs were, according to those interviewed, mainly assessed via essays, project work and theses. Nobody indicated a good mechanism which would show if the student is information literate or has attained IRCs. A senior manager notes: 'We have so many other dimensions on which we have to assess students, if you like, that I can't image that . . . information literacy is ever going to be the leading edge of a course assessment.'

A student indicates: 'Well, to be honest, it was slightly disappointing, I mean they gave you some tick boxes, we worked with tick boxes . . . and they rated you, I think out of three . . . achieved, well achieved . . . or something like that . . . .'

Role of the library in IRC development

Several respondents highlighted dramatic changes in libraries during the last decade and the increasing role of a university library. The discussion about changes in libraries focused most frequently on information and communication technology developments and the implications of information in digital formats. The role of the librarian, staff development initiatives and good contacts with librarians in their own institutions were highlighted. However, the general attitude towards librarians was not so positive and the need for a more proactive librarian was highlighted.

University managers and academic staff also expressed a concern that there is a lack of pedagogical skills among librarians in general, and in the context of ODL in particularly. The online learning environment requires new competencies and attitudes among librarians about the design and development of learning materials and how to support learners online. For example, in online courses with an IRC component the majority of students needed more interaction, a more research-based approach, personalized tasks and feedback from librarians. For example: 'I was rather disappointed with that [discussion forum] also because it was supposed to be students . . . you know, exchanging ideas and things about the course and trying, I suppose, to simulate what would you get if you work doing things face to face and it didn't really . . . .' Another view: 'The course seems to me not to have understood why somebody would want to be doing research, the model that they had of learning was "the knowledge is out there, all you have to do is to go and hunt for it". This is a librarian's view of the world, it's not the researcher's view of the world . . . .'

It should be said that distance students didn't visit the library very frequently. Several students noted that they contacted library staff only when there were serious difficulties in finding basic data, problems in accessing online resources or in cases of technical difficulties. The physical library environment was not always very encouraging (Virkus, 2006).

Conclusions

To map the extent of integration of IRCs into the European ODL, a survey was designed and delivered as an e-mail questionnaire to 163 EADTU member institutions in March 2003. Seventy-one respondents from 16 European countries submitted responses to the questionnaire, a total response rate of 43.6%. The respondents all reported some form of strategy for IRCs or were in the process of developing one. They referred to IRC initiatives at institutional policy level as well as at curriculum level and academic–librarian partnerships were indicated in the field of teaching, supervision, research and academic development. Librarians were to a certain extent involved in developing courses, providing online tutorial support, assessment and evaluation, assisting students in the preparation of their literature reviews and assessed work. Some of them were also involved in developing websites for courses and subjects, self-paced IL modules and web-based learning materials for staff and students. However, the number of institutions where librarians were always involved in these activities was much smaller than the number of institutions where they were sometimes involved. A brief tour of the library, a handout and/or map, verbal instructions from tutors or staff and a section in a student handbook were the most frequently mentioned ways of instruction or advice given students on finding information to support their studies. However, a lecture or seminar especially devoted to these topics, several lectures/seminars on using the facilities, a phased programme of detailed induction by staff, and a course or series of lectures devoted to these topics, were mentioned as well.

Many institutions referred to IL partnerships between academic staff and librarians supporting research and supervision. Several workshops and other activities were also arranged to introduce academics to the idea of IL.

72 interviews were conducted in the period August 2003 to October 2004. Case study interviews indicated that the importance of IRCs is acknowledged in European ODL institutions, but the term IL is not always clear and widely used. IRC development was at the early stages in all institutions where good practice had been identified in the period of the study. It was believed that students and staff do not possess adequate IRCs. Academic staff delivered some of these IRCs in their courses in collaboration with librarians, but there wasn't a solid enough framework for thinking about how students develop these competencies, how these are recorded, and of how students are made more aware of their IRC development and given a range of opportunities to develop those competencies. The main obstacles were a lack of awareness among teachers, lack of good and convincing examples of IRC development, lack of human resources and time, high workload of faculty and librarians, the modular nature of the programmes, the habits of providing the students with all the resources they need and difficulties in terms of pressure on students' and tutors' time and efforts. The role of the university library and good contacts with librarians within their own institutions were highlighted, but the general attitude towards librarians was not so positive. However, IRC initiatives in European ODL are quite fragmented and further exploration is needed.

References

Bruce, H. and Lampson, M. (2002) Information Professionals as Agents for Information Literacy, *Education for Information*, **20** (2), 81–107.

Correia, A. M. R. and Teixeira, J. C. (2003) Information Literacy: an integrated concept for a safer internet, *Online Information Review*, **27** (5), 311–20.

Johnston, B. and Webber, S. (2003) Information Literacy in Higher Education: a review and case study, *Studies in Higher Education*, **28** (3), 335–52.

Oberman, C. (1991) Avoiding the Cereals Syndrome, or Critical Thinking in the Electronic Environment, *Library Trends*, **39** (3), 189–202.

Ray, K. and Day, J. (1998) Student Attitudes Towards Electronic Resources, *Information Research*, **4** (2), www.shef.ac.uk/is/publications/infres/paper54.html.

Stern, C. (2003) Measuring Students' Information Literacy Competency. In Martin, A. and Rader, H. (eds), *Information and IT Literacy: enabling learning in the 21st century*, Facet Publishing, 112–19.

UNESCO (2006) High-Level Colloquium on Information Literacy and Lifelong Learning, Bibliotheca Alexandrina, Alexandria, Egypt, November 6–9, 2005: Report of a Meeting Sponsored by the United Nations Education, Scientific, and Cultural Organization (UNESCO), National Forum on Information Literacy (NFIL) and the International Federation of Library Associations and Institutions (IFLA).

Virkus, S. (2003) Information Literacy in Europe: a literature review, *Information Research*, **8** (4), http://informationr.net/ir/8-4/paper159.html.

Virkus, S. (2006) Development of Information-related Competencies in European ODL Institutions: senior managers' view, *New Library World*, **107** (11/12), 467–81.

13

Improving information retrieval with dialogue mapping and concept mapping tools

Virpi Palmgren, Kirsi Heino and Jouni Nevalainen

Introduction

Development of education practices and new education methods are increasingly important in Finnish universities. There is pressure because of internationalization and quality targets with no extra funding are to be expected. This can also be seen in training organized by the library.

The Library of Helsinki University of Technology (TKK) has almost 40 years' experience in teaching information retrieval. In these years several course models have been used and thousands of students have participated in the training (Palmgren and Heino, 2002, 197–207). The Bologna process (named after the University of Bologna, where the Bologna declaration was signed in 1999) aims to create a European higher education area by 2010, making academic degree standards and quality assurance standards more comparable and compatible throughout Europe. This has changed the situation at TKK and new courses have had to be planned. The library now has its own part in the student's seminar programme, where instruction has been planned to ease the writing of the thesis; for example, students undertake an exercise to search for information on the topic of their thesis. Library training reaches all students twice: at the beginning of the studies and then at the thesis writing phase.

Because the groups are large and the time to be used is limited, learning environments and other methods to ease tuition are being used. There is also less room for face-to-face teaching in the schedule (Heino and Palmgren, 2006).

In order to reach the goal of information literacy, students have to apply the basic skills they have learned in the library courses to their actual studies. TKK teachers are in a vital position, and so new training for teachers has actively been planned as a part of their pedagogical training. The new course presented in this paper combines different competences and allows for co-operation between different fields of knowledge within the university.

Mapping methods are being used for structuring the information search. Maps are known to be a good method for outlining things in general; however, piecing together information-searching exercises is difficult. When students receive the topic for their thesis they are often lost; they do not know about the topic, or how to search for information. Also, researchers need to familiarize themselves with their topic in order to make a thorough search. With the help of mapping software it is easier to analyse the topic and to choose relevant search terms and structures. At the same time the researcher's knowledge of the topic deepens. With the help of the maps, the information search is connected with the writing process, which is usually the ultimate objective.

Course arrangements

Mapping software details

The mapping software used on the course is freely available from the web and the course participants liked the idea of using free software. It is not fair to demand that course participants buy commercial software for only one course, although in the business world the use of commercial software is more understandable. To provide this software for students, it was agreed with the Computer Centre that the software could be included in the program packages installed on all computers in the computer rooms at TKK.

Mind maps are the best known, simplest and most used mapping method. FreeMind mapping software (http://freemind.sourceforge.net/wiki/index.php/Main_Page) was used for the course. It was used to plan the course and to present it to the course participants (see Figure 13.1). Mind maps have a major advantage compared with, for example, PowerPoint slides, which can only show a fraction of the topic at a time. However, mind mapping does not transform and improve the content of thinking in a similar manner to the more structured notations of dialogue mapping or concept mapping; the latter focus on essential building blocks of thinking, such as concepts, relations, questions and arguments (Nuutila and Törmä, 2007).

CmapTools software (http://cmap.ihmc.us/) is intended for making concept maps and Compendium software (http://compendiuminstitute.org/) for dialogue maps, which are used to help structure the search process. The aim is a dynamic search and structuring process with the help of the mapping software.

Concept maps enable identifying, widening and defining search terms which can be used in the search. At the same time the concept map outlines the relationship between different concepts related to the topic. It is possible to

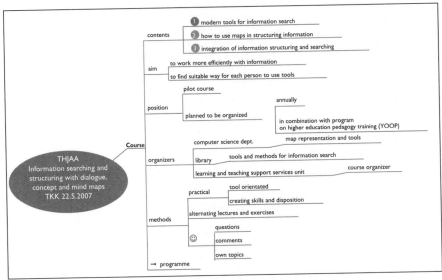

Figure 13.1 *Example of presenting the course programme by using a mind map*

define relevant broader and narrower concepts, partial and comprehensive concepts, other near concepts and synonyms. Course participants did some exercises where they analysed texts by choosing the relevant concepts and created relationships between them (see Figure 13.2).

With the help of dialogue maps it is possible to present questions, answers and solutions. They are suited for planning, problem-solving and knowledge creation. Information searching can be started by forming a question of the topic and finding answers and identifying useful ideas. It is also possible to develop critical questions concerning the information search (see Figure 13.3). Open rather than closed questions are used in dialogue maps. For example the question 'Is the project ready?' could be replaced with a question 'What are the deficiencies in the project?'

Course participants were advised to take their own laptops with them to the course so that they could start working at once. Maps are seldom completed during one session, as ideas may appear at random times. Attendees used laptops and WLAN when searching for information. They were, however, advised not to take laptops with them when doing the group work, in order to make it easier for them to concentrate on the actual group work.

The language issue

In concept maps, the sentence structures are split into two knots and the relationship between them. This is problematic when using the Finnish language

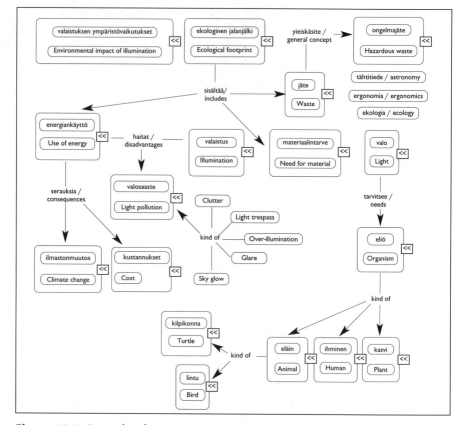

Figure 13.2 *Example of using a concept map for outlining search terms*

because of its complicated structure. Instead, English is much more suitable and adaptable for this purpose. English is used to a large extent in Finnish academia for both study and research. Today, the publication of key literature, and to an increasing extent teaching, is also in English. This is why many exercises were done in English. Finnish terms were translated into English and used in parallel with the English ones. See Figure 13.2 for an example.

Information retrieval

It is recommended on library courses to keep search diaries because often, when a researcher wants to continue an earlier search, its structure has been forgotten. Mapping software can be used for keeping a search diary. One can write down the search terms used and also make links to the search results, which is especially useful, as it helps to clarify the topic of the search. However, further development is yet to be done on this functionality, as the different programs cannot be completely integrated.

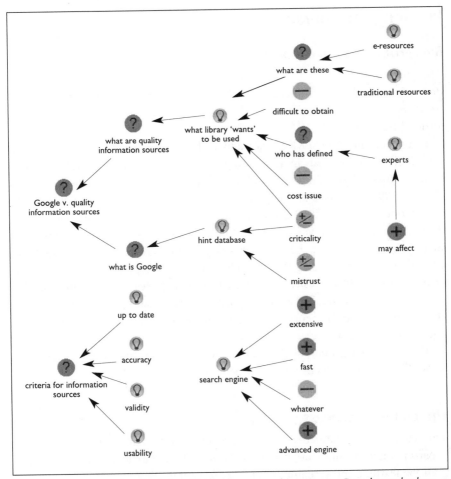

Figure 13.3 *Example of using a dialogue map: when to use Google and when to use quality information sources?*

Future challenges

The course held was the first pilot version and there is still a long way to go; a lot of questions need to be answered before these methods are in full use, for example:

- how to find teachers who are interested, motivated and have time for learning and applying these new methods
- how to find information search topics which are easy enough and suitable for everybody
- what kind of courses this method suits best
- about funding.

Planning the course

Background: a novel course

The library decided to start new courses aimed at TKK teachers as a part of the Programme on Higher Education Pedagogy Training (YOOP). This way the students would be the ones to get the final benefit from the extra information retrieval training.

During autumn 2006 TKK Library and TKK Department of Computer Science and Engineering started an interesting co-operative exercise (THJAA). New software for making mind maps (Margulies and Maal, 2002), concept maps (Novak, 1998) and dialogue maps (Conklin, 2006) will be used for structuring information retrieval. These methods have been taught on separate courses but there was a need for topics that would be of relevance to all. More information about these courses can be found at course sites created by the innovative education developers Esko Nuutila (Dr Tech.) and Seppo Törmä (Dr Tech.) http://tge.cs.hut.fi/Courses/KartatYOOP2007/. This project got a warm reception from the university because it can be adapted throughout the university and will benefit several departments. Teachers can also update their knowledge of information searching.

The chart in Figure 13.4 represents the channels of information training at TKK. This paper will focus on the left side of the map.

The planning process

The course was planned by two researchers from the computer science department, three information specialists from the library and a planning officer from the learning and teaching support services unit.

The course had to be planned so that the creativity of the course participants would be encouraged. This way the library training and the library teachers would develop and get new perspectives and ideas. The library staff have a certain way of thinking, and new views from the field can be very useful. Therefore model answers for the questions were not given out on the course, in order to encourage different ways of thinking; all unexpected answers were eagerly received. Naturally the exercises had been tested beforehand by staff to see what kinds of questions were best for the purpose. The use of the programs was easy, but analysing the topic was more complicated and took time. However, after the problem had been presented with the charts it seemed quite simple.

Free mind map software FreeMind was used for planning the course. During the intensive phase of the planning one-hour meetings were held once a week.

The members of the course planning group familiarized themselves with each

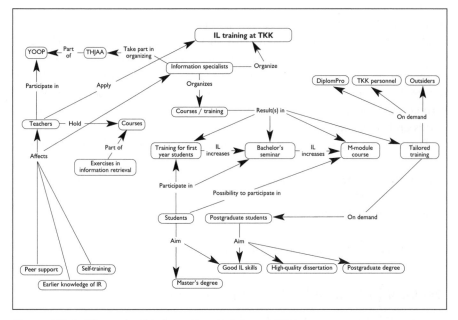

Figure 13.4 *Channels of information training at TKK*

others' fields of expertise; the computer experts studied the theory of information searching and the library staff made mind maps. It was necessary to select the best mapping software for different kind of tasks. It was not easy to know beforehand which would be the best choice. By trial and error it was soon possible to choose the best program for every task.

TKK was the first university in Finland to combine mapping techniques with information retrieval. In the beginning of the information search it is usual to face difficulties in understanding the topic and defining the need of information. The use of mapping methods combined with information search has also been of interest to other Finnish educational institutions (Kämäräinen, 2007).

The course

Participants

The course was aimed at teachers of the university. The interaction between teachers and the library is even more important after the changes caused by the Bologna process. The course was marketed especially to the TKK teachers who are undertaking pedagogic studies, who are actively interested in new teaching methods and who perform related teaching experiments.

Teachers are required to give information-searching assignments in their own courses where the application of basic searching skills would be directly connected to actual study. The teachers may have an insufficient knowledge of changing information retrieval methods or lack the experience necessary for applying them on the courses. Therefore the improvement of the information-searching skills of the teachers is a beneficial by-product of the new course discussed here. Almost without exception, teachers do their own research where they can take advantage of this update of their knowledge.

Teachers can use the mapping methods and information retrieval skills for:

- an analysis of the core substance in their own course material, for their own use
- use by students for exercises
- use as training materials.

Twelve people signed up and participated on the course.

The level of knowledge before the course

The course participants had to fill in a questionnaire about their experience and knowledge in information searching, library services and mapping software. The questionnaire also included links to extra information. The idea was that a certain level of knowledge would be guaranteed and no basic skills training would be needed.

The course participants were well aware of the essential information resources in their own field of study. It was noteworthy that young teachers were familiar with open access but it was quite surprising to discover their lack of knowledge in basic library services. The questionnaire was important in order to identify a level of knowledge before the course. Information-searching skills are important for teachers because students have already been taught these on the library courses. The questionnaire needs to be conducted in good time prior to the course, so that the results can be utilized in the planning of the course.

Conducting the course

The course was positioned at the end of May in order to get more teachers to participate. Other courses and exams had just ended and summer vacations not yet started. The course ran on four days: Tuesdays and Thursdays during two consecutive weeks. During the first course day, only the mapping software was presented. The library was responsible for the second course day and the topic covered was the basics of information retrieval. The responsibility for the two last course days was shared by the organizing parties. During these days, searches were undertaken and mapping software was used to help to define the search problem.

Because the days were so near to each other it was not possible to do any homework between the course days. This made the course very intensive, the active daily working time being about six hours.

There were five teachers working on this pilot course: two who knew mapping software and gave instruction on its use and three information specialists from the library. The size of the group (12 people) was ideal, as there were enough people for the discussions, yet everybody had an opportunity to give her/his opinion on the topic which was being dealt with.

The training sessions comprised a short lecture, lasting about half an hour and possibly also a demonstration on the topic which was followed by training in groups or pairs. Some of the exercises seemed to be too difficult, because the course participants did not yet know enough about the mapping software. The original idea was that in the beginning exercises should have been easy, i.e. hands-on. The exercises also had to be such that everybody was familiar with the topic (studying, university, information searching, etc.). The course participants were from different departments. Information specialists participated in the group and pair exercises when it was not their turn to lecture.

The method used was to display the chart on a computer screen so that everybody could see it. One person, a teacher or a course participant, acted as a facilitator and wrote down all the concepts. This is how Jeff Conklin advises meetings to be held (Conklin, 2006). All the exercises were also saved on the course pages (http://tge.cs.hut.fi/Courses/THJAA/).

Plagiarism is a problem in the academic world (Carroll, 2002). The practices concerning the handling of plagiarism seemed to differ substantially between various departments at TKK. Plagiarism and ways to avoid it were discussed. For example, exercises can and should be crafted so that they do not encourage plagiarism. The use of mapping methods makes plagiarism more difficult.

Because of the flexible timetable it was possible to fit an extra topic to the last course day. By request of the course attendees, this was bibliography management and in particular a RefWorks demonstration. It would have been useful to integrate bibliography management to mapping software and this will be a challenge for future courses.

Course feedback

We urged the course participants to give critical feedback on all aspects of the course (timing, structure, organizing, content). Because this was a pilot course it was necessary to get truthful feedback. The course is likely to run and perhaps be placed in optional courses, for example for postgraduate students.

We received feedback from seven course participants. They all thought that the course was useful or very useful for their work as teachers and also as researchers.

The implementation of combining the different mapping software and information retrieval was considered to need more planning, as it was not complete. However, completing a map takes a lot of time, and to master the mapping software to make it a routine tool takes a lot of personal practice.

Conclusions

A lot of time went into the planning of the course, but only a pilot course could show how it worked in practice. Next time, the course will have new participants and they may have different knowledge, skills or needs from those of the participants of the first course.

The course is certain to be unique every time. The objective is to have an innovative course with the aim of creating new insights into outlining information searching with the help of new tools. At the same time, the personnel of the library are in contact with the practical teaching and research done in the university. There has to be a learning process, during which different areas of expertise are brought together and new applications are built. The teachers of the course also learn when they are actually teaching the course.

The learning process should continue after this course and persistent work will be rewarded, as our students, who are assumed to be the ones to benefit in the end, will get better learning results and digest the core substance of a topic more thoroughly, making the studying process easier.

References

Carroll, J. (2002) *A Handbook for Deterring Plagiarism in Higher Education*, Oxford Centre for Staff Development.

Conklin, J. (2006) *Dialogue Mapping: building shared understanding of wicked problems*, Wiley.

Heino, K. and Palmgren, V. (2006) Embedding Library in Study Structure. In *Creating Knowledge IV: International Conference held on 16–18 August 2006 at The Royal Library and University of Copenhagen*, www.ck-iv.dk/papers/.

Kämäräinen, J. (2007) Tietoympäristö tuo Tekniikan Asiakkaan Tiedonhakuprosessiin – kokemuksia Hyvinkään Laurea-kirjastosta [Data environment brings technique to customer's information search process – experiences from Laurea library Hyvinkää], *Signum*, **40** (2), 5–10.

Margulies, N. and Maal, N. (2002) *Mapping Inner Space: learning and teaching visual mapping*, 2nd edn, Zephyr Press.

Novak, J. D. (1998) *Learning, Creating and Using Knowledge: concept maps (TM) as facilitative tools in schools and corporations*, Mahwah, Lawrence Erlbaum.

Nuutila, E. and Törmä, S. (2007) Lecture on 29 May 2007 at Helsinki University of Technology (TKK).

Palmgren, V. and Heino, K. (2002) Active Integration of Information Searching Skills into the University Curriculum. In Brophy, P., Fisher, S. and Clarke, Z. (eds), *Libraries Without Walls 4: the delivery of library services to distant users: proceedings of an international conference held on 14–18 September 2001 by CERLIM*, London, Facet Publishing, 197–207.

Rumsey, S. (2004) *How to Find Information: a guide for researchers*, Maidenhead, Open University Press.

THJAA course pages, http://tge.cs.hut.fi/Courses/THJAA/.

14

Public libraries, learning and the creative citizen: a European perspective

Robert Davies and Geoff Butters

Learning: the strategic background

European Ministers of Education have agreed on three major goals to be achieved by 2010 for the benefit of citizens and the EU as a whole. These goals are to:

- improve the quality and effectiveness of EU education and training systems
- ensure that they are accessible to all
- open up education and training to the wider world.

The 2006 EU Communication *Adult Education: it's never too late to learn* (European Commission, 2006a) calls on countries to promote adult learning in Europe and to place it firmly on the political agenda. A planned Action Plan on Adult Learning will aim to promote this goal, thereby contributing to personal benefits of development and fulfilment, raising skill levels, reducing social exclusion, promoting active citizenship and supporting employability and mobility in the labour market. Among the major challenges identified is lifting the barriers to participation affecting all groups, but especially the ageing population and migrants.

One of the major pillars of Europe's *i2010* (European Commission, 2006b) initiative calls for 'inclusion, better services for citizens and quality of life', and emphasizes the enhanced use of information and communication technology (ICT) for lifelong learning and social inclusion. A flagship initiative under this encourages a focusing of research and deployment efforts in the field of 'digital libraries', specifically to use high-tech tools to make Europe's rich heritage available to as many people as possible, in order to combine individual creativity with ICTs.

The European Union's e-learning initiatives also promote 'digital literacy' as one of the basic skills of all Europeans, alongside the contribution of ICT to learning in general, especially for those who, owing to their geographical location, socio-economic situation or special needs, do not have easy access to traditional education and training. 'Digital literacy' is sometimes held to encompass the following:

- knowledge about ICT components, operations, capabilities and limitations
- skills in using ICT to perform relevant tasks and retrieve and make use of digital content
- positive attitudes toward ICT use personally and in society.

In European society, it can be difficult to separate the processes of learning from the practice of education. Heavy investment in schools, colleges and universities leads to an almost inextricable relationship between the idea of learning and the issue of how schools should be organized, managed and run.

It is often held that in a 'knowledge economy' lifelong learning takes place in a range of sites and over sustained periods of time. Learning is seen increasingly to occur through the leisure activities that are now often mediated by digital technologies as part of young people's social and cultural lives, activities which are often viewed by formal educational establishments as being outside the realm of valued educational experience, such as children's playing of computer games, use of chat rooms, exploitation of digital media, digital television, and so on. This perception also focuses attention on what can be learned from these activities that may help in designing approaches to formal education and how this kind of learning may come to be valued by teachers, schools and the curriculum.

The role to be played by non-formal/informal learning institutions such as public libraries is an issue at the heart of this agenda. It is clear that learning is not confined to formal institutions such as schools, colleges and universities, supporting the concept of a wide 'ecology' of learning where education institut-ions, homes, families and friends, the workplace, consulting people in all walks of life and leisure activities, as well as interaction with libraries and other community and cultural organizations, all play their part.

An interest in informal learning has now become much more of a mainstream political concern at European level and among individual member states, although to date it has not on the whole been assigned sufficient resources or co-ordinated in such a way as to maximize impact. Policies have in the main not yet succeeded in overcoming the somewhat fragmented nature of adult education provision, in particular, and the optimal matching of high-quality provision to user demand remains some way off.

Today, the term 'informal learning' is used loosely to describe any or all of the following:

- learning which happens outside school in less formal, intermediate kinds of learning spaces such as libraries and museums or in families and groups of friends
- learning which is not about things which are learned in school
- learning which happens in a different way from that which occurs in school (e.g. is 'casual' or 'accidental' rather than 'organized')
- learning which has a different purpose (e.g. participation in leisure) from that which occurs in school (e.g. passing examinations).

Attention to informal learning is also inclined to make more evident the experiential nature of learning, involving notions of wonder, surprise, feelings, peer and personal responses, fun and pleasure.

Libraries and learning

The role to be played by non-formal/informal learning institutions, such as Europe's estimated 96,000 public libraries, is an issue at the heart of the strategic issues described. In order to optimize their potential to contribute to the goals of the Lisbon Agenda (European Council in Lisbon, 2000) and *i2010* (European Commission, 2006b), public libraries must offer new and innovative services and activities that empower citizens to successfully pursue lifelong learning, thereby helping to increase the number of qualified, skilled and fulfilled people in Europe of any age, class or gender, including those enrolled in recognized courses and those simply wanting to improve their skills at any time of their life, for any reason, while reducing the risk of creating a digital divide.

Europe's extensive network of public libraries, with a total membership of some 180 million people, is increasingly able to extend multiple learning experiences to visitors from all age groups and sections of society. An important question for the library community and its partners in the formal and non-formal education sectors relates to the role which libraries can play in delivering services in support of the new strategic agendas for learning.

In this context, there have been many calls for greater collaboration between libraries, schools and the adult education sector in the context of lifelong learning. However, such collaboration often takes place most effectively at local level, even where a broad national policy framework exists. Public libraries have a number of natural advantages, including their strong roots in local communities, a tradition of partnership with schools and provision of learning-oriented services of various kinds for children and an increasingly established role as part of the lifelong learning 'landscape'. However, while partnership frameworks and practice between government-run adult education institutions, the voluntary/NGO (non-governmental organization) and private stakeholders and between formal and the non-formal networks are well established in some countries, in others this trend remains nascent.

There is a strong political assumption, both implicit and explicit, that informal/non-formal learning organizations such as libraries have a vital job to do by supporting individual learners' needs, providing them with choices and flexibility, helping people to continue and return to learning, enabling adults to get a job or qualification, signposting and inspiring people to take up other courses, helping children to learn and supporting schools in diversifying children's experiences.

Accordingly, a significant amount of effort has been devoted at national and European levels to developing the learning role of public libraries for the digital era. Considerable investment by public libraries has already been made in training and equipment for services to support lifelong learning. Organizations such as IFLA (International Federation of Library Associations), www.ifla.org/; EBLIDA (European Bureau of Library, Information and Documentation Associations), www.eblida.org/; and EAEA (European Adult Education Association), www.eaea. org/, have helped to shape the professional and political discussion about the interrelation between public libraries and lifelong learning.

Numerous statements have also emerged as a result of EU programme-driven initiatives such as The Copenhagen Declaration (PubliCA, 1999), The Oeiras Manifesto (PULMAN, 2003) and CALIMERA, www.calimera.org/default.aspx, under successive IST Framework programmes. Projects in programmes now grouped together under the European Commission's Lifelong Learning Programme (LLP) such as: PuLLS (Public Libraries in the Learning Society), www.pulls.dk/; DILMULLI (Dissemination of Lifelong Learning activities in Museums and Libraries projects), www.dillmuli.feek.pte.hu/tool-kit.htm; PULIMA (Public Library Management and New Information Technologies); SLAM (School Libraries As Multimedia centres), www.karmoyped.no/slam/; and ISTRA (Improving Student's Reading Abilities), www.istranet.org/, particularly by using school/public libraries, have begun to create awareness of evolving findings and results, while projects such as e.Mapps.com, www.emapps.com/, under Information Society Technologies Framework Programme 6 (IST FP6), and AITMES, www.aitmes.org/, and IL Greco (Implementing Learning Game Resources based on Educational Content), http://ilgreco.europole.org/, under LLP, have contributed innovative environments for the use of new technologies such as games-based learning, involving public libraries to some degree. At national and regional level, networks of agencies such as the UK's Museums Libraries and Archives agency (MLA) have devoted substantial resources to work in this area.

Despite this, exploitation of project results, deployment and mainstreaming of innovative activities and services remains inconsistent across EU member states as a whole. Within many European countries, effective co-ordination in support of nationwide deployment is lacking. The specific case for investment in this area needs to be demonstrated more fully, conclusively and measurably to policy-makers and funders in the many and various national and local environments across the continent.

There is a need for further actions to support and extend the progress made to date by public libraries in supporting learning for all age groups and sections of society, for example by disseminating, consolidating and enhancing the work of key existing networks, projects and initiatives in this area, leading to the development of a framework which will help to convince education and cultural policy-makers that Europe's libraries have a key role and to determine where their major value lies in delivering new learning agendas. Libraries themselves need to embed more thoroughly into their policies a 'learning' culture and to find ways of measuring and demonstrating their impact on people's learning.

Opportunities through information and communications technology

Many people, perhaps especially children and young adults, are immersed in ICT-related activities in their homes and with their friends, supporting the concept of a wider 'ecology' of education, involving:

- parents, families, friends and homes
- clubs and community centres
- libraries
- museums, galleries, science centres and archives
- consulting people in all walks of life.

The home environment alone may offer a range of different digital experiences for young people, from watching DVDs to playing computer games, to using revision CD-ROMs to interactive voting with digital television, to editing digital photographs, to participating in 'social networking' environments.

Many of the transactions with ICT which allow people to experience activities that support learning do not take place in traditional educational settings; all sorts of learning goes on in a range of different settings, and this learning contributes to the capacity to learn the formal knowledge that is conventionally valued in society. In other words, it is possible to have both formal and informal learning occurring in both formal and non-formal spaces. Equally, some activities encourage informal engagement with socially valued information and resources but through non-curriculum-linked approaches. The experiences of public visitors to libraries, science centres and museums also fit into this category.

It is claimed by some that institutions such as libraries and museums have embraced new technologies and approaches to learning while schools have focused on delivering an outmoded curriculum.

New technologies also can offer all members of society the opportunity to match learning to their specific needs and circumstances. Learning is seen increasingly to occur through the leisure activities that are now mediated by digital technologies as part of young people's social and cultural lives. Increased recognition of the potential of ICT is refreshing the case that learning in out-of-school settings and in which the new opportunities and potential in a technology-rich world can be exploited needs to be accorded full status and understanding, even though some of these (such as children's playing of computer games, use of chat rooms, watching digital television, etc.) are sometimes viewed by formal educational establishments as being outside the realm of valued educational experience.

This is accompanied by significant debate over the value and utility of digital resources. Libraries (in the very broadest sense), archives and especially museums uniquely provide access to 'objects' in the digital and physical formats. By various means they seek to build learner participation, interactivity and collaboration between institution and learner.

A new set of relationships is emerging, between objects, learners and digital technology, in which cultural institutions are places of exploration, discovery and interpretation. This discussion is exploring how emerging standards allow 'chunks' of content to be cost-effectively used, adapted, shared, reused and developed by both teachers and learners.

Increasingly, significant levels of ICT integration are reported across European countries, especially within formal education and those institutions providing e-learning, whether as a specific subject, integrated within specific subject disciplines or as an enabling skill. Increasingly, higher education institutions and other training providers use ICT to provide resources to their students and for distance learning purposes. However, specific data and impact studies for the adult education sector in this area are not widely available, although a number of countries are examining the role of ICT in adult education curricula at a strategic level. Recent industry forecasts of future directions for e-learning have also indicated a significant increase in attention to support for informal learning.

Most available studies on the impact of ICT on teaching methodology and learning outcomes focus on secondary education. Impact study results where they exist point to a positive outcome in terms of schools managers'/directors' appreciation that ICT tools are making learning more efficient and teachers' work easier, facilitating both individual and co-operative learning and attracting pupils. The main impediments mentioned are technical problems (not enough computers, or old equipment) and insufficient educational tools (software applications).

In all, the ICT context for learning is evolving rapidly. Libraries have the potential to greatly enhance their role as centres of creativity and learning, by deploying new technologies. Broadband connectivity is spreading rapidly into all parts of Europe and is being extended to public education institutions of many kinds by a variety of means including the extension of access to academic 'backbone' networks and through radio, wireless and satellite technologies. While cost and coverage in some regions remain significant issues, it is becoming increasingly feasible to think in everyday terms about the practical applications of learning which rely upon internet and mobile communications for human and machine interaction and for the use of distributed digital content.

Some of the key technical developments which are likely to influence this context and to which libraries need to adapt in developing service provision are:

- personalization, enabling the individual learner to use technologies to exercise choice and to take responsibility for their own learning and provide a channel for the recording and sharing of personal experience
- new 'Web 2.0' delivery modalities such as mobile devices, blogging, podcasting, videocasting, the use of collaborative 'web spaces', multimedia content creation (e.g. mashups), location-based technologies (GPS and digital maps) and games technology – all of which are beginning to show signs that they are ready to move past the early adoption phase and into mainstream e-learning
- the enabling of ever more readily available user technologies for creation of animations, music, videos, graphic and web designs.

Games technology and learning

One important aspect of this issue is to investigate, with greater pragmatism, the value and potential of games in education, especially in conjunction with use of the other technologies described above. In most European countries, although the availability of ICT facilities and networks such as computer laboratories, high-speed internet connections and interactive whiteboards and networks is clearly growing, relatively few examples of sustained uses of ICT-based games in either formal or informal education are available.

The workshop at LWW7 to which this paper relates is based on the activities of several projects and activities which have set out to demonstrate on an experimental basis how in practical terms the role of libraries in this area may unfold and become explicit. These include games-based approaches such as eMapps.com, AITMES and Il Greco and the VeriaGrid, www.theveriagrid.org/. Established by Veria Public Library in Greece, the VeriaGrid is an innovative platform based on digital cartography linked to multimedia content which can be created using mobile devices and used by different audiences, for example in education and tourism promotion.

Video games have been around for nearly 30 years. Games have always been used in education. But for ICT-based games to take on a meaningful role in formal or informal education, the education sector and the wider public and media need to better understand the potential and diversity of such tools.

Recent research has investigated the integration of computer graphics with real-world environments. This new technology, called Augmented Reality (AR), blurs the line between what is real and what is computer-generated. Video games are driving the development of AR. Augmented reality games (ARGs) can transform interaction so that it is no longer simply a face-to-screen exchange but involves players in the 'real' environment. The term 'mixed reality' is also sometimes used in relation to these games: see, for example, The Harbour Game: a mixed reality game for urban planning.

For now, AR technology is still too complicated and expensive for many learning environments and may involve, for example, the use of 'wearable kit'. This is likely to change as computer hardware becomes smaller and less expensive. In the meantime, a partial solution is available in the form of augmented reality via Personal Digital Assistant (PDA), which provides a viable strategy being used with some success in learning, especially when combined with a game-based approach. It is held by many that it is these immersive environments that will help push gaming to the next level. Projects such as eMapps.com are experimenting with simplified and less high-tech approaches to ARGs in a schools context by integrating Web 2.0 and GPS technologies.

On a completely virtual reality (VR) plane, the success of Second Life, a 3-D virtual world entirely built and owned by its residents, should be noted. Since opening to the public in 2003, it has grown explosively and today is inhabited nearly 7 million people from around the world. Second Life is a digital continent, teeming with people, entertainment, experiences and opportunity in which residents retain the rights to their digital creations and can buy, sell and trade with other residents. The adaptation of this platform in an adult learning environment may be worth exploring.

The task remains to demonstrate how games-based learning through less formal (e.g. cultural) institutions can be used to complement the objectives of more formal skills agendas by reaching those people in the community which the formal sector does not reach in an innovative way. The work of projects such as eMapps.com, AITMES and Il Greco is beginning to address these issues.

Conclusion: looking forward

Public libraries potentially have a vital role in delivering European learning and skills agendas for adults and children by becoming centres for informal learning and creativity, using the potential of ICT in the process.

There is now a need to move forward this agenda in terms of enabling much wider dissemination, exploitation and take-up of innovative results across Europe, especially more recent developments in the deployment of ICT, and to create a usable means of evaluating comparatively and promoting a wider understanding of their overall impact and potential among different European countries. This should go hand in hand with increased consensus and adoption among the professional user communities involved and increasing value recognition among policy-makers. Work of this kind should among other things provide a focus for the development of guidelines, recommendations and frameworks for impact assessment.

In this process, the following areas are among those which will need to be addressed:

Learning management

- funding for the development of learning services
- staff competences and workforce development (including for learner support, mentoring and use of ICT)
- improving diversity of provision: types of learning services, especially ICT-based
- partnerships with schools, adult learning providers and employers: good practice
- increasing learner participation (re-engaging adult learners, including marginal groups, family and inter-generational learning)
- learner support methods
- accreditation: availability and demand for learning certification (including services currently provided, such as the European Computer Driving Licence – ECDL)
- development of an organizational learning and evaluation culture and practices in public libraries.

ICT

- creation of networked e-learning environments
- personalization of learning
- use of new tools (mobile learning, interactive TV, Web 2.0, computer games-based learning, etc.)
- designing inspiring, safe and accessible learning spaces and virtual environments.

Learning outcomes

- measuring impact: how public library services contribute to valid learning outcomes (knowledge, personal development, skills, inclusion, etc.)

- supporting basic skills (reading, numeracy, ICT)
- language learning
- digital literacy, creativity and content creation
- strengthening progression to other phases of learning and employment
- complementing and enriching formal learning (vocational and business education, homework, course and project support, and out of school and holiday activities).

There is in short a need to assess, bring together and disseminate the evidence relating to the e-learning approaches supported by public-library-based activity in a way which has not previously been achieved at European level, providing a sound basis for future comparative assessment, experience and learning between countries and regions through the provision of an impact assessment framework which is usable throughout Europe. This could have a significant and continuing effect on the development and assessment of new learning services provided by public libraries and on the development of fruitful relationships with learning partner organizations, based on emulation and a 'ripple effect' at both policy and practitioner level, and sustaining the sound establishment of a Europe-wide community of practice.

References

European Commission (2006a) *Adult Learning: it is never too late to learn*, http://ec.europa.eu/education/policies/lll/adultcom_en.html.

European Commission (2006b) *i2010 – a European information society for growth and employment*, http://ec.europa.eu/information_society/eeurope/i2010/index_en.htm.

European Council in Lisbon (2000) *Lisbon Strategy*, http://europa.eu/scadplus/glossary/lisbon_strategy_en.htm.

The Harbour Game: a mixed reality game for urban planning, www.havnespil.dk/graphics/havnebilleder/artikler/wbi_presentation.pdf.

PubliCA (1999) *The Copenhagen Declaration*, http://ec.europa.eu/education/copenhagen/copenhagen_declaration_en.pdf.

PULMAN (2003) *The Oeiras Manifesto*, www.pulmanweb.org.

Second Life, http://secondlife.com/.

15

A user-centred approach to the evaluation of digital cultural maps: the case of the VeriaGrid system

Rania Siatri, Emmanouel Garoufallou,
Ioannis Trohopoulos and Panos Balatsoukas

Introduction

In the European Union the digitization of cultural heritage resources has been promoted though various initiatives, such as the Lund principles, which resulted in a European wide framework for the digitization of cultural heritage (e-Europe 2001), the Information Society Technologies (IST) programme, which funded research on the digitization and access to cultural heritage collections through several projects (IST, 2006), and the European Library initiative, which developed a network of digital cultural heritage resources among the members of the European Union (The European Library, 2006). The digitization of cultural heritage resources (CHRs) has significant implications for the developing economy of digital cultural tourism in Europe. It implies the development of:

- the online availability and accessibility of digital CHRs
- the development of a network of digital CHRs
- the promotion of CHRs to a geographically dispersed audience of educators, learners and tourists
- the marketing and promotion of CHRs across the globe.

On the other hand, several factors can impede the development of digital cultural tourism in Europe, such as the shortage of technical infrastructure, the absence of a coherent cultural policy and the lack of innovation and knowledge transfer mechanisms, as well as the ignorance of users' needs and budget constraints (Manzuch and Knoll, 2005; Tanner and Deegan, 2003).

The Central Public Library of Veria (CPLV), a major provider of online inform-

ation services to the Greek public, has convinced cultural heritage institutions of
the city of Veria:

- to rethink their role in the society in the new electronic era
- to make their rich collections of CHRs easily accessible to the public via the
  internet and other technologies, such as laptops and mobile phones
- to compile an inventory of digital CHRs and other instruments useful to the
  public.

In particular, the CPLV, through the LIGHT project (www.light-culture.net),
developed the 'VeriaGrid', an online digital cultural map of the city of Veria to bring
to light the cultural resources managed by local museums, libraries and other
cultural organizations of Veria. The VeriaGrid system provides users with the
opportunity to navigate across the map and visit various cultural sites, such as
churches, museums, libraries and archaeological sites (see Figure 15.1). In addition,
the system provides an interactive search facility enabling users to search for
specific cultural sites and information about the city through the image, text, video

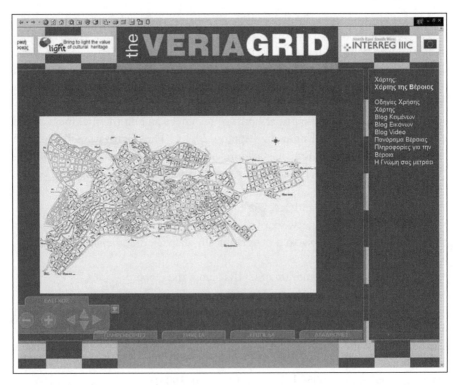

Figure 15.1 *The VeriaGrid System*

and panoramic photo inventories. As this is the first Greek digital cultural map, there was interest in investigating how users interact with this system. The investigation of the usability of this system could provide feedback to the designers of the VeriaGrid system, establishing some usability recommendations for the design of Greek digital cultural maps in the future, and help develop a methodological framework for the evaluation of the usability of digital cultural maps. The results of the usability evaluation and a list of recommendations for improving its usability can be found in Garoufallou, Siatri and Balatsoukas (2006). This paper focuses on the usability framework developed for the evaluation of the VeriaGrid system and provides some conclusions and recommendations for the usability evaluation of digital cultural heritage collections.

The evaluation methodology

Aim and objectives

To investigate the usability of the VeriaGrid system a usability test method was employed. In particular, the objectives of the usability test were:

- to investigate the time taken and errors made by users while using the system to accomplish a set of tasks, and measure user satisfaction in relation to the particular application
- to identify the usability problems impeding user performance
- to examine whether the level of IT experience (novice and expert users) has an impact on the use of the particular application
- to provide a set of recommendations to improve the usability of the system.

Defining usability

There are many approaches and definitions of usability. For example, the International Standards Organization (ISO) defines usability as 'the extent to which a product can be used by specified users to achieve specified goals with effectiveness, efficiency and satisfaction' (Usability Net, 2006). In another definition, Nielsen (1993) describes usability in terms of five constructs: Learnability, Efficiency, Memorability, Errors and Satisfaction.

Usability testing

Usability tests are formal, controlled and laboratory-based user studies that record user performance, while interacting with a product or prototype, in terms of the time needed to perform specific tasks, the number of errors performed and user satisfaction. Other measures recorded during usability tests include eye fixations and memorability. Users participating in usability tests are usually asked to perform a set of predetermined tasks. Their interaction with the system is recorded through screen-recording software, video and audio-recording devices or manual data collection forms. After performing the tasks users can be asked to complete a subjective satisfaction questionnaire. This questionnaire collects quantitative preference data about users' perceptions of the system's usability. Finally, participants may be also asked to participate in short structured or semi-structured interviews. The scope of these interviews or de-briefing sessions (Rubin, 1994) is to elicit qualitative data about users' experiences. These tests normally take place in usability laboratories. In many cases, however, more flexible and portable usability equipment exists that provides evaluators with the opportunity to set up a laboratory environment in locations where formal usability laboratories do not exist (Preece et al., 2007).

Although it is agreed that usability tests can be performed with a minimum of five users (Nielsen, 1993), this is not a general rule and in many cases more participants are required. This is important in the case of usability experiments. In this case, the number of participants should be more than five, to support statistical power and thus the validity of the results. Although usability experiments usually have a similar structure to that of the conventional usability tests, they differ in terms of the strength of statistical power needed to report the results and the focus of their inquiry, for example, hypothesis testing versus usability problem reporting (Morse, 2002).

Usability test frameworks

Several authors have proposed usability test frameworks. The purpose of these frameworks is to provide a general context within which decisions can be made on how the usability test should be designed and performed. For example, Preece et al. (2007) proposed the DECIDE evaluation framework, which contains six main constructs:

1   Determine the goals
2   Explore the questions
3   Choose the evaluation approach and methods
4   Identify the practical issues
5   Decide how to deal with the ethical issues
6   Evaluate, analyse, interpret and present the data.

A similar framework had been developed for the EBONI project (Wilson, Landoni and Gibb, 2002). According to the EBONI framework there are four main issues that need to be addressed for effective usability tests to take place. These are:

1   The selection of the systems under evaluation
2   The selection and recruitment of usability test subjects
3   The selection of the method of task testing
4   The data collection techniques employed.

The VeriaGrid evaluation methodology

The framework employed in this study amalgamates elements from the aforementioned usability frameworks. The main components of the proposed framework are:

1   The selection of participants
2   The selection of tasks
3   The selection of a task test design method
4   The selection of data collection techniques and analysis.

The selection of participants

A total of 10 subjects participated in the usability test. Usually the number of participants in usability tests varies from 5 to 12 subjects (Preece et al., 2007). Earlier, Nielsen (1993) had proposed that 5 usability participants can identify almost 85% of usability problems. Thus the use of more than 5 participants can increase the amount of redundant information. Other usability researchers have advocated that 10 participants are sufficient for any type of a usability test (Ahmed, McKnight and Oppenheim, 2005).

Because this research intended to investigate and analyse usability issues of an online service devoted to the cultural heritage of Veria, the testers of the system were Veria residents and higher education (HE) students: Veria residents would be interested in exploring the cultural sites of their region, while HE students are likely to visit them as part of educational programmes, or from personal interest, or both.

Furthermore, the usability subjects were divided into two categories: expert and novice users of the internet and the world wide web. In general, the recruitment of both expert and novice WWW users can facilitate the identification of different usability problems and inform the design of a cultural heritage application that can meet the needs of both categories of users (Faulkner and Wick, 2005).

The recruitment process was facilitated through announcements in the Technological Educational Institute of Thessaloniki departmental and faculty notice boards, newsletters and website. All candidates for the usability test were asked to complete a short background questionnaire. Following the analysis of the background questionnaire the final two groups of participants (novice and expert WWW users) were formed.

Before the task, test participants were reassured about the fair use of the data collected from their interaction with the VeriaGrid system. This was accomplished by requesting them to fill in a tape consent form and read the orientation script. The orientation script communicated the purposes of the usability test, the reasons why the particular subject had been asked to participate, and the participants' role in the test. In addition, the orientation script made explicit the fact that it was not the participant but the system that was being tested (Rubin, 1994).

The selection of tasks

The tasks developed for the purpose of this usability test reflected simple interaction scenarios between the user and the system. The selection of the tasks was influenced by criteria such as 'frequency', 'criticality' and 'vulnerability' (Rubin, 1994). In addition, the pilot study was critical for the formulation of the final list of tasks. This is the list of tasks performed by users during the usability test:

1 Find specific information using the help system/user guide
2 Access the map and zoom in
3 Use the control arrows to navigate across the map
4 Find on the digital map a specific cultural site by using the 'recommended points' functionality
5 Display and read the description associated with the specific site
6 Access the specific site for more information
7 Find the co-ordinates of the specific site
8 Choose a route and visit the sites of a particular route
9 Find textual information on a particular cultural site
10 Find and view the photos related to a particular site.
11 Find and view a video-clip about a cultural site.
12 Find and display a panoramic photo of the city of Veria.
13 Select a particular point in the panoramic photo and zoom in.
14 Find general information about the city of Veria.

Selection of the task test design method

For the purpose of the particular usability task testing, the 'within-subjects design' method was adopted (see Table 15.1). The 'within-subjects design' requires all tasks to be performed by all the participants of the usability test. This enables the maintenance of the validity and reliability of the task testing process as well as the prevention of bias from the results. While all subjects had to perform the same tasks using the VeriaGrid system the sequence of the tasks was counterbalanced among participants in order to minimize the effects of 'learning transfer'. However, where appropriate the sequential order of task presentation was preserved, as the provision of a realistic task order was critical (Rubin, 1994). For example, this was the case for tasks 2–8, where the sequential order of tasks was preserved.

Table 15.1 *The 'within-subjects' design*

Experts	System	Task order
2	VeriaGrid	1, 2, 3, 4, 5, 6, 7, 8, 9, 10, 11, 12, 13, 14
3	VeriaGrid	1, 9, 10, 11, 12, 13, 14, 2, 3, 4, 5, 6, 7, 8
Novices	System	Task order
2	VeriaGrid	1, 9, 10, 11, 12, 13, 14, 2, 3, 4, 5, 6, 7, 8
3	VeriaGrid	1, 2, 3, 4, 5, 6, 7, 8, 9, 10, 11, 12, 13, 14

Selection of data collection techniques and analysis

For the tasks specified above a number of performance and preference data were collected. The data collected corresponded to the three usability measures defined by Nielsen (1993). These were learnability, errors and satisfaction. Table 15.2 summarizes the different types of data collected, the three usability measures defined by Nielsen and the main data collection techniques employed in this study.

Table 15.2 *Summary of the data collection techniques, data collected and usability measures (Morris and Balatsoukas, 2006)*

Data collected	Task testing observation	Satisfaction questionnaire	Interview – debriefing session
1 Time needed for the completion of each task	Learnability		
2 Successful or unsuccessful completion of each task	Learnability		
3 Number of errors per task	Errors		
4 Nature of errors encountered	Errors		
5 Negative or positive comments	Satisfaction		Satisfaction
6 Ranking or rating of the system's particular tasks/tools		Satisfaction	

As seen in Table 15.2, three main data collection techniques were employed. These were observation; post-test subjective satisfaction questionnaires; and debriefing sessions or semi-structured interviews. In addition, a background questionnaire was administered at the beginning of each usability test to allocate participants to the two groups of expert and novice users of the WWW.

Observations took place during the task testing process. This was accomplished through the use of manual data collection forms, tape-recordings and screen-recording software. The data collection form provided the opportunity for researchers to gather important quantitative and qualitative data, such as the number and type of errors performed during the test, users' positive or negative comments and any questions raised by the participants in the usability test. The tape-recording device recorded users' think-aloud behaviour. During the task testing users were asked to think aloud and express verbally any thoughts or comments they might have on their interaction with the system. The tape recording device recorded users' think-aloud behaviour (where users verbalize their thoughts as they undertake a task), a Level 1 think-aloud protocol. It was anticipated that the concurrent think-aloud protocol would provide raw data on the user interaction with the system. This type of concurrent data is not subject to post-hoc rationalization and many scholars have argued that it does not increase users' cognitive load during the performance of the tasks (Ericsson and Simon, 1993; Van den Haak et al., 2003). A tape consent form signed by each participant in the test ensured the lawful and fair exploitation and dissemination of the recorded data. Observation techniques were coupled with the use of screen recordings. Unlike data loggers, the screen-recording software provides a perfect cinematic simulation of users' performance during the usability test and enables the interpretation and analysis of user actions in context. In addition, valid time data are recorded, giving the opportunity for exact estimations of the subject performance and the system's 'learnability'. After a comparison of different screen-recording applications against a set of functional requirements 'Camtasia Studio' version 4.0 was chosen.

A post-test satisfaction questionnaire was used to collect data on how users rated various interface tasks and objects against several measures such as, easy of use, learnability, effectiveness and efficiency (Nielsen, 1993; Rubin, 1994; UsabilityNet: subjective assessment, 2003). The questionnaire adopted items from the QUIS questionnaire (Shneiderman, 1998). In addition, a report by Vaki, Dallas and Dalla (2005) helped users to enhance the questionnaire with questions more relevant to cultural heritage applications. They were asked to indicate the level of their satisfaction, using a nine-point scale. The questionnaire evaluated various aspects of the interface, such as: the specific tasks performed by the subject during the usability test; 'interface metaphors' or 'screen issues'; clarity of output messages and 'design of displays'; visibility; situation awareness; adequacy of language; use of concepts familiar to the user; consistency; feedback; efficient error messages; and overall satisfaction. Each participant was asked to fill in a questionnaire after the performance of the tasks.

After the completion of the subjective satisfaction questionnaire, users were asked to participate in a short semi-structured interview. The interviews elicited further qualitative data on how users perceived the experience of using the VeriaGrid system. During the interview users were asked to specify likes and dislikes in using the system, the type of services or functionality that they preferred most and what other features they would like to see included in the system in future.

A pilot test was conducted to review the consistency of the usability test methodology. The pilot test took place during the first half of April 2006 in the Department of Library Studies and Information Systems of the Technological Educational Institute of Thessaloniki. A random sample of two participants participated in the pilot test.

Descriptive statistics, such as mean and standard deviation values, were produced for the time needed for users to complete the tasks, the errors performed and the data collected from the subjective satisfaction questionnaire. Statistical analysis was also conducted to test the null hypothesis that there was no impact of user WWW experience on the time and errors performed during the task test as well as on the user subjective satisfaction. Furthermore, a content analysis technique was applied in the case of the semi-structured interviews and the transcripts of the think-aloud protocol.

Conclusions

This paper reported on the design of a usability test that was employed for the evaluation of the VeriaGrid system. The implementation of the usability test was based on a framework that involved the definition of the selection of participants, the selection of tasks, the design of the task-testing process and the selection of data collection techniques. In particular we propose the following actions for the successful implementation of usability tests for the evaluation of web-based cultural heritage applications:

- Systematize the design of the usability test through the use of a usability framework.
- Recruit more than five participants, especially when the research design takes the form of a usability experiment. In this case a larger number of participants is required for hypothesis testing.
- Employ a 'within-subjects' design as opposed to a 'between-subjects' design. A within-subjects design requires fewer participants for tests of statistical signif-

icance and sample variability is less important. If it is used, however, counter-balancing the sequence of the tasks is important to minimize the learning transfer effects.

- When a think-aloud protocol is concurrently employed, it is suggested to choose a Level 1 think-aloud protocol. This type of think-aloud protocol normally does not modify user cognitive process and has a limited impact on user performance.

- Avoid the ad hoc use of general usability satisfaction questionnaires. As no usability satisfaction questionnaires are available specifically for web-based digital cultural heritage applications, enhancing existing general questionnaires, such as QUIS, with questions relevant to the applications under examination and the interface characteristics that apply to digital cultural heritage applications is recommended.

References

Ahmed, S. M. Z., McKnight, C. and Oppenheim, C. (2005) A Study of Learning and Retention with Web-based IR Interface, *Journal of Librarianship and Information Science*, **37** (1), March 2005, http://lis.sagepub.com/cgi/reprint/37/1/7 [accessed 10 September 2007].

eEurope (2001) *The LUND Principles: conclusions of experts meeting*, Lund, Sweden, 4 April 2001, http://dhc2006.salzburgresearch.at/images/stories/lund_principles_e.pdf [accessed 23 March 2006].

Ericsson, K. A, and Simon, H. A. (1993) *Protocol Analysis*, Cambridge, MA, MIT Press.

The European Library (2006) www.theeuropeanlibrary.org/portal/organization/about_us/aboutus_en.html [accessed 12 November 2007].

Faulkner, L. and Wick, D. (2005) Cross-user Analysis: benefits of skill level comparison in usability testing, *Interacting with Computers*, **17**, 773–86.

Garoufallou, E., Siatri, R. and Balatsoukas, P. (2006) *Usability Assessment of the VeriaGrid.org Online System*, Thessaloniki, Deltos.

Information Society Technologies (2006) DigiCULT Home Page, ISTweb, http://cordis.europa.eu/ist/digicult/index.html [accessed 4 May 2006].

Manzuch, Z. and Knoll, A. (2005) *Analysis of Research Activities and Requirements of the National Libraries of the New EU Member States, Deliverable 1.1. Final version, July, 2005*, http://digit.nkp.cz/CDMK/telmemor_final_July2005DFCorr.pdf.

MINERVA Working Group 5 (2003) *Handbook for Quality in Cultural Websites: improving quality for citizens*, version 1.2 (Draft), www.minervaeurope.org/publications/qualitycriteria1_2draft/qualitypdf1103.pdf [accessed 10 September 2007].

Morris, A. and Balatsoukas, P. (2006) Usability Evaluation of Ebrary and Overdrive E-book Online Systems. In: *Libraries Without Walls 6: evaluating the distributed delivery of library services: proceedings of an international conference held on 16–20 September 2005 by CERLIM*, London, Facet Publishing, 211–23.

Morse, E. (2002) Evaluation Methodologies for Information Management Systems, *D-Lib Magazine*, **8** (9), www.dlib.org/dlib/september02/morse/09morse.html [accessed 10 September 2007].

Nielsen, J. (1993) *Usability Engineering*, London, Morgan Kaufmann.

Preece et al. (2007) *Interaction Design: beyond human-computer interaction*, 2nd edn, Chichester, Wiley.

Rubin, J. (1994) *Handbook of Usability Testing: how to plan, design, and conduct effective tests*, New York, Wiley.

Shneiderman, B. (1998) *Designing the User Interface: strategies for effective human-computer interaction*, 3rd edn, Reading, MA, Addison-Wesley.

Shneiderman, B. and Plaisant, C. (2004) *Designing the User Interface*, London, Pearson.

Tanner, S. and Deegan, M. (2003) Exploring Charging Models for Digital Library Cultural Heritage, *Ariadne*, **34**, www.ariadne.ac.uk/issue34/tanner/ [accessed 12 April 2006].

Usability Net (2006) *International Standards*, www.usabilitynet.org/tools/r_international.htm#20282 [accessed 23 August 2007].

Vaki, E., Dallas, C. and Dalla, Ch. (2005) *Calimera: cultural applications: local institutions mediating electronic resource: deliverable D18: usability guidelines*, www.calimera.org/Lists/Resources%20Library/The%20end%20user%20experience,%20a%20usable%20community%20memory/Usability%20Guidelines.pdf [accessed 23 February 2006].

Van de Haak et al. (2003) Retrospective vs. Concurrent Think Aloud Protocols: testing the usability of an online library catalogue, *Behaviour and Information Technology*, **22** (5), 339–51.

Wilson, R., Landoni, M. and Gibb, F. (2002) A User-centred Approach to E-book Design, *The Electronic Library*, **20** (2), 322–30.

16

The process of assessment of the quality, usability and impact of electronic services and resources: a Quality Attributes approach

Jillian R. Griffiths

Introduction

As a profession we are constantly striving to ensure that we provide the best possible services and resources to our users. This concern has resulted in a myriad of approaches and methods being utilized in an attempt to establish the quality of services and resources and lead to improvements in them. Online resources in particular have been the focus of much research in recent years, with work being undertaken in many areas, including, for example, information retrieval, information-seeking behaviour and usability studies, different approaches which share the same ultimate goal of making resources and systems easier to use by end-users.

As a result of the shift in recent years from the use of performance indicators to measures of outcome and impact within libraries (Brophy, 2004), a Quality Attributes approach is proposed in this paper. This approach allows for a holistic assessment of the quality of services or resources and encompasses usability. The classic definition of quality as 'fitness for a purpose' was developed by Garvin (1987) into a model of eight dimensions or 'attributes' that can be used as a framework for determining the overall quality of a product or service. This approach has since been adapted for use in libraries and information services by Marchand (1990), Brophy and Coulling (1996), Brophy (1998) and Griffiths and Brophy (2002, 2005). Griffiths and Brophy adapted the Quality Attributes further by changing the emphasis of one attribute, changing the concept of one attribute, and introducing two additional attributes (Currency and Usability), thus producing a set of ten attributes which can be used to assess the quality, usability and impact of services and resources. These attributes are: Performance, Conformance, Features, Reliability, Durability, Currency, Serviceability, Aesthetics,

Perceived quality and Usability. Usability, often used as an assessment criterion in its own right, has been defined by ISO 9241-11 as 'the extent to which a product can be used by specified users to achieve specified goals with effectiveness, efficiency and satisfaction in a specified context of use' and, as Nielsen points out, 'It is important to realize that usability is not a single, one-dimensional property of a user interface. Usability has multiple components and is traditionally associated with these five usability attributes: learnability, efficiency, memorability, errors, satisfaction' (1993, 26).

This approach has been used to assess existing and developing services of the UK Joint Information Systems Committee (JISC) Information Environment, results of which can be seen in Griffiths and Brophy (2002, 2005).

This paper will discuss the use of these attributes within the context of the process for assessment of electronic services and resources.

The Quality Attributes

The following describes the Quality Attributes as further modified for the context of evaluation of electronic services and resources.

Performance is concerned with establishing confirmation that a service meets its most basic requirement. These are the primary operating features of the product or service. For example, an electronic information service would be expected to retrieve a set of documents that matched a user's query. The most basic quality question is then 'Does the service retrieve a list of relevant documents?'. In this study the Performance attribute was measured using the criteria 'Are you satisfied that the required information was retrieved' and 'Are you satisfied with the ranking order of retrieved items?' and is primarily concerned with eliciting information about the user's relevance assessment of the items retrieved.

With *Conformance* the question is whether the product or service meets the agreed standard. This may be a national or international standard or locally determined service standard. The standards themselves, however they are devised, must of course relate to customer requirements. For information services there are obvious conformance questions around the use of standards and protocols such as XML, RDF, Dublin Core, OAI, Z39.50 etc. Many conformance questions can only be answered by expert analysts, since users are unlikely to have either the expertise or the access needed to make technical or service-wide assessments: thus users in this study did not evaluate this attribute.

Features are the secondary operating attributes, which add to a product or service in the user's eyes but are not essential to it. They may provide an essential marketing edge. It is not always easy to distinguish Performance characteristics from Features, especially as what is essential to one customer may be an optional extra to another, and there is a tendency for Features to become Performance attributes over time – inclusion of images in full-text databases is an example of a feature developing in this way. The attribute was measured by asking participants which features appealed to them most on each individual service and by identifying which search option(s) they used to perform their searches.

Users place high value on the *Reliability* of a product or service. For products this usually means that they perform as expected (or better). For electronic information services a major issue is usually the availability of the service. Therefore broken links, unreliability and slowness in speed of response can have a detrimental affect on a user's perception of a service. Users were asked if they found any dead links while searching each service and, if so, whether these dead links impacted on their judgement of the service. Participants were also asked if they were satisfied with the speed of response of the service, a measure which has previously been reported as being important to users by Dong and Su (1997), who put forward the view that response time is becoming a very important issue for many users.

Garvin uses the term *Durability*, defined as 'the amount of use the product will provide before it deteriorates to the point where replacement or discard is preferable to repair'. In the case of electronic information services this will relate to the sustainability of the service over a period of time. In simple terms, will the service still be in existence in three or five years? This is more likely to be assessed by experts in the field than by end-users (although they may have useful contributions on the assessment of the attribute based on comparisons with similar services), and as such was not evaluated during this testing.

For most users of electronic information services an important issue is the *Currency* of information, that is, how up to date the information provided is when it is retrieved.

Serviceability relates to when things go wrong and is concerned with questions such as 'How easy will it then be to put things right', 'How quickly can they be repaired?', 'How much inconvenience will be caused to the user, and how much cost?' For users of an electronic information service this may translate to the level of help available to them during the search and at the point of need. The availability of instructions and prompts throughout, context-sensitive help and usefulness of help were measured in order to assess responses to this attribute.

While *Aesthetics* and image is a highly subjective area, it is of prime importance to users. In electronic environments it brings in the whole debate about what constitutes good design. In a web environment the design of the home page may be the basis for user selection of services and this may have little to do with actual functionality. A range of criteria were used to measure user responses to this attribute, these being satisfaction with the interface and presentation of features, familiarity with the interface or elements of the interface and how easy it was to understand the content of retrieved items from the hit-list.

Perceived quality is one of the most interesting of attributes because it recognizes that all users make their judgements on incomplete information. They do not carry out detailed surveys of hit rates or examine the rival systems' performance in retrieving a systematic sample of records. Most users do not read the service's mission statement or service standards and do their best to bypass the instructions pages. Yet users will quickly come to a judgement about the service based on the reputation of the service among their colleagues and acquaintances, their preconceptions and their instant reactions to it. Perceived quality in the studies undertaken by Griffiths and Brophy (2002) related to the user's view of the service as a whole and the information retrieved from it. This was measured twice, before using the service (pre-perceived quality, where participants were aware of the service prior to testing) and after using the service (post-perceived quality). This allows investigation of how a user's perception of a service changes pre- and post-searching.

The addition of *Usability* as an attribute is important in any user-centred evaluation. User-centred models are much more helpful when personal preferences and requirements are factored in and as such participants were asked how user-friendly the service was, how easy it was to remember what the features and commands meant and how to use them, how satisfied they were with the input query facility and how satisfied they were with how to modify their query.

The process of assessment

Initial steps can be critical in the success of any assessment of services and preparatory work should not be underestimated. And, of course, the first place to start is identification of the resource or resources to be assessed. Deciding if a single resource or several resources are the focus will impact on:

- Why you are assessing – are you concerned with how a single resource is performing? Are you trying to identify areas/elements where a single resource could be improved? Are you comparing resources to identify which is most effective, or best used, in order to inform collection decisions?
- How you assess – if assessing multiple resources the task undertaken on each resource needs, as much as possible, to be comparable.
- Who will assess:
    end-users – public, students, academic staff
    expert users – colleagues, usability/accessibility experts, you!
- How you handle the resultant data – how you analyse and work with your results will depend on what your focus is. Thinking about the sort of data you require, be it quantitative or qualitative, is essential in ensuring that the design

of the assessment captures the data which will provide you with the information you require about the resources you are investigating.

Design of tasks/test searches

In choosing the resource or resources it is most likely that consideration has been given as to why evaluation is being undertaken, and this in turn will affect the design of any tasks or test searches. As a general rule, if assessment is being made to gain an understanding of users' behaviour then participants should be allowed to use their own tasks or queries. If the evaluation is to assess the service then it will be necessary to design tasks or test searches.

A task-based approach can be very effective and can be: (a) very directed, as in McGillis and Toms (2001), who used this approach to assess the usability of an academic library website by faculty staff and students; or (b) looser simulations of real-world situations such as those proposed by Borlund (2003) and developed from work by Ingwersen (1992, 1996) and Byström and Järvelin (1995). Here, a short 'cover story' describes a situation that requires the participant to use the electronic resource. The 'cover-story' is a rather open description of the context or scenario of a given work task situation. Where directed tasks are used care must be taken to ensure that they are of relevance to users, avoiding 'tasks that focus almost exclusively on pet features rather than on goals that users really want to accomplish' (Nielsen, 2007). Tasks need to be piloted, timed, assessed and redesigned in an iterative cycle until you are satisfied that they test the service and all its aspects. They also need, as far as possible, to be of equal difficulty if assessing several resources.

Collection of qualitative transaction logging

Originally a feature of automated library management systems, transaction logging has been defined as 'the study of electronically recorded interactions between on-line information retrieval systems and the persons who search for the information found in those systems' (Peters, 1993) and typically consisted of data regarding:

- patron's entry
- date and time
- terminal identification
- search file
- number of hits
- system response (not all systems).

However, Griffiths, Hartley and Willson (2002) suggested that it is of more use to

capture the interactions between resources and the person searching for information on systems and resources, and proposed that qualitative transaction logging
ought to:

- show real time
- show elapsed time
- show mouse movement of the end-user
- show input of the end-user
- show response of the system, e.g. error messages, retrieved items
- be unobtrusive
- give control to the researcher
- synchronize the transaction log with verbal protocols
- be used across different interfaces.

While data of this type provides a very rich picture of the participant's interactions
it is important to consider that the data has to be transcribed by the researcher
before analysis is possible – a process which can be very time-consuming.
However, screen-capturing software is now widely available to collect this
qualitative data.

Advantages and disadvantages of multiple or single testing

Deciding on one-to-one testing or simultaneous multiple testing depends on a
number of factors, including why you are assessing, what you are assessing and the
resources and constraints within which you have to work. Single testing can yield
greater qualitative data through observation and/or transaction logging but it is
likely that fewer participants will be recruited , because of the time and resource
constraints. Simultaneous multiple testing is likely to yield more quantitative and
less qualitative data but has the advantage of being able to engage with a greater
number of participants.

Implementation of the testing

With the advent of a multitude of online survey tools, assessment need not be
undertaken face to face. Surveys can be designed in such a way as to provide links
to resources under assessment and descriptions of the tasks to be undertaken.
Such an approach was used in a recent survey of the assessment of the usability of
the European Internet Accessibility Observatory reported within these conference
proceedings (Craven and Griffiths, 2008).

Recruitment of participants has often been an area of difficulty for user studies
of many kinds and it is essential that careful planning is undertaken to ensure

adequacy of participation, be this by expert users, colleagues or contacts or end-users in the form of paid or rewarded volunteers. Marketing and advertisement through discussion lists, online newsletters, forums, personal contacts, posters, etc. are essential.

Focus groups to collect post-searching qualitative data

Holding a focus group is an excellent method for gathering input from several people at once, while benefiting from the interaction within the group, and can therefore serve to investigate a particular topic in great depth. They can provide information on subjective views and feelings as well as facts about experiences. Participants often stimulate each other to contribute with verbal cues (for example, 'Don't you think . . . ?'). They can also be used to reveal information about group processes, especially if using an established group.

However, an effective focus group needs a skilled facilitator (for example, to be able to steer without taking over and to ensure everyone contributes while no one dominates). If using established groups it is also important to remember that some groups can have hidden agendas, especially if the facilitator is seen as a threat to a service, and that transcription of the data can be very time-consuming.

Development of questionnaires for post-searching quantitative data collection

Questionnaires can provide large quantities of data, both quantitative and qualitative, in a relatively simple, structured and resource-efficient way. Their advantages are numerous. They:

- provide good structure
- are less expensive than many other methods
- are relatively easy to administer without special training
- are not subject to interviewer bias
- can produce quick results.

In addition, online survey systems can undertake basic analysis, but these are some of their disadvantages:

- It is more difficult than it appears to create a good, unambiguous questionnaire.
- Response rates may be low – people often suffer from 'questionnaire fatigue'.
- There is no chance to ask a follow-up question if the initial answer is not sufficiently revealing.

Table 16.1 presents examples of questions designed to provide responses for each of the Quality Attributes.

Table 16.1 *Examples of Quality Attribute question design*

Quality Attribute	Possible question
Performance Basic requirements, primary operating features	• Are you satisfied that you found the required information on this service? • How satisfied were you with the order of the items retrieved (e.g. most relevant first, least relevant last)?
Conformance Agreed standard	• Not evaluated by end-users, could be assessed by expert user
Features Secondary operating attributes, added value, subjective	• There can be many different search options that you could have used to search for the information on this service. Which did you use (please list)? • Were there any features that you particularly liked about this service?
Reliability High user value	• Did you find any dead links when using this service? • If Yes, does the finding of dead links in your search session make you think that the service is unreliable, or reliable, or doesn't it affect your judgement? • How satisfied were you with the speed of response of this service?
Durability Sustainability of the service	• Not evaluated by end-users, could be assessed by expert user
Currency How up to date is the information?	• Do you think that the information from this service is up to date?
Serviceability How easy will it be to put things right?	• Did you find on-screen instructions and prompts helpful or unhelpful? • Did you select Help at any stage? • If Yes, how helpful did you find it?
Aesthetics Highly subjective area of prime importance	• How satisfied were you with the interface and features of this service? • Were there any features or aspects of the interface that you were familiar with? • How easy is it to understand what each item is about from the retrieved list?
Perceived quality Users' judgements	• Please rate the overall quality of the items you found on this service

Continued on next page

Table 16.1 *Continued*

Quality Attribute	Possible question
Usability Important in any user-centred evaluation	• How user friendly did you think this service was? • How easy was it to remember which features to use? • How satisfied were you with the facility to input your query? • How satisfied were you with the facility to modify or change your query, e.g. find similar, related searches, refine search, etc.?

Analysis of the data and interpretation of the results

Analysis of the data can be undertaken in many ways, depending on whether qualitative or quantitative data has been gathered, and in many cases a combination of data types will be analysed. Large amounts of quantitative data are often analysed using a statistical package such as SPSS (www.spss.com), but with the increase in online survey services the basic descriptive analysis produced automatically is often sufficient for many evaluation activities. Qualitative data may be analysed using software such as NVivo (www.qsrinternational.com) or Atlas.ti (www.atlasti.com), or more simply through manual identification of

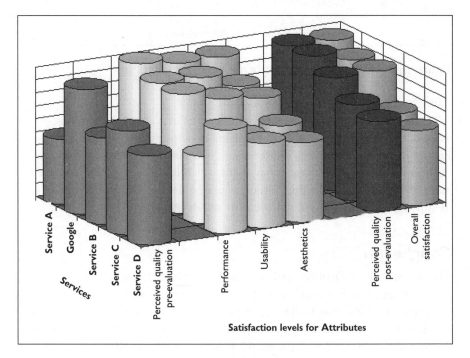

Figure 16.1 *Comparative assessment of resources*

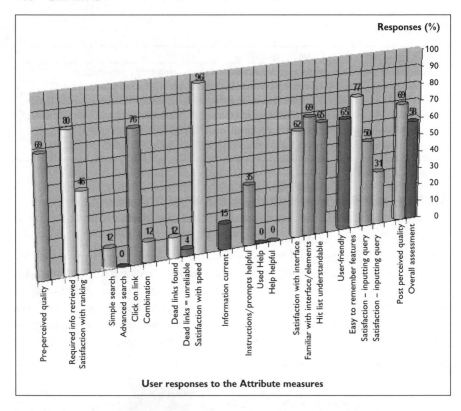

Figure 16.2 *Individual assessment of resource*

themes using a word-processing package.

Results from analysing data from assessments of a number of resources can assist in the identification of those which are underperforming. In the example in Figure 16.1 (looking just at performance, usability, aesthetics and perceived quality) it is possible to make comparisons which can inform collection development and retention. Individual resources can be assessed in greater detail, thus identifying specific areas for improvement and development (Figure 16.2).

Conclusion

The usefulness of Quality Attributes as evaluation criteria is that they allow investigation of how a user's perception of a resource changes pre- and post-searching, and show that while preconceived notions of a service can be negative it is possible to change these perceptions if the resource performs well across a number of the Attributes. If pre-search perceptions do not alter it is possible to identify which aspects of a resource need to be improved by examining those

Attributes that users have scored lower. In addition, because these results demonstrate that measures other than performance play an important role in student evaluation, it is vital that resource developers, providers and educators understand that a range of Attributes affects resource evaluation.

References

Borlund, P. (2003) The IIR Evaluation Model: a framework for evaluation of interactive information retrieval systems, *Information Research*, **8** (3), paper no. 152, available at http://informationr.net/ir/8-3/paper152.html.

Brophy, P. (1998) It May be Electronic but is it Any Good?: measuring the performance of electronic services. In *Robots to Knowbots: the wider automation agenda, Proceedings of the Victorian Association for Library Automation 9th Biennial Conference*, 28–30 January 1998, Melbourne, VALA, 217–30.

Brophy, P. (2004) The Quality of Libraries. In Hilgermann, K. and te Borkhorst, P. (eds), *Die Effective Bibliothek: Roswitha Poll zum 65 Geburtstag*, Munich, Saur.

Brophy, P. and Coulling, K. (1996) *Quality Management for Information and Library Managers*, Gower.

Byström, K. and Järvelin, K. (1995) Task Complexity Affects Information Seeking and Use, *Information Processing & Management*, **31** (2), 191–213.

Craven, J. and Brophy, P. (2004) Evaluating the Longitudinal Impact of Networked Services in UK Public Libraries: the Longitude II project. In Parker, S. (ed.), *5th Northumbria International Conference on Performance Measurement in Libraries and Information Services. An IFLA Satellite pre-conference sponsored by the IFLA Section on Statistics*, 28–31 July 2003, Durham, UK.

Craven, J. and Griffiths, J. R. (2008) Involving Users in a Technical Solution to Help Assess the Accessibility of Websites. Chapter 23 of this book.

Dong, X. and Su, L. (1997) Search Engines on the World Wide Web and Information Retrieval from the Internet: a review and evaluation, *Online & CD-ROM Review*, **21** (2), 67–81.

Garvin, D. A. (1987) Competing on the Eight Dimensions of Quality, *Harvard Business Review*, **65** (6), 101–9.

Griffiths, J. R. (2003) Evaluation of the JISC Information Environment: student perceptions of services, *Information Research*, **8** (4), http://informationr.net/8-4/paper160.html.

Griffiths, J. R. and Brophy, P. (2002) Student Searching Behaviour in the JISC Information Environment, *Ariadne*, **33**, www.ariadne.ac.uk.

Griffiths, J. R. and Brophy, P. (2005) Student Searching Behaviour and the Web: use of academic resources and Google, *Library Trends*, Spring, **53** (4), 539–54.

Griffiths, J. R., Hartley, R. J. and Willson, J. P. (2002) An Improved Method of Studying User–System Interaction by Combining Transaction Log Analysis and Protocol Analysis, *Information Research*, **7** (4), http://InformationR.net/ir/7-4/paper139.html.

Ingwersen, P. (1992) *Information Retrieval Interaction*, Taylor Graham.

Ingwersen, P. (1996) Cognitive Perspectives of Information Retrieval Interaction: elements of a cognitive IR theory, *Journal of Documentation*, **52** (1), 3–50.

McGillis, L. and Toms, E. G. (2001) Usability of the Academic Library Web Site: implications for design, *College and Research Libraries*, **62** (4), 355–67.

Marchand, D. (1990) Managing Information Quality. In: Wormell, I. (ed.), *Information Quality: definitions and dimensions*, Taylor Graham.

Nielsen, J. (1993) *Usability Engineering*, Academic Press.

Nielsen, J. (2007) Should Designers and Developers Do Usability?, *Alertbox*, 25 June, www.useit.com/alertbox/own-usability.html.

Peters, T. (1993) The History and Development of Transaction Log Analysis, *Library Hi Tech*, **11** (2), 41–66.

17

Reaching the unreachable in India: effective information delivery service model of DELNET and the challenges ahead

Sangeeta Kaul

Introduction

India has a long history of libraries that were established during the ancient medieval and modern periods. It also has a diverse socio-economic and cultural environment with varying levels of literacy and an uneven spread of ICT infrastructure. It is estimated that about 50,000 libraries exist in India, comprising academic libraries, public libraries, special libraries and libraries attached to research and development institutions, government departments and ministries, industries, etc. The ICT revolution has brought about a radical change in some of the major libraries in India. This technological change is not witnessed uniformly in the wider cross-section of the libraries, as libraries are at varying levels of transformation. They have to use ICT effectively to help the users. The country has also witnessed the growth of library networks during the last 20 years. A number of city library networks were conceptualized through institutional and governmental initiatives but only a few were able to survive. The rest failed to make progress and were shut down.

The paper highlights the pioneering work being done by Developing Library Network (DELNET), a non-governmental, non-profit-making organization supported partly by the Ministry of Communications and Information Technology of the Government of India. It is a major resource-sharing library network in South Asia, connecting more than 1150 libraries in 30 States and Union Territories (UTs) in India and six other countries (see Tables 17.1–3 and Figure 17.1). DELNET serves its member libraries, which are located within and outside India, and offers inter-library loan/document delivery services (ILL/DDS), one of its most popular services.

Library networking in India

The genesis of library networking in India can be traced back to the late 1980s. The National Information System for Science and Technology (NISSAT), a body under the Department of Scientific and Industrial Research (DSIR) of the Government of India, took the initiative of supporting the city-based library networks. This led to the establishment of city library networks such as Bombay Library Network (BONET), Calcutta Library Network (CALIBNET), DELNET (Delhi Library Network, which became Developing Library Network in 2000), Madras Library Network (MALIBNET) and Pune Library Network (PUNENET). The University Grants Commission also established the Information and Library Network (INFLIBNET) in 1988 to network the university libraries in India. Only a few networks were able to work on a self-sustainable model and continued to exist after the initial phases of implementation and functioning. DELNET, which started as a project in 1988, became a national library network in India by the year 2000. The University Grants Commission continues funding INFLIBNET to provide support to the university libraries in the country. The remaining city library networks were shut down due to the lack of planning and financial resources.

DELNET – Developing Library Network

DELNET – Developing Library Network – has emerged as a major resource sharing library network in India. It networks more than 1050 libraries in 30 States and UTs in India and six other countries. DELNET was conceived as a city-based library network in Delhi in 1988. It was known as the Delhi Library Network, established primarily to network libraries in Delhi, and was registered as a society in 1992. When DELNET services were made available on the world wide web, accessibility was soon transformed from the local dial-up connectivity for the Delhi region's institutions to the global access through the web. This gave a great boost to DELNET and soon it crossed geographical boundaries within the country and also became accessible from outside India. It was on 13 September 2000 that its name was changed from DELNET: Delhi Library Network to DELNET: Developing Library Network. The main objective of DELNET is to promote resource sharing among member libraries by collecting, storing and disseminating information and by providing networked services to the researchers and scholars to supplement their research activity.

Development of library resources

For any library network, the greatest concern is the consolidation of catalogue information of the resources lying scattered across the member libraries. This ensures a wider access to the resources as catalogue information in digital form is converted into union catalogues and made accessible online. Since its inception DELNET has been actively engaged in developing union catalogues and union lists, which became a major strength. Between 1992 and 1993 DELNET had saved Rs10 million in foreign exchange by rationalizing the acquisition of periodicals in the libraries in Delhi. The number of records in the DELNET databases has been growing since then and as a result more and more resources are becoming accessible to the member libraries. These union catalogues are the major tools for resource sharing, as they contain location data for each item and we get to know where the document is physically available.

The data collection methodology of DELNET includes the electronic transfer of exported records through e-mail and FTP protocols. Also, the data is sent physically on CDs by the member libraries. The data back-ups are also physically taken by DELNET staff during their visits to the respective libraries. It should be mentioned that in a country like India, co-operative cataloguing or co-operative collection building still does not exist. There is a lot of duplication of effort in the libraries; the same title is catalogued again and again in different libraries. The libraries in the country are also using various software packages which range from commercial packages like Libsys, Alice for Windows, Virtua, etc., which may be adhering to international standards, to software developed in-house with the back-end on SQL, Access, Excel, Oracle, Sybase, etc. DELNET collects the records from its member libraries in the default exported format, and conversion programs are being developed to convert the base records into the standard ISO 2709 format before they are finally merged into the union catalogues. Databases like union lists are also updated by DELNET, as data is not always available from the libraries in database format. In this case the whole task of data inputting is done by DELNET. Information on current subscriptions to periodicals is also collected from prominent libraries that may not be members of DELNET but can be approached for the desired references.

Challenges for resource creation in the libraries

In India a large number of libraries, especially those with small and medium annual budgets, are struggling to create their records in machine-readable form using standard library software. Commercial software is expensive and out of reach for many of them and the annual maintenance cost is often not affordable by the management of the institutions. Another form of slackness is the adoption of open-source, low-priced library management software. This often leads to in-house development of the software or that produced by local vendors, which does not conform to any bibliographic standards such as MARC 21. This leads to the creation of sub-standard records. A further challenge to modernization of libraries is the lack of availability of trained staff. Professionals need to be fully trained to get acquainted with MARC 21 record creation, Dublin Core metadata, the use of the standard thesaurus, etc. Also the creation of bibliographic records in Indian languages is of major concern. Some of the commercial library software packages provide UNICODE compliance for multilingual record creation.

DELNET databases and their significance

Union catalogue of books

DELNET provides access to more than 6 million bibliographic records of books in English available at various member libraries located in and outside the country. The databases can be accessed by any of the desired fields, including title, author, subject and date of publication. Boolean operators can also be used for refining the search queries. Sorting can be done on the searched results. Searching uses 'Phrase Searching', 'Any Words' and 'Includes'. The records can also be retrieved using specific indexes, including title, author, subject, etc. The database size grows with each passing day as more and more data from the member libraries are being merged in the centralized union catalogues. DELNET has developed its own modules on Basisplus software, a relational database management system (RDBMS).

The member libraries using the ILL facility can place requests online through the system for obtaining books on loan. The ILL loan is one of the most popular services of DELNET. The resource sharing is done not only between libraries located within the country, but also outside India. It is quite heartening to note that DELNET has evolved a very successful functional model of ILL/DDS. Through these services, the users – faculty, researchers and scholars of the member libraries – are able to obtain and refer to books which are not readily available in their own libraries. At times books are out of print and are not even available from the publishers themselves. In special cases, reference books are lent out, although this is for a shorter loan period. It is worth mentioning that certain reference libraries in the country, such as the Central Reference Library, Delhi University and the Indian Institute of Advanced Study, Shimla do lend books to DELNET. This is possible only due to the mutual co-operation between DELNET and such other important libraries. Such libraries also benefit from this method of resource sharing. It demonstrates a win-win situation. DELNET charges only for the actual courier costs for sending the books on loan to the borrowing library and it is the responsibility of the borrowing library to return it back to DELNET at its own cost. In India, where both users and libraries have limited resources, using this method of resource sharing helps users a great deal.

DELNET is also in the process of creating a database of e-books that are available in the public domain. The database will be accessible in a few months time.

Union list of current journals and e-journals consortium in India

Journals are a vital source of current information for the scientific community. It is worth noting that the number of journal titles is growing threefold every 15 years whereas their cost increases 2.5 times every 10 years. Information on the availability of current journals is a great support to the document delivery services. DELNET is maintaining an online union list of current journals available in the fields of science and technology, social sciences and humanities. This database has more than 25,000 unique titles of current journals available in member libraries as well as the non-member libraries. The database is updated continuously by receiving lists of currently subscribed journals. For each request, photocopies of journal articles are obtained from the libraries and are then supplied to the requesting libraries. It is also one of the most popular services of DELNET.

In India, a major e-journals consortium was formed in 2000, the Indian National Digital Library in Science and Technology Consortium (INDEST), with a financial contribution of Rs200 million from the Ministry of Human Resource Development (MHRD) of the Government of India. The India Council for Technical Education (AICTE) has also contributed Rs37.5 million to it. Thirty-seven centrally funded government institutions, including the Indian Institute of Technology (IIT), the National Institute of Technology (NIT), the Indian Institute of Information Technology (IIIT), the Indian Institute of Management (IIM), the Indian Institute of Science, Bangalore (IISc) and a few others, are the core members of INDEST. Private institutions are self-supported, and nearly 500 institutions have joined so far. Under the consortium, access is given to more than 6500 journals from various publishers. Another consortium of e-journals is the UGC Infonet e-journals Consortium, which covers 4453 plus e-journals and offers services to nearly 100 university libraries. It has been noticed that private institutions that are not able to afford membership of the consortiums are heavy users of DELNET Document Delivery Services. Moreover, at times, the members of the Consortium also approach DELNET for the delivery of journal articles, since the desired journals may not be the ones that are covered under the access agreement, or specific issues may not available online. At this stage there is a lot of speculation about the extent of utilization of e-journals in the institutions and a few studies are being carried out to understand the patterns of accessibility. It has been noticed that if an institution ceases to be a member of a consortium because of the non-availability of the digital archiving facility, the users are deprived of browsing the issues for which the institution had paid the consortium.

Union catalogue of journals

DELNET has also created a database of the holdings data of journals available in the member libraries, which contains complete bibliographical information on the journals. At present the database contains 19,289 titles of journals with holdings data. It is a good resource for tracking down the articles from rare, old issues of journals dating back to late 19th and 20th centuries. DELNET receives a number of requests from libraries for locating journal articles from very old issues of journals. The union catalogue of journals has proved to be a good resource for locating the articles from rare and old issues.

Database of journal articles

There are a number of libraries, though not many, in DELNET that are involved with the indexing of articles in machine-readable form. For these libraries, a large proportion of the library budget is annually spent on subscribing to journals, either in print or online mode, but they index important journal articles for their own users. DELNET has been collecting articles and storing them in a machine-readable form and has created a database of select articles. This specific database contains more than 800,000 records and is growing in size. For journal articles, users and researchers send requests through e-mail and DELNET arranges delivery of the full text of the article to them. DELNET also helps users by collecting full-text copies of selected articles from other networked and commercial resources and supplies the articles to the users.

Databases of non-print materials

DELNET maintains databases of CD-ROMs, video recordings and sound recordings available in the member libraries. The non-print materials are not loaned out of the libraries, but the video recordings and sound recordings are being taken on loan, in special cases, for short periods of time. The CD-ROMs are generally used for keyword searching and the bibliography containing the abstracts is provided to the requesting library. The records of 2281 CDs, 748 sound recordings and more than 5000 video recordings are available in the respective DELNET databases.

Database of theses and dissertations

This database contains records of around 45,000 theses and dissertations submitted to various universities and institutions. Since theses and dissertations are available for reference only, researchers and scholars use this database in the libraries only to find out about work being carried out in their specific fields. There have been some projects in India concerning the digitization of theses and dissertations, mostly initiated by the University Grants Commission and the University of Mysore (Vidyavahini project). However, they have not taken off, copyright restrictions being one of the possible reasons for their non-implementation.

DELNET's network operations

The DELNET services are accessible through the world wide web by the registered member libraries. The DELNET databases are hosted on Basis web server and are connected with an 11 mbps RF link offered by National Informatics Centre, Ministry of Communications and Information Technology of the Government of India. The network remains functional 24/7. The web tracking software installed at the DELNET servers gives a day-to-day picture of the use of the DELNET services by the member libraries.

DELNET's services

Interlibrary loan (ILL) and document delivery services (DDS)

DELNET's ILL and DDS services are two of the most popular services among the member libraries located in different parts of India as well as outside the country. The requests for the supply of books on ILL or the requests to arrange for journal articles are received by DELNET through various modes, including the DELNET Online System (options are available through online databases), e-mail (one of the methods most used by the member libraries), by fax and at times by post. DELNET promotes electronic communication, since it is faster and interactive and it facilitates the quick and safe delivery of the ILL/DDS items. DELNET has a separate ILL tracking system in which every transaction is recorded and the status of its date of dispatch, date of return, etc. is recorded. DELNET is able to reach out to the users of the member libraries located in remote parts of the country as well as those from the mainstream cities. The material is sent through insured courier services. DELNET not only provides the ILL/DDS to its member libraries located in various parts of the country but is also engaged in international inter-lending, sending books on ILL to member institutions outside India. Photocopies of journal articles are also provided to member libraries outside India. DELNET is working towards the implementation of ISO ILL protocols. The member libraries of DELNET save a lot of revenue by making use of the inter-library loan and document delivery services of DELNET.

DELNET has also opened up a co-ordination unit in Bangalore (Karnataka) in the southern part of India. The unit co-ordinates the ILL/DDS services and provides a nationwide catalogue of member libraries, which is available on the DELNET system.

DELNET membership

The details of DELNET membership are available at www.delnet.nic.in. At present DELNET has 1150 libraries as its members located in 30 States and UTs in India and six other countries. This includes those within and outside the South Asian Association for Regional Cooperation (SAARC). A detailed breakdown of the members (regionally, by subject, etc.) is provided in Tables 17.1–3 and Figure 17.1 shows the growth in DELNET membership from 1992 to the present.

Table 17.1 *Geographical membership of DELNET*

India

Andaman and Nicobar Islands	1	Kerala	39
Andhra Pradesh	114	Madhya Pradesh	45
Arunachal Pradesh	1	Maharashtra	111
Assam	6	Manipur	1
Bihar	7	Meghalaya	1
Chandigarh	5	Orissa	31
Chhattisgarh	7	Pondicherry	6
Delhi	177	Punjab	44
Goa	6	Rajasthan	37
Gujarat	34	Sikkim	2
Haryana	37	Tamil Nadu	158
Himachal Pradesh	6	Tripura	1
Jammu and Kashmir	9	Uttar Pradesh	95
Jharkand	9	Uttarakhand	13
Karnataka	93	West Bengal	38
		Total	**1134**

Other SAARC countries

Nepal	2	Sri Lanka	5
		Total	**7**

Outside SAARC

Oman	2	United Arab Emirates	2
Philippines	1	United States	4
		Total	**9**

Grand Total	**1150**

Table 17.2 *DELNET membership by subject*

General	184	Science and technology	811
Social science	126	Humanities	29

Table 17.3 *DELNET membership by types of library*

Academic libraries	
Universities	59
Colleges/Institutes/ Dept/Centres	911
Total academic libraries	**970**
Research/special libraries	96
Public libraries	5
Government libraries	29
Libraries of diplomatic missions/UN agencies	10
Miscellaneous, including trusts	40
Total	**1150**

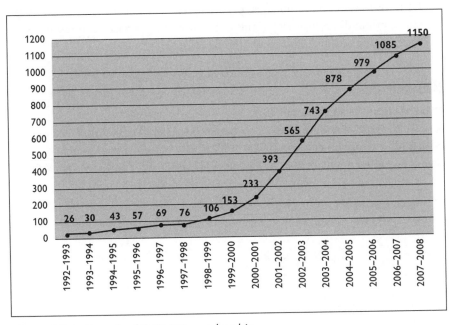

Figure 17.1 *Growth of DELNET membership*

Challenges ahead

DELNET wants to undertake projects in a variety of areas, including the following:

1   DELNET intends to network both libraries and knowledge in the integrated

network model. The National Knowledge Commission of the Government of India has identified DELNET as one of the major library networks which will network more than 25,000 libraries in India in the near future.

2   DELNET is planning to open knowledge centres in India with the support of the Government of India and the State Governments. This approach is being taken in order to convert public libraries in the country into knowledge centres. As a result, the general public can have access to a variety of knowledge resources. DELNET is providing consultancy to the State Government of Gujarat for transforming its State Central Library into a Knowledge Centre. DELNET will soon be launching a national knowledge gateway. Plans are under way to develop local content in various states in India and then make them accessible through the National Knowledge Centre.

3   DELNET is also keen to open state centres and regional centres in order to provide training to library professionals, to promote the use of network resources and also to help local libraries in the development of digital content.

4   DELNET wants more libraries, especially those specializing in South Asian studies from different parts of the world, to use its services and resources for their researchers and scholars at affordable costs.

References

INDEST, http://paniit.iitd.ac.in/indest.

Kaul, H. K. (1992) *Library Networks : an Indian experience*, New Delhi, Virgo Publications.

National Knowledge Commission (India) (2007) *Libraries: gateways to knowledge*.

Rao, N. L. (2006) Knowledge-sharing Activities in India, *Library Trends*, **54** (3), 463–84.

18

Breaking through the walls: current developments in library service delivery: observations from a Sri Lankan perspective

Kamani Perera

Introduction

Libraries, which have been repositories of knowledge for hundreds of years, now need to make major changes in their operations and the means by which they make information and knowledge available. The world is moving rapidly towards the model of the digital library, which provides wide opportunities not only for efficient retrieval and access to knowledge, but also creates avenues for taking libraries far beyond the buildings and structures in which they are housed. Digitization makes it possible to read material that may physically be housed thousand of miles away.

The internet has added a new dimension to information technology and knowledge-sharing platforms, giving rise to rich concepts such as e-learning, knowledge management and archiving of indigenous culture and heritage. Digital libraries can help the move towards realizing the enormously powerful vision of 'anytime' access to the best and the latest of human thought and culture, overcoming all geographical barriers, so that potentially no classroom or individual needs to be isolated from knowledge resources.

Information provision is not the only important role for the library in the transmission of information through the value chain from author to end-user. The individual library also needs to consider tasks in relation to e-publishing and e-learning as being as important as the more traditional role of information provision. The task of information provision remains central but should probably be organized in a new way, changing the role of the individual library.

Technological progress has changed *how* libraries do their work, not *why*. But the most profound technological development, the connection of computer to computer in an unbroken chain around the world, may alter the fundamental concept of the library in the 21st century. Librarians may discover that 'Libraries without Walls' are actually only libraries with new walls, technologically bounded, legally and administratively restricted.

With the advancement of ICT, most of the libraries in Sri Lanka, such as the National Archives and those of government organizations and non-governmental organizations (NGOs), have focused their attention on digitization. Digitization provides a convenient mode of storage, quick retrieval of information and preservation.

Developing countries such as Sri Lanka, India, Pakistan and Bangladesh use languages other than English for communication. Their semantic networks act as a bridge between these communities and the knowledge they need. They can access whatever information they need globally anytime, anywhere, without any geographical barriers but may encounter semantic difficulties. At the same time, financial constraints make it very difficult to access the information needed physically in developing countries. Thus new information technologies help people in third-world countries to gain access to knowledge otherwise unavailable.

However, due to the day-to-day information explosion, digital libraries need to continue to provide new information access facilities to their users. The metadata standards used by libraries in Sri Lanka are different from worldwide standards. At this stage, semantic web services infrastructure offers the potential to provide more flexible services to users to enable them to get what they need.

Library automation: the Sri Lankan scenario

There are three main organizations in Sri Lanka involved in information development in general and library automation in particular. They have made significant impacts on the library and information field. They are the National Science Foundation (NSF), the Sri Lanka National Library and Documentation Centre (SLNLDC) and the Sri Lanka Library Association (SLLA).

The National Science Foundation

The National Science Foundation undertakes a number of relevant activities:

- distribution of CDS/ISIS and WINISIS software
- compilation of a common data format for the exchange of data among libraries
- distribution of turnkey library system to help library automation
- conducting workshops on CDS/ISIS, WINISIS, the internet, e-mail and electronic publishing
- preparation of manuals
- managing a computer training centre for library professionals

- hosting library web pages
- maintaining the online Union Catalogue of Books (PURNA).

The National Library and Documentation Centre

The National Library and Documentation Services Board (NLDSB), established in 1970, is the apex organization in the library field in Sri Lanka. The National Library and Documentation Centre (NLDC), which functions under the NLDSB, was established in 1990.

The NLDSB is the national agency for the International Standard Book Numbering (ISBN), International Standard Serial Numbering (ISSN) and International Standard Musical Numbering (ISMN) projects. All the statistics and data of the projects have been maintained as databases since 1989.

The catalogue of the National Library is also computerized and can be accessed through its OPAC. The National Union Catalogue (NUC) has been compiled and maintained by the NLDC since 1986. Among the main libraries, 75 participate in the NUC project, which was automated in 1996.

The major bibliographic and documentation projects of the National Library, i.e. bibliographies, directories and indexes, are either kept in both print and digital formats or in digital format only. The Sri Lanka National Bibliography (English Section), Sri Lanka Postgraduate Thesis Index, Sri Lanka Conference Index and Government Publications Directory, Index on Devolution of Power and Ethnic Conflict (DEPEC) and National Conference Index are in digital format (Wettasinghe, 2006).

The NLDC has commenced a document scanning project and is in the process of developing a digital library. NLDC has unique and rare collections. Out of these collections, the folklore collection which reveals Sinhalese culture and indigenous knowledge of Sri Lanka is being digitized. A flat-bed scanner and a high-resolution digital camera are used for image capturing. Each volume of the folklore collection has been stored on CD-ROMs as an e-book. It is planned to develop a database and link the full text to the database.

The Sri Lanka Library Association

The SLLA is responsible for conducting a course on library automation (COLA) and organizing workshops and seminars to promote ICT.

Most of the universities, research institutes and NGO libraries in Sri Lanka have now developed information skills using ICT applications. Four out of the 13 universities in Sri Lanka have developed web catalogues and provide remote access to their collections. All universities provide electronic reference services using CD-ROM databases, access to online e-journals, online databases and internet access. Leading organizations such as SLLA, the University of Colombo and the University of Kelaniya have revised the syllabi of their courses to accommodate ICT.

Observations from the Regional Centre for Strategic Studies Library

In Sri Lanka, 95% of the libraries use either CDS/ISIS or software based on it. In this system, DDC or UDC classification systems are used to classify the books. Downloaded online documents are classified using traditional approaches and kept ready for physical access in the library. At the same, time e-documents are preserved using PDF/JPEG or HTML. Thus users can locate the documents they need physically or electronically. Users who cannot visit the library physically can make queries by e-mail, telephone, fax, etc. and have e-documents delivered by e-mail or paper documents through snail mail. Most users in Sri Lanka have e-mail facilities and can also use e-documents once mailed.

The RCSS library is fully automated and provides online databases and internet access. The library is very popular among researchers, university lecturers, undergraduates, military personnel and South Asian scholars, because of the way it is organized. Keyword indexing saves users time.

Conclusion

Modern society is an information-based society. Libraries, being part of the society, are gradually bringing changes to their structures, functions and services. Traditional libraries in Sri Lanka are shifting their budgets to electronic services, CD-ROMs, online access, etc. Libraries are gradually getting connected to networks, nationally and globally.

Reference

Wettasinghe, S. (2006) Digitization of Documentary Heritage in Sri Lanka. In *International Conference on Digital Libraries 2006: information management for global access*, 5–8 December 2006, New Delhi, India, Conference Papers, 2, 935.

19

Meeting users' needs online in real-time: a dream of librarians in the developing world

Anusha Wijayaratne

Introduction

Since the internet has broadened its scale and dissolved physical boundaries, there is huge competition among professionals to bring their business to cyberspace. There is plenty of evidence in the literature to confirm that librarians have also marched into this new space, particularly in their effort to reach their clients to provide a much-needed online real-time reference service. Coffman (2003) describes this new trend: 'In a little less than 4 years, thousands of librarians got out from behind the desk, opened up their shops on the internet, and made ready to answer patron questions live and in real time.' Bakker (2002) states that 'since the year 2000 there's been an explosion of interest in the library world of adapting chat technology'. However, this explosion has hardly travelled beyond the northern hemisphere and most of these librarians who have shops in cyberspace are from developed countries. Therefore, in spite of the abundance of literature on online real-time reference, very little has been published on such efforts in the developing world.

The statement by Alemna and Cobblah (2005) that 'information technology is expanding throughout Africa but at a slower pace, yet with intense efforts directed towards training and implementing more automation' describes a situation common to most countries that suffer from shrinking library budgets, technological drawbacks, user resistance, etc. E-mail versions of online reference services may have been tried by quite a number of librarians in these countries, but there is hardly any evidence of evaluation studies being undertaken to identify the usability and effectiveness of such a service. The time has arrived for librarians in the developing world to think seriously about how they can actively participate in the investigation of technological alternatives to in-person, face-to-face reference, which is becoming obsolete at a rapid pace.

Why do librarians have to go online?

The number of questions coming in to library reference desks is declining and more and more of our patrons are turning to the web to look for their answers (Bakker, 2002). A discussion has already commenced, and is continuing, on whether libraries could be replaced by the internet and its commercial reference service providers such as AskJeeves and WebHelp. Fortunately, there are a significant number of scholars who do not believe in technology to that extent. Ming (2000) lists several common and persistent problems of the internet:

1   Documents are poorly organized. Hence, they are difficult to retrieve and produce unsatisfactory results.
2   Search tools are inadequate to facilitate speedy information retrieval.
3   Documents on the internet are transient.
4   The bewildering mass of updated documents causes users to lose track of the original sources.
5   Users often encounter restricted access or denial of access to information.

It is obvious that thousands of our patrons are suffering in the electronic world due to the lack of the gentle and careful hand of reference librarian. That is why Francoeur (2001) points out, 'So if users are out in cyberspace struggling alone to find answers solely in online sources, then it is worth wondering what is to become of libraries with their vast repositories of print.' Lipow (1999) notes that 'if librarians are not online to assist users in cyberspace, then there is not likely to be anyone else there to recommend printed resources found only in a library'. Therefore, librarians have a war to win not only for mere survival but for the sake of their clientele and for the invaluable printed collections stored in libraries. Broughton (2001) points out another good reason for librarians to go online: 'Providing users with access to remotely available electronic resources without providing assistance and instruction on how to use them is like telling them which airport they are scheduled to depart from, but not giving them a flight number, airline, or gate number.' If we do not take immediate action, our clients are going to miss their flights – and we will too.

Furthermore, there are signs of a bright future for digital virtual reference, where the patrons expect us to wait for them in their desktop whenever they need help. Bailey-Hainer (2005) stated that 'teens are an especially ripe market for chat reference services owing to their personal online habits . . . as today's children mature, the trend will be toward increased use, with younger children added as new users'. Why are we waiting?

There are number of excuses which can be brought forward to postpone this phenomenon. Real-time chat reference is too challenging for the Third World when considering the numerous difficulties faced by the developed world during the initial breakthrough. Radford and Kern (2006) conducted a multiple case study to investigate the discontinuation of nine chat reference services in the USA. They identified six major reasons for discontinuation: funding problems, overall low volume, low volume from target population, staffing problems, technical problems and institutional culture. However, they have learnt from their mistakes and now large numbers of libraries in the developed world are providing 24/7 digital/virtual reference services, not only for their own clientele but also for external information seekers.

Costly mistakes are even more critical in the Third World but we should not remain idle due to fear of failure. The literature provides many examples of pilots and experiments in taking reference into cyberspace (Bakker, 2002). Many models have been developed to overcome the inherent barriers of virtual reference, such as time, language, staffing and so on. In addition, many professionals have recommended this approach highly and stated it as a key component of future librarianship. Let us try. If we can stick to the mantra 'start SIMPLE', we will not lose too much.

Digital reference (DR)/virtual reference (VR)

There are different interpretations of these terms. Berube (2003) tries to distinguish between them:

1   Digital reference: any reference over the web, including e-mail, web form and virtual
2   Virtual reference: real-time reference on the web, using chat, voice or video.

Online reference services are again divided into two categories, according to the time between request and response:

1   Asynchronous: based on e-mail, delayed response because the user is not addressing an individual librarian in real time
2   Synchronous: text-based, digital reference or chat, where the user receives the response in the same session when addressing an individual librarian in real time.

There are a fairly large number of critical topics to be resolved, such as new trends in the web contact centre software market; various models to solve time, language and staffing issues; privacy of patrons; copyright law and intellectual property issues; licensing of electronic publications; and standards and guidelines to facilitate virtual reference. All are being discussed in professional forums worldwide.

However, the scope of this paper is limited to an exploration of the possibilities of introducing synchronous forms of reference service to library user communities in developing countries. This paper focuses on five components of the successful digital reference service process, namely: preliminary surveys, staff training, user orientation, promotion and evaluation. The reason for concentrating on these topics is that they are the most neglected areas in the libraries of developing countries, owing to the biggest hindrance of the developing world – lack of finance. Efforts undertaken by the Open University of Sri Lanka Library to use technology to break the physical and time barriers to reach its remote users are also discussed in this paper.

Preliminary surveys

Chat technology is changing rapidly and in order for services to ensure long-term sustainability, additional research is needed to bridge the gap between the expectations and preferences of the service users and those of the information providers who staff these services (Radford and Kern, 2006). We still know very little about the information-seeking behaviour of our patrons in the e-environment. They may be behaving in a quite different way when they are in cyberspace.

One of the librarians who participated in the Radford and Kern (2006) study stated, 'I think most people are willing to wait. Some just want to drop off the question and get on with life and then come back later for the answer.' Broughton (2001) has come to a similar conclusion after observing her teenage daughter's multitask behaviour (listening to music, surfing the web while chatting). On the other hand librarians think that they have to respond quickly, otherwise the user will leave. Quality and accuracy of the answer may be affected due to this unnecessary rush.

Staff training

Librarians have practised the primary forms of reference, in person and by telephone, for decades but there are many weaknesses. A significant percentage of participants in the 'Visit Study' of Nilsen (2006) saw the reference librarians as a rude, cold and ignorant set of people. It is important for us to change this negative attitude. The best mechanism to produce user-friendly, warm and knowledgeable reference librarians is training and retraining.

VR is a new and challenging role for librarians. They have to deal with users whom they cannot see or hear, although this situation is changing due to the development of VoIP (Voice over Internet Protocol) and webcam technology. In addition, they have to use technology which is not always robust. Furthermore, in many cases they are dealing with patrons with two deficiencies: information illiteracy and computer illiteracy.

Therefore strong and effective training programmes are necessary to prepare our librarians, who may be suffering from 'technostress' (the inability to cope with greater demands of service and increased use of computer-based technology) to meet the demands of this new endeavour. The question is where we can obtain such training. Our training budgets are certainly insufficient for overseas training. Nevertheless, there are a number of options, including finding rare resources such as experts whom we may have in our countries; looking for volunteers (professional colleagues or international organizations who will extend a helping hand by offering free training sessions or consultancies); and donor agencies who will come forward to sponsor a training program.

In addition, we will be able to design an effective training program based on RUSA (Reference and User Services Association) guidelines such as 'Guidelines for Implementing and Maintaining Virtual Reference Services', 'Guidelines for Behavioural Performance of Reference and Information Service Providers', 'Professional Competencies for Reference and User Services' (American Library Association, 2007) and free learning materials available on the web, together with a small amount of outside consultancy.

User orientation

The next demanding issue is familiarizing our users with the electronic world. As the Chinese proverb says, 'Give a fish to a man and he will eat for one day; teach him to fish and he will feed himself for a lifetime.' It is the librarians' duty to develop the information literacy skills of their patrons. Online tutorials and virtual literacy training sessions have been used by librarians worldwide for many years. Numerous libraries provide free access to these educational materials. For example, Edinburgh University Library provides free access to 21 training modules created using Macromedia Flash (see www.lib.ed.ac.uk/howto/flash). There is no need to re-invent the wheel. We can study, adopt and translate these resources to serve our own needs. In addition, the need for user training can be minimized with user-friendly websites which explain themselves (and hundreds of brilliant sites are available on the web to take as examples).

Librarians also should be careful to select software which does not need to be downloaded or configured by patrons and which does not require them to remember passwords. A comprehensive frequently asked questions (FAQs) database is another tool to reduce user traffic at the reference desk.

Promotion

Bernie Sloan, one of the renowned professionals who laid the foundations for DR/VR, stated that 'a system will not be effective until a critical mass of possible users is aware of the potential benefits of the service' (Sloan, 1998). Promotion and marketing can be achieved very cost-effectively by utilizing existing resources such as in-house publications and e-mails. The following tactics would also be very effective in raising awareness among users:

1   Moving the physical location of the online librarian into the public arena.
2   Demonstrating the service at all library training sessions.
3   Encouraging academic staff to use the service and promote it to students. (Fletcher, 2004).

Above all, practitioners have always stressed the importance of giving the live chat link a prominent, highlighted place in the library website. For example, on all web pages of the library and the home page of the parent organization, on the library catalogue, on subscribed databases, etc. This would make it appear that the reference librarian is accompanying each individual user to provide a helping hand at any time. In addition, depending on the capability of chat software, the librarian may be able to ask the question 'Can I help you?' This would give a warm welcome and comfortable feeling to our patrons during their virtual visit to the library.

Evaluation

Evaluation takes time and resources but it can produce data that are very useful to improve the service quality and to help identify cost-effective mechanisms to maintain the service. So it can recover its own cost and save a lot of time and money in the long term. Evaluation of VR is relatively easy, as Web Contact Centre software automatically collects the majority of the data needed for successful evaluation. What librarians have to do is to devote sufficient time to analysing the data in respect of outcomes (quality of answers), processes (effectiveness and efficiency of the process), economy (cost-effectiveness) and user satisfaction. Occasional user surveys can be used to fill the remaining gaps.

The Open University of Sri Lanka (OUSL) Library

The OUSL, which was established in 1980, is the first and the only single-mode distance education university in Sri Lanka. The library network, which consists of the main library, two regional centre libraries and mini-libraries in study centres, is the key information provider to OUSL's population of around 25,000 students, spread all over the country. This is an uphill task as the resources, in terms of funds and staff, are very limited. Although Sri Lanka is a small island (65,525 km^2), a significant number of students are unable to come to the library on a regular basis because of job commitments (80% of students are employed), household commitments and transportation difficulties. Therefore the OUSL Library is always alert to find new technological developments with the potential to enable us to go the extra mile to meet users' needs.

OUSL Library is one of the first academic libraries in Sri Lanka to start automation with the CDS/ISIS package (see http://portal.unesco.org/ci/en/ ev.php-URL_ID=2071&URL_DO=DO_TOPIC&URL_SECTION=201.html). The Library took another step forward in 2000 by shifting to an integrated library management software system (Alice for Windows). Simultaneously, the Library has managed to publish a website as a page of the OUSL main site – www.ou.ac.lk. The web page was redesigned in 2006 (see http://lib.ou.ac.lk/). The website now provides access to online public access catalogue (OPAC) and e-journal databases including H. W. Wilson, Blackwell Synergy and EBSCO Host, which the library accesses through the INASP (International Network for the Availability of Scientific Publications) Project. In addition, the library has started a digitization project to provide online access to past examination papers and course materials. The 'Virtual Information Resource Centre', with 15 terminals, printers and scanners, was opened in April 2006 to provide free access to the internet and the e-resource collection.

After years of hard work the OUSL Library has been able to take the first few steps of transferring a traditional library to an electronic library. The next target is to take the service component into cyberspace. The library has provided e-mail based digital reference services since 2000. A 'Live Chat' service based on Skype (www.skype.com) was launched in late 2006 as a pilot project. However, we have not really done a full planning exercise before launching the service nor have we yet made serious efforts to promote it. The service is still in its infant stage and available only on one day a week. Our next goal is to re-launch the service in a more dynamic fashion.

Conclusion

We must go into cyberspace in one way or another to ensure our patrons are receiving their share of e-information. VR has proven to be a wonderful solution to two reference problems: serving distance learners and troubleshooting remote access problems (Ciccone and VanScoy, 2003). So it is obvious that VR is going to be a leading part of tomorrow's reference services. Nevertheless, librarians cannot do this alone, since the contributions of administrators, policy-makers and e-resource publishers are needed. The information communication technology

(ICT) status of the country is also a determining factor in the feasibility of the service. Despite recent developments in the telecommunication industry, the current ICT status of Sri Lanka is not very encouraging. According to the annual report of the Central Bank of Sri Lanka (2006), internet and e-mail connectivity is only 6.5 per 1000 persons and fixed-line telephone density is 9.5 per 100 persons. The situation would be more or less similar in the majority of developing countries.

However, as librarians we have a duty to do what we can. We, in the developing world, have proved on many occasions that we can do wonders with minimal resources. It is true that VR is very expensive but the major portion of the cost is for the software package. A software package with fabulous features, such as page pushing, co-browsing, escorting users, sharing files, e-mailing the session transcripts and queuing of users, is certainly very attractive. However, when considering the cost factor (for example, according to Broughton (2001) the price of the Virtual Reference Desk software is US$8000 for setup and training and US$500 per month for maintenance), such a system is out of our reach. Fortunately, there is a wide array of free software systems such as MSN Messenger, SIP Communicator, WengoPhone, Ekiga, AOL Instant Messenger, Netscape Chat and Skype. So the cost factor cannot stop us from going into cyberspace. Dedication, commitment and hard work can make online real-time reference a reality for the developing world. Many librarians have described their virtual reference experience as exciting, though they have felt a little nervous during the first few sessions. If we are bored with day-to-day routine duties, something exciting is waiting!

References

Alemna, A. and Cobblah, M. (2005) Relevant Issues in the Provision of Digital Information in Africa, *Library Hi Tech News*, **22** (9), 18–20.

American Library Association (2007) *RUSA Reference Guidelines*, www.ala.org/ala/rusa/protools/referenceguide/default.cfm

Bailey-Hainer, B. (2005) Virtual Reference: alive and well, *Library Journal*, 15 January 2005, www.libraryjournal.com/article/CA491140.html.

Bakker, T. (2002) *Virtual Reference Services: connecting users with experts and supporting the development of skills*, www.igitur-archive.library.uu.nl/DARLIN/2005-0520-200224/2002-2-bakker.pdf.

Berube, L. (2003) Ask Live! UK public libraries and virtual collaboration, *Library and Information Research*, **27** (86), 43–50.

Broughton, K. (2001) Our Experiment in Online, Real-Time Reference, *Computers in Libraries*, **21** (4), 26–31.

Central Bank of Sri Lanka (2006) *Annual Report 2006*, www.cbsl.gov.lk/pics_n_docs/10_publication/_docs/efr/annual_report/Ar2006/Content.htm.

Ciccone, K. and VanScoy, A. (2003) *Managing an Established Virtual Reference Service*, Binghampton, NY, The Haworth Press.

Coffman, S. (2003) To Chat or Not to Chat: taking another look at virtual reference, *Searcher*, **12** (7), www.infotoday.com/searcher/sep04/arret_coffman.shtml.

Fletcher, J. (2004) *Online Librarian Real Time/Real Talk: an innovative collaboration between two university libraries*, http://vala.org.au/vala2004/2004pdfs/20FIHaMc.pdf.

Francoeur, S. (2001) An Analytical Survey of Chat Reference Services, *Reference Services Review*, **29** (3), 189–204.

Lipow, A. G. (1999) Serving the Remote User: reference service in the digital environment, *Ninth Australasian Information Online & On Disc Conference*, Sydney Convention and Exhibition Centre, Sydney, Australia.

Ming, D. C. (2000) Access to Digital Information: some breakthroughs and obstacles, *Journal of Librarianship and Information Science*, **32** (1), 26–32.

Nilsen, K. (2006) Comparing Users' Perspectives of In-person and Virtual Reference, *New Library World*, **107** (3/4), 91–104.

Radford, M. L. and Kern, M. K. (2006) A Multiple-Case Study Investigation of the Discontinuation of Nine Chat Reference Services, *Library & Information Science Research*, **28** (4), 521–47.

Sloan, B. (1998) Service Perspectives for the Digital Library: remote reference services, *Library Trends*, **47** (1), 117–43.

20

Information Central: a service success case study

Susan Robbins

Background

The University of Western Sydney (UWS) is the ninth-largest university in Australia, with over 35,000 students, including some 5000 international students. Its six campuses, served by seven libraries, are responsible for students over an area of 9000 km², a footprint roughly the size of the Netherlands. A large proportion of UWS students study through off-campus and offshore multimodal delivery. 'Two thirds of our domestic students live in the region, which has a population of 1.8 million and the third largest economy in Australia' (Pavincich, 2007, 1).

The UWS library is committed to ensuring that it provides an equitable approach to all services across all campuses, and all modes of study. The challenge of providing high-quality client services to such geographically dispersed and disparate groups of academics and students has been in part met through a service we call Information Central, which is a single receipt and response point for all incoming queries (telephone, online and e-mail). Information Central is staffed by a small team throughout the library's extensive opening hours, including evenings and weekends.

Previous remote client services

Prior to 2006, the library ran an e-mail enquiry service (Contact Us) and virtual reference service (Online Librarian), operating as adjuncts to an individual library's desk and phone services. Contact Us, although popular, suffered from a lack of consistency of responses and the 24-hour turnaround key performance indicator (KPI) was not always met, particularly on weekends and evenings. While the more traditional universities were cancelling their virtual chat subscriptions due to poor use, ours was flourishing, although once again consistency of responses was an issue, and the service operated for very limited hours. All queries to the service desks were received and responded to at a campus level. A complex face-to-face reference query could be interrupted at any time by a phone enquiry involving a loans dispute, resulting in interruption of service for all parties concerned. An integrated approach to service delivery was clearly required. Kortz, Morris and Greene (2006) assert that from a client perspective it is good practice to have a number of access options available, such as face-to-face, live chat, e-mail and phone, and integrate them in a meaningful way so that the client can choose the method most comfortable and useful to them. We took this one step further and chose to integrate several of these options into a central receipt and response point.

In 2005 an internal initiative was generated from within the library's quality management processes. Staff brainstormed suggestions for improving the quality of client service within the library. The ensuing service, Information Central, is an amalgamation of separate suggestions for a call centre for phone enquiries, extended hours of operation for our online service and a desire to improve response times for Contact Us. This holistic approach to 'virtual' queries has now been operating successfully for over a year. It has ensured that there is a standardized and rapid response to client queries, has enabled a systematic analysis of these queries and resulted in subsequent improvements to service delivery.

A literature search revealed that if other libraries were operating such a service, they were not publishing on the subject, although some were utilizing a modified version of a centralized phone service (Burke and Beranek, 2006). Commercial companies, however, were embracing the type of centralized service we wanted and a checklist of issues based on their experiences was developed (Anton, 2000). These included where the service would be based, how it would be staffed, what software would be used and how to manage workflow, given peaks and troughs and service parameters (Pavincich, 2007). Once these issues were resolved the pilot could begin.

The pilot project

The pilot was scheduled to commence at the beginning of first semester 2006, to capture the intake of new students. It was to be staffed from the Ward Library, as the library with one of the longest opening hours and decreasing numbers of face-to-face clients on weekends and evenings. Systems and resources management staff were also located within the Ward Library and the university call centre nearby. Q-Master telephone software was already being used by the call centre and considerable troubleshooting expertise had been developed. The library systems team and the university's IT department worked together to install the hardware and software. Extensive testing was required and several technical issues took longer than anticipated to resolve, mostly involving scheduling the hours of operation. Reportage was determined and procedures established. A new phone number was set up and advertised on the library web page. Individual campus numbers were removed from the front screen of the library contacts page. A recorded message gave clients the option of listening to opening hours, or speaking to a librarian.

Expressions of interest were sought for secondment to the position of Information Central librarian. A very experienced liaison librarian with an extensive systems background was selected for the position.

The Information Central librarian and a small pool of Ward Library staff were trained in Q-Master software, Online Librarian and Contact Us. An Information Central office was created away from the public area of the library and an Information Central computer was designated at the service desk for after-hours use. The service hours were established, operating from the Information Central office between 9 a.m. and 4 p.m. weekdays and from the service desk before 9 a.m., after 4 p.m. and on weekends and public holidays. Seamless weekday changeover techniques were developed and refined.

The possibility of offering a 24/7 service via a consortial arrangement was considered but rejected. Most queries received by the library are specific to our client base, either reference queries relating to assignments, lending services queries relating to student records, or various booking needs. The literature supported our decision, as the University of Strathclyde in Glasgow, Curtin University in Perth and the University of Technology in Sydney had considered such consortial arrangements but did not proceed beyond the pilot stage due to concerns similar to those raised at UWS (Davis and Scholfield, 2004).

A few weeks into first semester, Information Central was operational. In addition to being advertised on the library website, the new service was publicized during presentations at college and library orientation sessions and within all information literacy classes. University switchboard staff were also informed.

The Q-Master telephone system presented the most 'teething' problems, and these took several weeks to resolve. Scheduling (opening and closing of queues at the beginning and end of each day) was a major issue and resulted in disruption to the service on a regular basis. Changing the announcements and schedule to reflect changes in opening hours outside of semester times was particularly problematic.

Initial anecdotal feedback indicated that the new service was well received by clients and refinements continued. Protocols determined that calls would only be transferred to a specific campus for lost property, for study room or training session bookings or when a particular staff member was required. Complex reference queries requiring specialized assistance were referred on. Initially some continuing clients were reluctant to accept assistance from a librarian not based at their home campus, being unaware that our library services are centralized with a unified catalogue, circulation system and policies and procedures. These misgivings were rapidly overcome as clients found their enquiries responded to professionally and in a timely manner.

Developing the service

Once the service had been operational for a few months, areas for improvement were identified. Strategies were developed and refined to manage multiple online and phone queries. This was the service issue of most concern for librarians staffing Information Central. Online Librarian queries were to be kept to 30 minutes where possible. When juggling multiple clients the time spent on each query was often longer, owing to the time delay in the librarian getting back to the client. Statistics were skewed by this and do not necessarily reflect the actual time spent assisting each client. Early online transcripts, particularly during busy times, were analysed and discussed to ascertain ways to improve our responses. Particularly when juggling multiple online clients and the phone, librarians' responses became briefer and more streamlined and, although we knew why, clients occasionally perceived them as abrupt. Paterson (2000) asserts that librarians are taught attributes of helpfulness and approachability through interpersonal skills such as smiling and nodding, and these skills need to be adapted to the virtual environment. Human interaction is difficult online. Simple techniques such as using the client's name in a welcome greeting at the beginning of each session, and the use of emoticons (Paterson, 2000), are effective.

Other strategies were discussed, including transferring phone calls, calling for another librarian to take on additional online queries and not picking up additional online clients immediately, leaving them with the message that their query had been placed in a queue. These measures successfully alleviated many of the multiple client issues.

Basic scripts were already in place for Online Librarian queries and these proved invaluable. For consistency and expediency, clients were referred where possible to our online Successful Searching tutorial and Library FAQs. A knowledge base was created for Contact Us for this same purpose. In-house manuals and procedures were produced.

Further strategies were required when face-to-face clients were added to the mix. As this occurred in the evenings and at weekends, it was not possible to transfer calls to another librarian and a system of prioritizing each encounter was established. It was determined that simple queries should be attended to first, followed by more detailed ones. Clients with complex enquiries could therefore receive more comprehensive assistance without compromising the rapid response requirements of clients with simple queries.

Another issue of concern was the length of time spent on some phone queries. Q-Master software was not initially loaded on the service desk computer and so desk staff could not use the call queue, resulting in the abandon rate (number of callers who choose not to wait in the queue) being higher on the desk. This situation was later rectified by installing Q-Master on the service desk computer.

The literature suggests (Kortz, Morris and Greene, 2006) and experience mirrors that often clients do not choose the most appropriate medium to ask their questions and this can lead to frustration for the librarian and the client. A Contact Us e-mail query saying 'Please send me 5 articles for my biology assignment', and yes, this was a real query, obviously cannot be answered in one exchange as all the necessary information is not contained within the e-mail. As David Lankes (2007) remarked, 'the reference interview is putting the client on a rack and stretching them until they tell the truth', and e-mail is not the best forum for this. It is our philosophy to assist clients to locate their own material. In such instances, the client is referred to more suitable mediums of assistance.

In July 2006, as the result of a takeover, our Online Librarian software ceased to be supported. The new package did not have the co-browsing functionality we had been using successfully to answer reference questions. Co-browsing allowed the librarian's browser and client's browser to share a connection to the world wide web. This functionality enabled clients to interact with staff and received much positive feedback. The lack of it resulted in more online queries being referred on to other methods of assistance, resulting in a time lag in service provision. Recently we upgraded our online software to a package that supports co-browsing, so this situation has been resolved.

A central receipt and response point for all library contact has many and varied advantages. Previously a library-wide technical problem would typically be reported in person at one campus, by phone to another and online at another. This often resulted in delays in resolving the issue. With Information Central these problems are identified almost immediately and rectified rapidly, resulting in better client service.

Complex and difficult assignment questions are also identified rapidly and strategies for assisting students developed in conjunction with the relevant liaison librarian. This ensures a greater consistency of response to the client. Feedback from the Information Central librarian has resulted in the development of additional FAQs, fine tuning of a number of procedures, amendment to some web content and revision of some library publications (Pavincich, 2007).

The centralized system also limits clients who want a service outside our normal parameters. Some ask the same question via e-mail, online, then by phone and are surprised to discover the same librarian responding to each query. A single staff member responding to all contact points ensures that policies are adhered to in an equitable way.

The initial impetus for Information Central, the timeliness and consistency of responses to clients, has proven to be one of the major successes of the service. Once the service had been operational for a few months a number of additional scripted messages were added to the Online Librarian menu and the Contact Us knowledge base. Expediency and consistency are well served by these expanded 'shortcuts'. Early, Japzon and Endres (2006) suggest that knowledge bases are also an excellent solution for assisting new or less experienced staff and relevant knowledge needs to be identified, captured and made accessible. Transcripts from Online Librarian and Contact Us are a useful training tool as they study both user and staff behaviour.

Some interesting patterns of use behaviour emerged. Clients regularly logged on to Online Librarian from within the library. When they were asked why they did not go to the service desk a variety of responses were obtained. Some users did not want to 'lose' their computer by leaving it to go to the desk. Others felt more comfortable remaining anonymous, especially if asking a question they felt they should know the answer to. Others from non-English-speaking backgrounds felt they communicated better in a written context. This was reinforced by a study undertaken in Vancouver University libraries, where Curry and Copeman (2005, 409) claim international students 'struggle to engage in the reference process using a language in which they often lack fluency'. A written transcript is generated and e-mailed to the client for each Online Librarian session making it an even more appealing mode of contact. Net generation clients are often more comfortable in the virtual arena (Gardner and Eng, 2005). Weekends and evenings saw increased usage of Online Librarian by full-time workers who study part-time. These time-poor clients find travelling to the physical library difficult and the range of virtual options available for service delivery has been expressed by many as most appreciated.

From pilot to permanent service

Once the service had been operational for a year, it was thoroughly evaluated and deemed sufficiently successful to move from pilot to permanent status. The position of Information Central librarian was advertised and the seconded staff member became the inaugural incumbent.

The quantitative success of Information Central was measured by key performance indicators, such as requiring a 1% increase in Online Librarian sessions. The figures in Table 20.1 illustrate the improvement in all Information Central activities from March 2006 to March 2007.

Table 20.1 *Information Central activities from March 2006 to March 2007*

	2006	2007	Increase
Telephone	339	1598	+79%
Online Librarian	201	284	+29%
Contact Us	169	304	+44%

It was more difficult to measure the success of the service qualitatively. The Online Librarian software provided a satisfaction measure at the end of each session but it was not compulsory, and consequently rarely completed. The number of repeat users could have been a measure of satisfaction but statistics were extremely difficult to obtain. Anecdotal evidence from the transcripts indicated a high level of satisfaction, the following response indicative of many: 'your assistance was very much appreciated thank you for your time' Guest (Customer).

The library does measure client satisfaction and benchmarks against other Australian universities through the externally administered Rodski (now InSync) Student Satisfaction Survey. This survey is carried out biannually and is scheduled to be next administered in August 2007. The University of Western Sydney library has shown extraordinary improvement since undertaking the survey in 2001, having jumped from the lowest quartile to the top quartile in 2005. This remarkable achievement received a commendation from the Australian Universities Quality Agency (AUQA), an independent national agency which audits and reports on quality assurance in Australian higher education (Australian Universities Quality Agency, 2007). It is with keen interest that we await the results of the 2007 survey, hopeful that along with other service improvements, the implementation of Information Central will raise our status to the top decile.

Rigorous evaluation by the Information Central team has resulted in additional service delivery improvements. The phone call abandon rate of 4% is within the call centre industry standard of 3–4%. To further reduce this rate it was determined that more complex calls would be transferred to a nearby extension to keep the Information Central line open. Transferred clients could be placed on hold if the Information Central staff member was required to answer the main number, and assistance resumed when the other call was completed.

Each phone and e-mail query was assigned a wrap-up code, used to generate reports which identified the exact nature of our client's inquiries. The wrap-up code categorized each query by subject. Recently the wrap up codes for the phone and e-mail services were standardized, enabling more accurate evaluation of the total service. This function is not available through the Online Librarian software and so currently substantive data is unavailable for this contact point. Reports are also generated indicating when clients use our virtual services. These reports assist us to know our clients better and ascertain ways to assist them in a more targeted manner.

The future

The future of Information Central lies in the hands of the stakeholders. Library staff are committed to placing clients at the core of all endeavours. The 2007 to 2009 Library Strategic Plan reflects this commitment through an innovative set of initiatives, reflective of and responsive to clients' needs for flexible delivery of service and resources. While Information Central continues to be a valuable and valued service to our clients it will continue to evolve and through constant evaluation and assessment ensure it meets the needs of our clients.

References

Anton, J. (2000) The Past, Present and Future of Customer Access Centres, *International Journal of Service Industry Management*, **11** (2), 120–30.

Australian Universities Quality Agency (2007) *Report of the Audit of the University of Western Sydney*, AUQA Audit Report Number 51, Melbourne.

Burke, L. and Beranek, L. (2006) Call Us: development of a library telephone enquiry service, *Australian Library Journal*, **55** (3), 211.

Curry, A. and Copeman, D. (2005) Reference Service to International Students: a field stimulation research study, *Journal of Academic Librarianship*, **31** (5), 409–20 [retrieved 6 September 2005 from ScienceDirect database].

Davis, K. and Scholfield, S. (2004) Beyond the Virtual Shore: an Australian digital reference initiative with a global dimension, *Library Review*, **53**, 61–65 [retrieved 16 July 2007 from Emerald database].

Early, C., Japzon, A. and Endres, S. (2006) Creating a Knowledge Base: analysing a veteran reference librarian's brain. In Lankes, R. D. et al. (eds), *The Virtual Reference Desk: creating a reference future*, London, Facet Publishing, 55–167.

Gardner, S. and Eng, S. (2005) What Students Want: generation Y and the changing function of the academic library, *Libraries and the Academy*, **5** (3), 405–20.

Kortz, L., Morris, S. and Greene, L. W. (2006) Bringing Together Teens and Chat Reference: reconsidering the match made in heaven. In Lankes, R. D. et al. (eds), *The Virtual Reference Desk: creating a reference future*, London, Facet Publishing, 3–23.

Lankes, R. D. (2007) Virtual Reference Will Rule the World, seminar presented at *Information Online 2007*, Sydney.

Paterson, L. (2000) Definitions of Personal Assistance in the New Millennium: philosophical explorations of virtual reference service. In Lankes, R. D., Collins, J. W. and Kasowitz, A. S. (eds), *Digital Reference Service in the New Millennium: planning, management and evaluation*, New York, Neal-Schuman Publishers, 37–46.

Pavincich, M. (2007) Information Central: not just a call centre, paper presented at *Information Online*, 30 January 2007, Sydney, www.information-online.com.au/docs/Presentations/pavincich__online_2007_paper_1.pdf [retrieved 1 August 2007].

21

Discrete library services for international students: how can exclusivity lead to inclusivity?

Moira Bent, Marie Scopes and Karen Senior

Introduction

This paper reports on research being undertaken for the UK Society of College National and University Libraries (SCONUL) to investigate how UK university libraries can best support international students, culminating in guidelines which will be published by SCONUL in December 2007. The research examined the issues surrounding the debate over exclusivity versus inclusivity that affect the provision of library services for international students. Results include what techniques UK university libraries are currently employing; feedback from international students about their priorities for library support and how that matches library staff perceptions; and with whom university libraries need to work to improve service provision. The research identified examples of good practice in providing a truly inclusive library service for international students and explored whether issues faced in UK libraries are reflected by experience in other developed countries.

Background to the study

International students make up 13.4% of the total UK higher education institution (HEI) population, and, in addition to enriching cultural diversity and providing essential income, they also bring a wide variety of needs, experience and expectations. In recent years the international student profile has become increasingly diverse, as in other developed countries, with students worldwide having a diverse range of abilities and subject interests and hence a broader scope of teaching and learning experiences. These changes are reflected in the issues faced by all libraries striving to support international students effectively.

Findings of a major survey of more than 28,000 international students confirmed that the UK is still 'a close rival to the US as the best study destination in the world' (Tysome, 2006, 3). However, if UK universities are to maintain their place in the global market, they need to respond to changing needs to attract students from abroad. Academic libraries have an important supporting role in this. Andreas Schleicher, head of the Indicators and Analysis Division at the OECD, warns that 'the global educational landscape has changed fundamentally' and UK universities must face challenges from China and India, in particular, as well as from other European countries now offering degrees taught in English. He says, 'Success will go to those institutions and countries that are swift to adapt, slow to complain and open to change' (Schleicher, 2007, 3).

Globalization also means that universities need to equip all their graduates with the appropriate attributes for employment and citizenship through internationalization of the curriculum. As well as providing resources and teaching information skills, academic libraries can foster an international ethos in the library that enriches the experience of both home and international students.

Definitions

International students

For the purposes of this research we have used the definition of international students given by Carroll and Ryan (2005, 3): 'we speak of international students when we mean students who have chosen to travel to another country for tertiary study . . . most of their previous experience will have been of other educational systems, in cultural contexts and sometimes in a language that is different from the one in which they will now study'.

Internationalization

Internationalization is a term used increasingly by universities. Knight and de Wit (1995) define it as 'the process of integrating an international/intercultural dimension into the teaching, research and service of an institution' and David Coyne, the Director of Education for the European Commission, says 'higher education in Europe, if it wants to retain both the reputation and the reality of excellence in its teaching provision and its research, must open itself up to the wider world. It must internationalize . . . If universities cannot manage that adaptation and transition . . . then they have lost what they should be about' (Coyne, 2003).

The international student profile

It is predicted that by 2020, global demand for HE international student places will increase from 2.1 million in 2003 to 5.8 million. In the five major English-speaking destination countries (USA, UK, Australia, New Zealand, Canada), the forecast is for an increase from 1 million to 2.6 million places, with Asia dominating the demand. Some of this demand will be catered for by in-country collaborative agreements (Bohm et al., 2004).

Perceived issues

This research was undertaken against a background of perceived issues, derived both from experience and a review of the literature. We have considered issues from the perspectives of library staff and international students separately, in order to recognize congruencies and conflicts in approaches.

Library staff perceptions

Numbers of international students are increasing in all countries, while at the same time UK student numbers are rising. In addition, statistics show that UK student mobility has continued to decline since 1994/5 in comparison with growing figures from other European countries (Erasmus, 2007). The cumulative effect is that libraries are dealing with increased demand with frequently declining budgets.

Incoming international students may sometimes harbour unrealistic expectations, both of the university and the library. Students are now travelling from a much wider range of countries, as more developing nations want to educate their students elsewhere. Furthermore, it is no longer just high achievers who are funded by their governments; now opportunities are available for a wider range of abilities and ages. International students are not a homogeneous group; students from the same country may still have different cultural backgrounds and experiences. Sunuodula (2006) comments, 'In China . . . the disparity between its east and west and between urban centres and countryside is reflected in the students' knowledge of information resources and information skills.'

Student perceptions

It is well documented (Carroll, 2005; Hughes, 2001; McNamara, 1997) that international students face additional challenges to those faced by all new students and these can affect both the academic and social aspects of their study in the UK.

Language barriers

In her survey of incoming international students at San Jose State University, Jackson (2005, 199) says that 'English language proficiency is a difficulty widely documented in the literature on international students. Both librarians and students encounter verbal and written language barriers and non-verbal communications problems.' International students may feel self-conscious about speaking English, afraid of making mistakes or not being understood, and this may discourage them from approaching library staff for help. They may find it difficult to understand regional accents and colloquialisms. Reading and writing Roman script may be a problem and students may also experience difficulties in following what is happening in class, and keeping up with academic work because of constantly having to refer to dictionaries.

Previous library experience

In her review of the literature, Jackson (2005, 198) reports, 'It is well documented . . . that students from other countries are accustomed to different library services and varying degrees of access to information . . . .' In a similar study of incoming international students at Deakin University, McSwiney (2006) also comments on the diversity of students' previous library experience. Problems include unfamiliar classification systems and confusing library terminology. Some international students may be used to closed access libraries and to having materials brought to them by library staff. They may need more help in finding information independently and in using self-service systems. Books and other resources may have a Western or UK-centric perspective which international students may find difficult to relate to their own experience. Length of opening hours throughout the year, including vacations and public holidays, is important to many international students, who are often more dependent than home students on the library for access to e-mail and the internet and as a place to study.

Levels of computer literacy vary among international students and assumptions should not be made. Some students may not be able to make full use of computers because of language difficulties. In addition, there may be issues regarding access to computer programs to enable the reading and writing of non-Roman scripts, such as Chinese, and this may also mean difficulties in communicating with relatives and friends back home.

Culture

International students may feel overwhelmed by differences in culture and may experience the stress often described as 'culture shock', the symptoms of which can include frustration, mental fatigue, loneliness, boredom and lack of motivation, as well as homesickness. Pace of life and differences in food are often highlighted by students. They may encounter well intentioned ignorance which could cause offence. Yoshino (2004, 18) comments: 'All too often, [university staff] seem to be left to their own devices, with little back-up or systematic information, when dealing with students from fundamentally different cultural and academic backgrounds from their own.' Both McSwiney (2006) and Sunuodula (2006) recommend library staff development that includes cross-cultural awareness.

Teaching methods

Differences in educational culture can be a major issue for international students. They may be used to more formal teaching methods and unused to critical thinking, group work and independent learning. Tweed and Lehman explore the influence of culture on academic learning by examining the Western approach, characterized by questioning and evaluating accepted knowledge in which students are expected 'to generate and express their own hypotheses' in contrast with the Eastern approach which values 'effortful, respectful, and pragmatic acquisition of essential knowledge' (2002). They suggest the development of a flexible approach to teaching and learning which combines the advantageous elements of both approaches.

Another important issue is plagiarism and research has found a high incidence of it among international students. Swain suggests that this may be due to language, stress and different cultural traditions or simply because more international students are actually caught plagiarizing (Swain, 2004, 23) but Jackson (2005, 198) comments that 'many authors suggest that the concept of plagiarism is a Western academic value'. However, home students also plagiarize, so this is not solely an international issue.

SCONUL project research methodology

Commencing with a comprehensive literature survey, the research focused initially on a survey of SCONUL member institutions. Due to the short timescale and practical nature of the outcomes, a mixed methodology was used to collect data. Quantitative data was collected in January 2007 using the Bristol Online Survey (BOS) software by sending a request for participation to the SCONUL Directors mailing list. Qualitative data, from other surveys undertaken by project group members using focus groups and interviews with students, supplemented the comments also collected in the BOS survey. A stratified random sample, representing different types of UK university, assessed the visibility of services to international students on their library and general university websites and gathered examples of best practice. Selected university and library websites were also looked at in Australia, New Zealand, and the USA, and personal visits were made to libraries in these countries.

Preliminary results of the SCONUL UK Directors' survey

The results of the Directors' survey painted a disappointing overall picture for the UK, with some areas of good practice in evidence, while the literature search and other methodologies revealed good practice being undertaken elsewhere in the world. The Directors' survey elicited a 33% response rate (50 libraries).

Strategy

While 72% (36) of respondents had university-level international strategies, only 8% (14) had an international library strategy or action plan in place. However, the majority of libraries collaborated with other university departments in the support of international students, including:

- academic departments
- international offices
- language centres
- international student associations
- students union
- departmental committees
- faculties or colleges.

Designated staff support

Just over 25% of respondents (13) had a designated member of staff within the library supporting international students and delivering services to them. Of these, only one was working full-time in the post, and ten estimated that up to 25% of their time was spent on such activities. Jackson advocated that 'the library should appoint a librarian responsible for international student outreach and instruction' (2005). In Jackson's Library at the University of San Jose in California, the role has now been defined as that of an overall co-ordinator, albeit with some discrete research and teaching, with subject librarians looking after the international students in their own subject areas. In the UK, existing posts also tend to be combined with other responsibilities, such as those of a subject librarian, e.g. at Hertfordshire (Singer, 2005), and Exeter (Gale, 2006).

Staff development

It is encouraging to note that 70% [35] of respondents have staff development for library staff addressing international student issues and services. The areas covered include:

- cultural awareness (32)
- customer care skills (27)
- language problems (20)
- staff communication skills (20)
- strategies dealing with problem solving (19)
- learning styles (15).

Jackson (2005), Mu (2007) and others discuss these issues as they affect all international students, while Li (2006), examines the challenges posed specifically by East Asian students. Training library staff effectively will have other benefits. As Li says, 'these special customers have offered librarians challenges and opportunities in exploring and addressing information needs of people from other cultural backgrounds. The knowledge and skills gained from helping this customer group will not only benefit the library's clientele, but will also advance librarians' professional development' (Li, 2006, 3).

Library web pages

In the survey, only four libraries had specific library web pages aimed at international students, and when the project group accessed over 30 UK library websites, the pattern was similar. Elsewhere in the world, there is evidence of good practice. For example, the University of Technology Sydney (UTS) library site details services for international students from a prominent link on their main page. The services include an international students orientation programme; access arrangements including a library guide in Chinese; information skills sessions; a resources section which references the International and Cultural News Centre (ICNC) situated in the library; and MyLanguage.gov.au, an online service providing information links and search engines in nearly 60 languages other than English. Singer (2005) comments that websites can go a long way towards managing pre-arrival student expectations: 'I felt strongly that the support structures should be clearly visible on the website in order to "sell" the facilities and also to enhance the student experience before arrival.'

Publications

Publications aimed specifically at international students were produced by 13.7% (7) of libraries, and three of these provided them in languages other than English. These were mainly general library guides. However, some libraries do produce other resources, such as the University of Birmingham, which is producing a multilingual audio tour of the main library in English, French, Arabic and Mandarin.

Services provided

Most libraries in the survey provided some discrete services for international students. These were:

- an induction (45)
- information skills (37)
- one-to-one consultations (36)
- non-English newspapers and magazines (25)
- computing support for non-English languages (12).

Emerging themes

Preliminary analysis of research results is producing a number of prominent themes which need addressing if library staff are to contribute to a positive learning experience for international students, and for home students:

Managing expectations

- communication before arrival
- clear information on university/library web pages
- library induction
- information skills teaching.

Staff development

- including cross-cultural awareness in regular 'customer care' training for all library staff
- encouraging library staff to learn a language or brush up existing language skills
- training in using jargon-free English for library publications, including web pages
- encouraging participation in university initiatives on diversity and international themes.

Stock management

Although libraries may feel their main responsibility is to provide access to materials on reading lists, there is a need to consider the provision of resources which enable all students to develop a wider international perspective. In addition, many libraries provide leisure literature and access to other media such as newspapers and TV in a wide range of languages, which can also be relevant to home students.

Information literacy

- library induction
- measuring competencies in information literacy
- subject-specific training in information skills delivered at an appropriate time in the curriculum
- one-to-one tutorials
- understanding scholarly communication and how it works
- ethical use of information including copyright and plagiarism issues
- continuing support mechanisms which students understand and find easy to access.

Social space

Survey results indicate that many international students value the library as a neutral, non-threatening, safe social space, as well as a key resource for learning. This view is enhanced by long library opening hours. Library staff may need to consider how much they would like to adopt practices which attract international students to use their space, even though they may not have a direct 'library' role. Services such as the provision of Skype on library PCs, notice boards for international student use, world time clocks, national flags, the celebration of important national festivals on display screens and the watching wall of international TV programmes at Canterbury University of Technology are just a few examples.

Communication

- library publications – jargon-free in 'plain English'
- clear guiding.

The survey flagged up useful areas and the literature cites many suggestions on how communication can be improved.

Student feedback and involvement

Libraries must establish mechanisms for obtaining the views of international students, as well as networking and liaising with relevant sections of the university in developing and evaluating library services and facilities.

Conclusion

Jargon-free library publications improve access to library facilities, and good customer care benefit both home and international students. Information literacy skills which are embedded in study programmes and based on an understanding of different learning styles are equally relevant to all students. It is not just about improving the library for international students; it is also about appreciating cultural diversity and creating an international, multicultural ethos which will prepare all students for life in a globalized world.

However, it is also important that international students realize that their needs are recognized and addressed. As social networking websites show, joining groups which create a sense of identity is an important communication issue. International students often face greater challenges in using the library than home students and it is sometimes necessary to provide 'exclusive' services to achieve equity. Therefore it is helpful to badge certain services and facilities which help international students adapt to the host country's libraries. Information skills sessions which have been tailored to the pace and specific needs of international students, glossaries explaining library terms and sections on library web pages are all good examples of these. A welcoming and informative approach will create a positive library experience for international students. However, it is important to treat all students as individuals without generalizing too much; if we can do this successfully, then exclusive activities will enable all students to be included.

References

Bohm, A. et al. (2004) *Vision 2020: forecasting international student mobility; a UK perspective*, British Council.

Carroll, J. and Ryan, J. (2005) Canaries in the Coalmine: international students in Western universities. In Carroll, J. and Ryan, J. (eds.), *Teaching International Students: improving learning for all*, London and New York, Routledge.

Coyne, D. (2003) Internationalization at Home and the Changing Landscape, *Internationalization at Home Conference*, Malmo University, Sweden, 26 April 2003.

Erasmus (2007) *Timeseries Erasmus Student Mobility: 1987/88–2005/06*, http://ec.europa.eu/ education/programmes/llp/erasmus/stat_en.html.

Gale, C. (2006) Serving Them Right? How can libraries enhance the learning experience of international students: a case study from the University of Exeter, *Sconul Focus*, **39** (Winter), 36–9.

Hughes, H. (2001) The International-friendly Library – customising library services for students from overseas, *ALIA 2001 TAFE Libraries Conference*, August 2001, Australian Library and Information Association, http://conferences.alia.org.au/tafe2001/papers/hilary.hughes.html.

Jackson, P. A. (2005) Incoming International Students and the Library: a survey, *Reference Services Review*, **33** (2), 197–209.

Knight, J. and de Wit, H. (1995) Strategies for Internationalization of Higher Education: historical and conceptual perspectives. In de Wit, H. (ed.), *Strategies for the Internationalization of Higher Education: a comparative study of Australia, Canada, Europe and the United States of America*, Amsterdam, European Association for International Education.

Li, Z. (2006) Communication in Academic Libraries: an East Asian perspective, *Reference Services Review*, **34** (1), 164–76.

McNamara, D. and Harris, R. (1997) *Overseas Students in Higher Education*, London and New York, Routledge.

McSwiney, C. (2006) *Academic Library Experience and Expectations: a study of incoming international students at Deakin University English Language Institute (DUELI)*, report submitted to the Deakin University Librarian.

Mu, C. (2007) Marketing Academic Library Resources and Information Services to International Students from Asia, *Reference Services Review*, **35** (4), 571–83.

Schleicher, A. (2007) Universities Must Face the Chinese Challenge, *Independent Education Supplement*, 7 June, 3.

Singer, H. (2005) Learning and Information Services Support for International Students at the University of Hertfordshire, *Sconul Focus*, **35** (Summer/Autumn), 63–7.

Sunuodula, M. (2006) *Supporting International Students in Durham: a library perspective*, unpublished report, Durham University.

Swain, H. (2004) I Could Not Have Put it Better so I Won't, *Times Higher Education Supplement*, 25 June, 23.

Tweed, R. G. and Lehman, D. R. (2002) Learning Considered Within a Cultural Context: Confucian and Socratic approaches, *American Psychologist*, **57** (2), 89–99.

Tysome, T. (2006) Brits Popular but Posh, *Times Higher Educational Supplement*, 8 December, 3.

Yoshino, A. (2004) Cue the Praying Hands and Ill-informed Bow, *Times Higher Education Supplement*, 16 July, 18.

22

Are we ethical? A workshop on the ethical challenges of providing library services to distance learners

Gill Needham and Kay Johnson

Introduction

This paper reports on discussions drawn from a workshop on the ethical challenges of providing library services to distance learners, which was undertaken at the Libraries Without Walls conference in September 2007 (www.cerlim.ac.uk/conf/lww7/).

Drawing on our respective experience at the UK's Open University and at Athabasca University, Canada's Open University, we engaged in a dialogue about ethical challenges in providing library support to distance learners. We felt it would be valuable to have a framework of ethical principles to guide our practice. Unable to locate an existing framework, we devised our own, influenced by the UK and Canadian professional codes of ethics for librarians (Canadian Library Association, 1976; CILIP: the Chartered Institute of Library and Information Professionals, 2006), as well as by the Society of College, National and University Libraries' briefing paper *Access for Distance Learners: report of the SCONUL task force* (SCONUL, 2001) and the Canadian Library Association's *Guidelines for Library Support of Distance and Distributed Learning in Canada* (CLA, 1993 [2000]).

The purpose of the workshop was to test a set of ethical guidelines proposed in an article we wrote for a special issue on ethics in *Open Learning* (Needham and Johnson, 2007).

The workshop scenario

The following scenario was enacted as an opener to the workshop; the characters are a librarian on a helpdesk telephone (L) and a distraught student on the telephone (S):

L: Hello. Library Helpdesk. Susan speaking. How can I help you?

S: I'm a student on the Science and Society course and I have a real problem with my assignment.

L: What's the problem?

S: Well, it's due tomorrow. I was supposed to do it over the weekend, but the children wanted to go shopping and my mum's not been too well, and then my partner had to work. You know how it is . . .

L: Well, yes . . . . So can you get it done tonight?

S: I've written a lot of it, but my computer has just blown up, just when I was going online to look for some literature.

L: Shouldn't you have done that first?

S: Yes, maybe, but I didn't and now I'm really stuck. I wondered if you could do a search for me and fax me a list of references and some articles. I've got a fax machine. It's really important. We get marks for the bibliography.

L: Well then, it wouldn't be very fair if I did it for you, would it?

S: Nothing's fair, is it? Some of the students on my course don't have kids. They have a lot more time than I do . . .

L: That's not really the point.

S: . . . and they live near libraries where they can go in and find stuff on the shelves and get help there. We're miles from the nearest library. PLEASE help me!!!!

L: Perhaps you could plan the literature search and talk me through it, and I could just carry it out as you would have done it yourself?

S: But I don't know how to do it. I've never done a literature search. I was just going to put some words into Google.

L: Didn't you learn it as part of the course?

S: No, we didn't. They just seem to expect us to know it – and some of the students have done it in another course.

L: Why didn't you contact the Library for help earlier?

S: To be honest, I didn't really think of it. I only found your number because there was a leaflet in one of the mailings I got. We weren't told anything about the Library in the course. Look, it's getting late and I'm beginning to panic. My kids will be waking up in a few hours. Are you going to help me or not?

The situation of the distraught student certainly raises ethical questions as the librarian finds herself juggling principles of equivalence, personalization and fairness. What are the responsibilities of the institution and of the student in her predicament? How will the librarian resolve the situation? What would you do?

Distance education institutions provide library support to their students, to varying degrees, but there appears to have been very little discussion about ethical principles or critical reflection on the impact of our practice. This is despite the fact that there are obvious obstacles to providing distance learners with an equivalent library experience to that offered to campus-based students. While it may be argued that these challenges are significantly reduced by the opportunities provided by access to technology, this can itself be seen to raise a further set of ethical issues. Library support is an essential component in creating a successful educational experience for distance learners and providers of this support cannot underestimate the challenges of, or miss the opportunities for, helping and empowering distance learners to overcome barriers.

In examining the ethics of providing library support to distance learners we feel that we have taken on a topic that requires more attention in the library and distance learning literature. Our hope in the workshop was to open a wider dialogue. Participants were encouraged to engage with our ten proposed ethical guidelines for library support to distance learners and to reflect on them in the context of their own practice. The set of ten proposed guidelines (Needham and Johnson, 2007, 119) is reproduced below:

1 Ensure that each originating institution takes responsibility for providing library support for its own distance learners.
2 Provide distance learners with access to equivalent levels of library services, resources and support as students at campus-based universities.
3 Treat all information users equitably – all users to receive the highest quality service possible.
4 Acknowledge the reality that distance learners may need library services that are more personalized than those for on-campus students.
5 Respect and provide for user diversity.
6 Promote awareness of distance library services and resources.
7 Respect confidentiality, privacy and dignity.
8 Defend intellectual freedom, and avoid bias.
9 Respect the integrity of information and intellectual property.
10 Ensure that professional development of distance education librarians is an ongoing process.

The 52 workshop participants represented library services from 16 countries. Given time constraints, six of the ten guidelines were selected randomly for discussion. Participants broke out into six groups of eight or nine members to discuss and give feedback on one of the selected guidelines. Each group had 20 minutes to work together and then had five minutes to report back in the plenary session. Some of the ensuing discussion is captured here.

Guideline 2

Provide distance learners with access to equivalent levels of library services, resources and support as students at campus-based universities.

We have identified providing distance learners with access to equivalent levels of library services, resources and support as students at campus-based universities as perhaps the most difficult ethical challenge, particularly in terms of learner access to physical library resources and in the provision of information literacy instruction (Needham and Johnson, 2007). The group who took on this guideline agreed in principle that libraries should be providing an equivalent standard of service (particularly where students are paying the same fee), but that this was not always possible. They suggested that there were particular challenges in providing physical resources at a distance with costs of postage and risks of losing stock presenting problems.

While some distance education institutions such as Athabasca University have been able to provide students with postal book loan and photocopy services, at no cost to the student, this is not always feasible for libraries. Examples were given of strategies to overcome challenges to delivery of materials; in particular, reciprocal arrangements with local libraries such as the Canadian University Reciprocal Borrowing Agreement (CURBA), which extends in-person borrowing privileges to students, faculty and staff at university libraries across the country. Interlibrary loan services such as those provided by DELNET in India have also been quite successful. DELNET is a very impressive collaborative network of libraries providing services over a vast area (see Chapter 17).

While the group felt that in theory it was far easier to provide access to electronic resources, some libraries had difficulties in securing licensing arrangements which gave access to off-campus users. It was also pointed out that success is dependent on access to broadband, the internet and an uninterrupted power supply, which is not always the case for some libraries. This was particularly the case in Africa: see Chapter 4, where Pauline Ngimwa describes the challenges of providing services in Kenya. It was felt that innovative use of electronic environments should facilitate service provision to distance learners, but this requires significant investment in time and resources. A wide range of examples was cited, including providing access to computers on rickshaws in India, using an integrated one-stop-shop helpdesk in Australia, using podcasting at the London School of Economics and various virtual reference services.

Guideline 3

Treat all information users equitably – all users to receive the highest service possible.

In proposing this guideline our concern had been to address the inequities that distance learners experience for a variety of reasons, such as the different levels in library service a student located outside the country might receive (Needham and Johnson, 2007). The participants who discussed this guideline were not fully in agreement with it. They felt that treating all information users equitably, and ensuring that all users receive the highest service possible, was so obvious that it should be part of the institution's overall strategy. Nevertheless, as shown in the scenario above, where the librarian is under pressure to provide 'extra' support to compensate for the student's situation, it is not always easy to do this. Apart from an obvious conflict between delivering service demanded by the student and the responsibility to educate, there are additional constraints. The group suggested that it was important to manage users' expectations of the service to be provided and to set clear boundaries, determined by capacity and cost in many cases. An example of this might be the amount of time spent with individuals making enquiries. Their needs will vary according to their experience, knowledge, confidence and motivation. The library must respond to those varying needs within what is reasonable and it may not always be easy to articulate this.

The group suggested that service standards and service level agreements are very important here. They did point out, however, that they will sometimes 'bend the rules' to meet particular circumstances and it may not be entirely ethical to do so. A number of arrangements were cited as examples of attempts to ensure equity of provision. For example, in one Canadian university special services were available to students who registered as distance learners. It is important to find alternative means of supporting students who, as in Africa (see Chapter 4), may have difficulty in accessing the library. Course packs and peer mentoring schemes were mentioned here as possible solutions.

Guideline 4

Acknowledge the reality that distance learners may need library services that are more personalized than those for on-campus students.

The group who discussed this proposed guideline agreed that it is important to acknowledge that distance learners may need library services that are more personalized than those for on-campus students and thought the guideline was well illustrated by the scenario. They felt that the lives of distance learners, the majority of whom juggle work, home, family and study, necessitated a personalized approach to enable them to succeed in their studies. With increasing emphasis on student retention, libraries must take steps to ensure that the particular needs of learners are addressed. Information literacy was seen as a challenge when libraries may not have access to distance students early in their studies. This means that instruction may often be remedial and has to be tailored to individual needs. Where instruction is provided early in the course it is often the case that busy distance learners forget what they have learned by the time they need to implement it.

The group pointed out that distance learners often have more complex circumstances or problems than on-campus students. They may be studying in this way because they have disabilities or illness, they may be carers or be housebound for many reasons. Language my also be an issue. All these circumstances will influence the kind of service they require.

These challenges can be addressed in a variety of ways. Help desk hours need to be flexible and offer a choice of means of contact. More frequent or systematic contact with students may be required, using e-mail, chat or discussion forums.

Guideline 5

Respect and provide for user diversity.

The group working on this proposed guideline endorsed it and suggested that respecting and providing for diversity would be an integral part of policy in the majority of institutions. They felt, however, that the practicalities were less easy to address. The challenges were summarized as addressing diversity in language, culture, skills and learning styles.

Many universities provide learning materials in one language only and cultural issues are difficult to take into account always. The UK Open University, for instance, used the abortion debate as an example of a controversial topic in their information skills tutorial. This had to be changed in the version being made available in the Middle East. Skills tutorials may be provided at level one for first-year students, but many distance learners may have skills at a lower or a higher level, depending on their previous education or work experience. It can be difficult for libraries to anticipate or meet the diverse needs of distance learners.

The most important intervention here was felt to be staff development on the subject of diversity. It was thought that this should be reinforced at regular intervals. Some interesting examples were described. At the University of Bath, international students have been actively involved in library staff development sessions. The Universitat Oberta de Catalunya provides search facilities in multiple languages. Bolton University provides a detailed guide for its off-campus students and also talks to its lecturers about the suitability of some assignments for distance learners with diverse needs.

Guideline 7

Respect confidentiality, privacy and dignity.

While the participants who discussed this proposed guideline agreed that respecting confidentiality, privacy and dignity is important in principle, they acknowledged a number of circumstances in which this might be difficult to maintain. The situations they highlighted are fairly extreme. They discussed a scenario where a student had been accused of plagiarism and library staff were asked to give evidence to support the case. Here the librarian's respect for a user's confidentiality is clearly being compromised. Other extreme examples cited were users presenting a potential terrorist threat or users with serious psychological problems. In some cases librarians have been asked to supply information to students which they suspect is going to be used in a business context. In the case of electronic collections this contravenes licensing agreements which state that the material is for educational use only. Similarly, the infrastructure in the UK, the Joint Academic Network (JANET), is provided for educational use only. If students make use of resources and the system for their businesses or their employers' businesses the library should be taking action. This is a particular issue in distance education, where the majority of students are in full-time employment.

In drafting this principle we had considered a more mundane challenge to the privacy principle, which was not raised in the workshop (Needham and Johnson, 2007). We suggested that pressures on resources for library services in higher education, and a growing emphasis on targets and performance indicators, could mean that library staff are being expected to collect a great deal more information about their users than might have been the case in less cash-strapped times. Frequent surveys are carried out and libraries are required to demonstrate which groups of students they are reaching, which may necessitate collecting various types of personal data. This can be seen to compromise the privacy of users. On the other hand, the popularity of personalization in services such as eBay and Amazon (now being replicated by libraries) may be seen as a sign that users are happy to trade a certain amount of privacy in order to enjoy a higher level of service.

There was some discussion in the workshop about techniques such as the use of emoticons (influenced by the world of gaming), which could be seen to 'insult users' intelligence' and hence raise dignity issues. This may be culturally and age-determined.

Guideline 8

Defend intellectual freedom and avoid bias.

Although this group felt that defending intellectual freedom and avoiding bias is an ethical essential for libraries, they struggled a little with the concept. They concluded that they would expect this to be embodied in the culture of the university. They suggested that cultural and religious differences could present problems here. With distance teaching universities increasingly seeking international markets, the principle may need to be compromised if, for example, the library were under pressure not to hold materials which are unacceptable to some groups. The Chinese market could present particular problems, for example.

In discussing the difficulties of upholding this principle we had suggested that distance education libraries are unlikely to have collections which could be regarded as balanced and therefore unbiased. Collection development policies are driven by the curriculum and specific research interests rather than a responsibility to present a balanced overview of the world of knowledge (Needham and Johnson, 2007).

Conclusion

The workshop was an interesting exercise, which gave some useful feedback on the proposed guidelines and raised some further questions. The opportunity to gather comments from a multinational group was particularly valuable. It is, however, important to emphasize the limitations of the process. The restricted time available (we were grateful to be granted an hour in a busy and excellent conference programme) meant that only six of the guidelines could be addressed and that discussion was limited. We were impressed by the extent to which participants engaged with the issues and many said that they found it particularly challenging, suggesting that as a profession we do not address ethical issues on a regular basis. We suggest that the results of the workshop demonstrate the value of exploring these topics more widely in the future.

References

Canadian Library Association (1976) *Code of Ethics*, www.cla.ca/Content/NavigationMenu/ Resources/PositionStatements/Code_of_Ethics.htm.

Canadian Library Association (1993/2000) *Guidelines for Library Support of Distance and Distributed Learning in Canada*, www.cla.ca/AM/Template.cfm?Section=Position_ Statements&Template=/CM/ContentDisplay.cfm&ContentID=3794.

CILIP: the Chartered Institute of Library and Information Professionals (2006) *Ethical Principles and Code of Professional Practice for Library and Information Professionals*, www.cilip.org.uk/policyadvocacy/ethics [retrieved 27 October 2007].

Needham, G. and Johnson, K. (2007) Ethical Issues in Providing Library Services to Distance Learners, *Open Learning: the journal of open and distance learning*, **22** (2), 117–28.

SCONUL (2001) *Access for Distance Learners: report of the SCONUL task force*, www.sconul. ac.uk/publications/pubs/index.html [retrieved 27 October 2007].

23

Involving users in a technical solution to help assess the accessibility of websites

Jenny Craven and Jillian R. Griffiths

Introduction

The European Commission Communication on e-accessibility aims to move forward recommendations to address accessibility and inclusion and to achieve 'an "Information Society for All", promoting an inclusive digital society that provides opportunities for all and minimizes the risk of exclusion' (European Commission, 2005a). The measures recommended by the Commission include Design For All methods in the design of products and services, including the design and evaluation of websites and drawing on recommendations made by the World Wide Web Consortium/Web Accessibility Initiative (W3C/WAI). As a result of these activities, a range of projects have been funded to address the issues raised (see for example, Klironomos et al., 2006).

The Design for All approach refers to the way content and structure are applied to web-based resources and services so that they can be developed and delivered in a way that reaches as many people as possible. This is in alignment with various e-inclusion activities under way within Europe, such as the e-Europe accessibility action plan (European Commission, 2005a) to address the i2010 strategy for creating a 'European society for growth and employment' (European Commission, 2005b). The i2010 strategy, for example, places a particular emphasis on accessibility requirements for public procurement of ICT, accessibility certification, and web accessibility assessment methods and tools.

A new technological solution to assessing the accessibility of websites over time is being developed by the European Internet Accessibility Observatory (EIAO) project team. EIAO is funded by the European Commission and runs from 2004 to 2007 (with a proposed extension within the existing budget until 2008). It involves partners from six countries across Europe. The aim of the project is to develop an online service, via a user interface, which will provide regular (e.g. monthly) updates of the general accessibility of websites by country, sector (for example, the library sector) and on an individual basis. The 'Observatory' is different from other automated checkers (such as LIFT and Cynthia Says), because it aims to aggregate individual tests for large-scale benchmarking and to evaluate the development of the results from one period to the next to indicate where improvements have been made and/or to alert to possible problems which have arisen.

The EIAO project has adopted an iterative user-centred approach to the design and development of the system, the results of which have been used to influence the technical development of the project in terms of interface and schema design. This approach is a well documented one (for example, Gulliksen et al., 2003; Maguire, 2001; Van House, 1995), the merits and challenges of which will be discussed further in this paper. Traditional user-centred design methods include user panels, formal case studies and individual user assessments (Newell and Gregor, 2001). It could also include more formal user testing, which can be achieved through structured or semi-structured task-based exercises with a variety of users employing observational and interview techniques, followed by query techniques such as focus groups or questionnaires (Craven and Booth, 2006). User testing protocols can include remote and face-to-face user testing. Both methods can produce useful input to the user-centred design approach, and there are advantages and disadvantages to both (Petrie et al., 2006).

User testing should include people representatives of the intended target audience and should also include people with different access requirements, such as disabled and elderly people and people using alternative devices such as a mobile phone. In order to try to consider the needs of the typical user, people with different levels of skills and expertise should be included. For usability testing, Nielsen recommends at least 15 users to discover all the usability design problems; however, he also suggests that excellent results can be gained from using as few as five users (Nielsen, 2000).

The EIAO user-centred approach has involved end-users and stakeholders using the following methods:

1   End-users (in particular people with disabilities such as visual, aural, physical and cognitive impairments) were involved to inform the selection of accessibility elements to be tested by the EIAO system, and to evaluate the accuracy of the automated testing so that any necessary adjustments could be made to the algorithms (see Craven and Nietzio, 2007).

2   Stakeholder groups (in particular web designers, web developers and web-related policy-makers) were involved first to establish the need for such an observatory, to identify any relevant issues or concerns, and then to evaluate

the functionality of the Observatory, the user interface (UI) and the content provided.

Focusing on the stakeholder activities, this paper will describe how the user-centred approach was used to inform the technical development of the project and the design and appearance of the UI.

The involvement of users at iterative stages of the technical development has provided the project with rich data relating to the awareness stakeholders have of accessibility issues, and the involvement they have in accessible website design, the functionality of the Observatory's UI, and their perception of its usefulness. The user-centred approach has not been without its difficulties, and various challenges have arisen during the project, such as dealing with the late delivery of software releases, technical–non-technical liaison and terminology, a lack of understanding of user testing, and the unpredictable nature of involving humans! Despite this, the project team have striven to ensure technical developments are continuously improved in a way that is user-led.

This paper will provide an overview of the EIAO project, placing it in context with other approaches to web accessibility assessment and e-accessibility activities. It will then describe the methods used to involve users in the development of the Observatory, focusing in particular on the involvement of stakeholder groups, including some examples of how the results were used. The paper will then discuss the advantages and disadvantages of the user-centred approach, drawing from experiences documented in the literature and on some of the challenges faced by the EIAO project team. It will finally provide some key points to be considered by anyone wanting to adopt a user-centred approach to inform the technical development of a web-based product or service.

Overview of EIAO

The evaluation of the accessibility of websites is the focus of the European Internet Accessibility Observatory (EIAO) project (www.eiao.net), which is developing an online tool that aims to provide policy-makers with a tool to observe and improve the effect of accessibility. The results can also be of interest for web designers, web editors, website commissioners, etc., with different levels of data according to their needs and depending on different circumstances. This may vary between a brief report on the accessibility of a particular website to a full-blown report on the position of a website's accessibility in relation to a particular sector, region or country. The final version of the EIAO tool or 'Observatory' will publish monthly updated measurements from around 10,000 websites. The results will be available online via a user interface.

The data collected by the Observatory represents barriers detected when accessing a website. Many existing web accessibility evaluation tools can evaluate one web page and indicate detected barriers for that page. In contrast, the Observatory will present data representing the likely barriers of a website or a group of websites by evaluating a sample of pages from the website or group of websites.

Involving users throughout the EIAO project has provided the project team with feedback from each user group to influence the technical development of the project in terms of interface and schema design. It has also provided the team with a clearer picture of what users actually want to get from the Observatory and what the potential concerns about such a system might be, which could then be addressed in FAQs, disclaimers and promotional materials relating to the Observatory.

The aim of the user testing of the Observatory and UI with stakeholder groups was to establish whether the EIAO service offered potential stakeholders a tool which would be useful to, or may even enhance, their job performance. In essence, we were testing the usefulness of the reports offered by the EIAO service as well as the functionality of the interface (i.e. did it perform in a way that was intuitive, were there any issues with the speed data was retrieved, was the website robust, etc.).

The initial user requirements gathering exercise provided the project team with some rich data relating to stakeholders' awareness and involvement in accessibility and website design, development, procurement, etc. It also provided the team with a better idea of what stakeholder groups might want from the Observatory in general and in relation to specific features. The findings characterize current needs and concerns related to an Observatory and define the work needed to progress. It was considered important to be able to establish general levels of awareness, together with the main difficulties developers, owners and decision-makers face when dealing with accessibility in their context. It was important to gain users' approval in order to reach high credibility and achieve the aims in delivering the Observatory, namely to develop the right tool to fulfil the target users' needs and to make them feel that the Observatory was doing a useful and strategic job for them. For these reasons the findings were used to inform the work of the project and shape future decisions.

An initial user-testing phase, with a small sample of stakeholders evaluating the UI, revealed a positive reaction to the Observatory, the majority of participants responding that they thought the Welcome Page was informative and that they all understood the purpose of the Observatory. The main issues raised by participants, which required further consideration, related to the language used, which was felt to be too academic, and a need to improve instructions and prompts, error messages and the Help function.

These results aided the development of the next version of the Observatory and UI, which was then tested on a much wider group of stakeholders. The UI and an online survey were distributed to 160 individuals and to 14 e-mail lists and newsletters over a period of two months. Participants were asked to undertake a set of tasks using the Observatory and report on their impressions of the Observatory via an online questionnaire. Additionally, they were queried about the ways in which they use web accessibility data.

During the development stage of the testing framework, the development team asked participants to try to evaluate as many functions of the Observatory as possible, which led to a task-based approach to the design of the survey. Despite some concerns that the scope of the survey was beginning to evolve into a full-blown user-testing activity rather than the evaluation of the interface and the Observatory functions, it was agreed that the survey would go ahead using the task-based approach. A task-based approach can be very effective. For example, McGillis and Toms (2001) used this approach to assess the usability of an academic library website by academic staff and students. Another example is the Non-visual Access to the Digital Library Project (NoVA), where tasks were developed to provide comparative data of the user seeking experience of a group of 'sighted' and 'visually impaired' people (Craven, 2003). However, care needs to be taken that the tasks are of relevance to users rather than, as Nielsen puts it: 'tasks that focus almost exclusively on [developers'] own pet features rather than on goals that users really want to accomplish' (Nielsen, 2007).

The task-based approach for EIAO was employed to evaluate the user interface, and elicited some very useful comments and feedback, but it was evident that some of the EIAO survey respondents struggled with the tasks set because – according to their comments – they could not see the relevance of what they were being asked to do in relation to their work experience:

> [Overall] I found it difficult to use because there is too much jargon; too much on the home page even, before you begin to try to use it
>
> [Statistical Report] Afraid I didn't understand it!
>
> [Indicator's Report] Far too complicated for me to understand. Who would want this level of detail? Not a policy-maker, one of his/her minions perhaps

From a total of 74 initial respondents, over half dropped out before completing the survey (this could be tracked by the system), and although exact reasons for non-completion could not be confirmed, comments suggest a lack of task relevance may have been a strong factor. Despite this, it was possible to provide recommendations for improvements to the next iteration of the UI. These included improvements to the overall information provided about the Observatory, the structure and navigation, language used and accessibility.

Drawing on the experience of the task-based method, the next iteration will use a different approach. Instead of creating tasks for each and every function, a general 'scenario' has been created which participants can use – if they wish – to help with their evaluation:

> Imagine you have been asked to investigate the accessibility of websites across Europe, to be used in a report to demonstrate whether or not web accessibility (in general) is improving as a result of various e-accessibility training and awareness raising activities that have been held across Europe over the last two years. The aim could be to justify funding for accessibility training, to make a case for a website re-design, to demonstrate the accessibility of websites in a particular sector, to compare accessibility across a number of regions, etc.

> To help gather the information for this report you have been asked to try out the Observatory, which provides assessments of the design of websites by country, by region and by sector, to see if they are being designed in a way that is accessible for different groups of people – in particular people who have disabilities and/or use assistive technologies such as screen readers and screen magnification.

The aim of this approach is to *suggest*, rather than *lead*, how the Observatory might be used and to gently direct participants to try out the different functions it provided. At the time of writing this iteration has not been undertaken but it is hoped that it will provide the project team with further suggestions to improve the user interface.

Involving users: challenges

The involvement of users in the design process can be challenging at times. Nielsen (2007) recommends, where possible, having 'dedicated usability specialists perform your project's usability activities', some of the disadvantages of designers and developers undertaking their own usability testing being that they:

- might be less willing to admit [design] deficiencies
- can be too willing to dismiss user complaints or problems as minor or unrepresentative
- can get so caught up in their own theories about how users ought to behave that they forget to test for cases in which people behave differently.

The EIAO project used a mixed approach to its user-testing activities, with a user-testing team dedicated to these activities, but also working in liaison with a development team. The development team were very enthusiastic about the involvement of users in the design and development of the Observatory and were open to feedback from end-users and stakeholders throughout the life of the project. However, it has not always been an easy process to maintain user involvement in a technical process of design and development, because of the nature of technical development. Problems which arose with this will now be described.

For the user-testing project team responsible for identifying stakeholder groups for the evaluation and establishing contacts for the wide distribution of the survey, it was vital to have a reasonably clear timeframe to work within. For example, to distribute a survey via an appropriate online newsletter or discussion forum (EDeAN or e-Access Bulletin, for example) it was necessary to meet the deadline set by the respective editors or list owners.

For the project team responsible for technical development, it was vital to release a product that was in a fit state to be evaluated, having undergone all the necessary quality checks and bug fixes (some of which might only become apparent at the final pilot stage). The project development team would therefore not release the Observatory to the user-testing team if it was still below a standard acceptable for public inspection. This decision was perfectly understandable as, potentially, negative feedback from respondents would be likely to be about issues the development team were well aware of, but had not been able to fix because the user-testing team had a tight timeframe in which to distribute the survey.

However, this decision presented problems for the user-testing team because survey release dates had to be constantly put back, which had a potentially negative impact on the likely response rate, and could damage relationships developed between the user-testing team and any participants who agreed to take part in the iterative stages of the evaluation. The knock-on effect of this was to extend the deadline for survey responses, which then put enormous pressure on the user-testing team to gather, analyse and report the findings (according to deliverable deadlines set at the beginning of the project and in agreement with the funding body).

At the time of writing the final evaluation of the Observatory and UI has not taken place, despite the framework being in place. A recommendation was made to undertake this evaluation during the six-month extension to the project, when there will be sufficient data in the Observatory to allow the technical development team to present a more relevant tool for potential stakeholder groups to evaluate.

User involvement in the EIAO project has been an iterative process; the responses gathered from user requirements, user testing and feedback has provided the project team with valuable data which have been used to inform development from the start of the project.

Conclusions

The EIAO project sought to involve users in the design and development of the Observatory at iterative stages throughout the project and included two specific areas of user involvement: comparison of user and automated results, and stakeholder testing of the Observatory content and UI. The experience of working with the development team was at times a challenging one. However, lessons learnt from it have been positive and have provided the team with some key points which should be helpful for anyone considering the involvement of users in the design and development of technical products and services. These are listed below:

1   Be very clear of the purpose of the user involvement; for example, if the evaluation needs to include accessibility testing a sample of users with different access methods should be included.

2   Be very clear how the results will be used – is the development team prepared to act on the results even if they are not what was expected (e.g. very negative)?

3   Decide on an appropriate approach to user testing; for example, if using a task-based approach, ensure that the tasks or scenarios for evaluation will be of relevance to the users.

4   Avoid trying to user-test all elements available. Instead, think about how the users might want to use the system and develop the testing framework accordingly.

5   Linked to the above point, be realistic about the timeframe for testing. Most users will not spend more than 15–30 minutes on an evaluation if they are not being remunerated. If remuneration is offered, a time-frame of up to two hours is generally seen as acceptable.

6   The technical development and user-involvement teams need to be prepared to be flexible in order to achieve the goals of the exercise.

7   Joint planning meetings are helpful, of course, but it is also useful to attend planning meetings specific to both groups – for example, the user-testing team attended some of the development team meetings, which provided more of an insight into the process of technical development and associated problems.

The authors wish to extend their grateful thanks to all the 'users' who participated in the EIAO project.

References

Craven, J. (2003) Access to Electronic Resources by Visually Impaired People, *Information Research*, 8 (4), paper no. 156, http://informationr.net/ir/8-4/paper156.html.

Craven, J. and Booth, H. (2006) Putting Awareness into Practice: practical steps for conducting usability tests, *Library Review*, **55** (3), April, 179–94.

Craven, J. and Nietzio, A. (2007) A Task-based Approach to Assessing the Accessibility of Web Sites, *Performance Measurement and Metrics*, **8** (2), 98–109.

European Commission (2005a) *Communication from the Commission to the Council, the European Parliament, the Economic and Social Committee, and the Committee of Regions: eAccessibility*, COM (2005) 425.

European Commission (2005b) *Standardization Mandate to CEN, CENELEC and ETSI in Support of European Accessibility Requirements for Public Procurement of Products and Services in the ICT Domain*, M 376-EN, Brussels, 7 December 2005.

Gulliksen, J. et al., (2003) Key Principles for User-centred Systems Design, *Behaviour & Information Technology*, **22** (6), November–December, 397–409.

Klironomos, I. et al. (2006) White Paper: promoting Design for All and e-accessibility in Europe, *Universal Access in the Information Society*, **5**, 105–19.

Maguire, M. (2001) Context of User Within Usability Activities, *International Journal of Human-Computer Studies*, **55**, 453–83.

McGillis, L. and Toms, E. G. (2001) Usability of the Academic Library Web Site: implications for design, *College & Research Libraries*, **62** (4), 355–67.

Newell, A. F. and Gregor P. (2001) User Sensitive Inclusive Design, *JIM 2001 Interaction Homme/Machine & Assistance*, 4–6 July, France, 18–20.

Nielsen, J. (2000) *Designing Web Usability: the practice of simplicity*, Indianapolis, New Riders Publishing.

Nielsen, J. (2007). Should Designers and Developers Do Usability? *Alertbox*, 25 June, www.useit.com/alertbox/own-usability.html.

Petrie, H. et al. (2006) Remote Usability Evaluations with Disabled People. In *Proceedings of CHI 2006*, CHI (Computer–Human Interaction).

Van House, N. (1995) User Needs Assessment and Evaluation for the UC Berkley Electronic Environmental Library Project: a preliminary report. In *Digital Libraries '95: the second international conference on the theory and practice of digital libraries*, June 11–13, 1995, Austin, Texas, www.dlib.org/dlib/february96/02vanhouse.html.

24

The reality of managing change: the transition to Intute

Caroline Williams

Introduction

In 2003 the UK's Joint Information Systems Committee (JISC) funded eight internet gateways or hubs within a collective named the Resource Discovery Network (RDN). Their brief was to identify and catalogue the best websites relevant to university and college work. The teams of people who developed the hubs were dispersed geographically across UK universities. They all worked on different subject areas and had unique identities. They had their own websites, databases, strategies and plans. But JISC was concerned: it wanted more value for money. In other words, it wanted the RDN to be used more, to be more widely known and to cost less. The hubs needed to change.

This paper tells the story of that change. It shares the experience of the transition of the RDN to Intute, and explores the cycle of organizational renewal which began in 2003 with the creation of the RDN Executive at Mimas, at the University of Manchester. As library and information professionals, managers and leaders, we operate in an environment where new technologies, shifting organizational priorities and evolving user needs are pervasive. We respond with projects and initiatives which deliver new services to our users. However, developing them in the first place can be relatively easy compared with ensuring that they are embedded in our wider operations. So we grapple with the organizational and people issues of change, perhaps taking a systematic considered approach or, more likely, relying on our enthusiasm to guide us through. Change is not easy. In the words of William Bridges (2003), 'It isn't the changes that do you in, it's the transitions. They aren't the same thing. *Change* is situational: the move to a new site . . . the reorganization of the roles of the team . . . . *Transition*, on the other hand, is psychological; it is a three-phase process that people go through as they internalize and come to terms with the details of the new situation that the change brings about.' Without transition change is not sustainable. This paper describes the tools and techniques used in the move to Intute and shares lessons learnt. It gives a strategic management perspective, and describes the Office of Government Commerce's (OGC) Managing Successful Programmes (MSP) approach, before going on to outline the complex people, political, cultural and leadership aspects.

Strategic management

On taking up the role of Executive Director of the RDN, like any new starter I wanted to find out everything I could about my new organization and its situation. So I met with staff. I asked questions such as 'What do you do, who are your users, and what do they want?' I read dense technical reports about search engines, portals, enterprise systems and digital libraries. I found out about similar services in other countries, e.g. Education Network Australia (EdNA) and Multimedia Educational Resource for Learning and Online Teaching (Merlot). I read past reviews and analysis, and looked at statistics of students by subject. In short, I did what management textbooks call an environmental analysis. From the discipline of management, I found the most helpful things to be the diagrammatic representations of key theories. They acted as checklists and prompted me to consider things from a number of angles. I referred specifically to the Johnson and Scholes (1993) model of the strategy process and Grant's (2002) work linking resources, capabilities and competitive advantage. The former describes three overlapping areas of strategic analysis, implementation and choice. Within each area we are invited to examine: organizational resources and capability; organization structure and culture; and strategy in relation to stakeholder expectations, environmental conditions and available strategic options. All of which take us through the cycle of thinking: Where am I now? Where to I want to be? How am I going to make it happen? The Grant model was a useful complement in its focus on the resources of the organization, i.e. what we have, what we do with it and how that makes us different.

Once completed, the analysis formed the basis for a new organizational vision and strategy, without which it would have been impossible to move forward. The vision was grounded in the environmental analysis but was kept deliberately broad so that it could survive as the context changed. The strategy was clear and certain in its aims for improved communication, technical consolidation, better performance measurement and renewed focus on stakeholder needs. However, to realize the strategy it became apparent that as an organization made up of eight separate entities, we would be faced with significant hurdles. It looked likely that the barriers would be in communication, decision-making and technical standardization and that our organizational structure and ways of working would not be pliable enough.

So a change programme was born. Now, three years later, the vision and strategy have undergone several iterations and become the cornerstone of our planning and development. They are the foundation for decision-making and prioritization, and evolve in response to the changing environment. Adam Lashinsky, a writer for *Fortune*, recently reported that Meg Whitman, CEO of eBay, 'says she's spending the bulk of her time these days on people . . . and on strategy. She notes . . . that on the internet "the landscape changes quarterly," elevating strategy to a mission-critical task' (Lashinsky, 2006). Later in the paper I will consider 'people' in depth, but now will move from strategy to planning.

MSP and project management

The challenge ahead was to plan and manage at least four major strands of work: organizational restructuring, marketing review, technical integration and performance measurement. Within each segment of activity there was a whole host of projects with many interdependencies, e.g. organizing the Intute launch event, revising the collection management policy and rewriting the cataloguing guidelines. However, established project planning techniques did not fit well with the complexities of wholesale organizational change. We were striving for outputs which were often intangible or highly dependent on other strands of work. Risk was difficult for us to deal with. Our risk registers identified and prompted descriptions of mitigating action, but within a culture of autonomy, identifying 'risk owners' was awkward. The executive team was small, and a great deal of responsibility remained with the geographically distributed managers of the hubs as they formed the new subject groups.

In such a situation, the extent of comprehensive planning was at first inadequate. However, the Executive, as part of Mimas, was able to tap into a wealth of expertise. A lead from a Mimas colleague opened the door to programme management techniques. Programme management proved to be the perfect match for our situation. With the help of Ruth Murray-Webster of Lucidus Consulting we created the overarching planning documents needed. These were based on the OGC's MSP approach. One of the most significant documents was the 'blueprint', as its role was to outline the characteristics of our desired 'future state'. The document was 26 pages long, and arranged in five main groupings of activity: 'one organization', service development, performance measurement, branding and marketing, and other funded projects. It contained details of 19 projects (four of which had attracted additional funding) and specified what we were hoping to achieve at breakpoints in four tranches from 2006 to 2008. Project briefs were written and management of the projects divided between all available managers. A detailed overarching project plan was created for the first tranche of work which was constantly revised in the lead up to the Intute launch. All of this worked well in practice. Staff were clear about their roles and they understood how their work fitted in to the big picture. Delegation improved and there was a clearer understanding of what was required from everyone by when.

Intute was launched on time on 13 July 2006 at the Wellcome Trust in London and received a warm welcome from the community. However, we didn't stop working on our programme. We carried on using MSP techniques in order to meet the JISC requirement to produce a business case and business plan, and strategic technical development plan, by November 2006.

Creating a business case demands research, evidence collection and analysis, and it is used to validate the ongoing viability of a programme of work. For us it was crucial to get this right in order to secure continuing funding. We commissioned a series of 'strategic stakeholder' interviews and ran a survey of academic use of the internet. Technical staff undertook an analysis of the technical environment, other staff developed scenarios of use attributable to different groups and others looked closely at internet research skills and information literacy. Everything was scrutinized; we went back to our 'unique selling point', core competencies and capabilities, and asked ourselves, 'Does this remain valid?' Our university library supporters allowed us to quote their financial savings accrued by using Intute (as opposed to creating and maintaining subject lists of recommended websites themselves), and we attempted to quantify our benefit to the community. We built up a body of evidence and reflected on our strategy and vision . . . and we changed it. The business case and plan, new strategy and vision, and strategic technical development plan were submitted to JISC and we received confirmation of success with a commitment to a further five years of funding.

People

'[People] struggle to protect their world and the meaning and identity they [get] from it . . . People have to bring their hearts and their minds to work' (Bridges, 2003).

People are the life-blood of academic institutions. Every library and information service will employ teams of people who are experts in purchasing, licence negotiation, cataloguing, website design, authentication, information literacy, subject coverage, etc. In order for an organization or a service to change, it is necessary for groups of people to move out of their established patterns and be recast. This process is often referred to as the phases of transition; Bridges defines it as: 1. ending, losing, letting go; 2. the neutral zone; 3. the new beginning.

The reality of this is more complex. People respond to and approach change in different ways. In 'Who moved my cheese?' Spencer Johnson (1999) describes personal responses to change in an amusing way by telling the story of four characters who live in a maze and look for cheese to feed them and make them happy. Cheese is a metaphor for what you want to have in life and the maze is where you look for what you want. However, these characterizations are of extremes. In reality, boundaries are blurred, and managing people with different and inconsistent responses takes dexterity in communication and negotiation. The following quotes from staff illustrate the complexity of feelings at the prospect of the end of the RDN hubs, and the beginning of Intute:

> It was accompanied by internal staffing changes at our hub, so that was a little bit traumatic, but once that had been sorted out, I felt a lot happier. I never had any real attachment to the RDN, but a strong attachment to the hub . . . I saw how the hubs could combine to the benefit of the user.

> The RDN had evolved piecemeal from a range of earlier JISC initiatives . . . policy as such was a compromise of the individual policies of the various hubs. The hubs were successfully creating their own customer and marketing bases and were effectively services in their own right (at least that's how their customers saw it). Individually too small to survive, but struggling to find a truly collective perception, you had the impression of tremendous potential in danger of disappearing.

Communication was at the crux of the transition. This communication took numerous forms and had different purposes at different times, from formal meetings, e-mail correspondence and facilitated 'coping with change sessions', to staff questionnaires and simply giving staff the space, time and opportunity to express concerns. We employed an experienced staff training and development management consultant, Deborah Dalley, to run workshops. Some staff expressed concerns and asked questions, others were quiet and adopted a 'wait and see' attitude. At the time I felt that there was resistance to change but now I recognize it as doubts about the future and people protecting the needs of their existing user communities. The things that staff say helped through difficult times were:

> A lot of moaning! It helped when there were specific things to tackle.

> Basically we kept doing what we did best. Keeping the services . . . going; looking after the customer base.

> I think just trying to hold onto a coherent view of the aims of the service, and also concentrating on developing skills, and encouraging staff to see this as an opportunity to develop skills and expand their work experience helped . . . . Grasping onto any positive feedback also helped morale.

In addition, the first significant communication challenge was to secure senior support through Board approval, and then the most senior institutional represent-atives of all hubs (the hub directors). Once support, however reservedly, was secured then the work of getting staff to embrace and implement the changes began.

Uncertainty was inevitable but as the new vision, strategy, brand identity and planning documents emerged we began to implement change. It was clear that involvement was vital to staff motivation and to facilitate this Intute managers took on delegated responsibility for cross-service work. Management text books would call them 'change agents', but they were existing managers with new project briefs and the will to forge working relationships in the new subject groups. However, there were some shaky starts. There were lots of questions, particularly about levels of autonomy and delegated decision-making. There were human resource management issues to cope with; some people moved on, others were working exceptionally long hours. Within a university environment it is almost impossible to use some of the techniques of industry to help manage and motivate in this kind of situation, e.g. bonuses, so we relied on regular communication and meetings and verbal commendation and praise. We continued to utilize all lines of communication and were able to invest in staff development and training and support.

A low point was reached when we had to make a decision about the new name of the organization. With the strategic rebrand consultants The Big Idea (TBI) we had achieved consensus on moving to one name for the whole organization built around the concept of an identity we called the 'authoritative mentor'. When choosing a name that summed this up, we had four possible approaches. Our new name could be one which was evocative of personality, descriptive, conceptual or unique. We drew up a short list of names and consulted users, ran legal checks and were left with nothing definitive. But knew we wanted something unique, fresh, short, which would not date. The decision was made to go with Intute. It wasn't a popular decision at the time. One member of staff reflected 'We just didn't like it. Nor did any of the academics we asked.' However, Intute has grown on us and we've grown into it. In the words of another member of staff, 'With the wisdom of hindsight Intute is a good brand identity, but the leap of faith had to be made by the Executive and forced through.'

Now, we are in our new beginning and striving to be an organization which con-stantly renews itself in response to community needs and technological innovation. The next steps for us as an organization are to enable codetermination in decision-making and further develop shared control. In our environment, we see the potential for a more sustainable future if we continue to innovate. Our barri-ers have been broken down; our staff have responded to, and embraced, change in such a way that our hearts and minds are free to realize our ambitions for the future. As Deborah Dalley observes,

I have worked as the training and development consultant for Intute during the transition from RDN to Intute and I can hardly believe how far people have come. In the early sessions with staff it was clear that levels of trust were low and there was a high degree of uncertainty and concern about the future. Now in 2007 groups are displaying many of the characteristics of high performing teams, morale is significantly higher and there is a much stronger sense of a shared identity.

Politics, culture and leadership

Leading the Intute transition in the beginning (2003/4) was like walking a tightrope between the hub cultures, priorities, identities, resources and capabilities; the changing environment; and the need to realize synergy and economies of scale, and so build a strong foundation for the future. Different people (e.g. JISC stakeholders and hub managers) had different views on the direction they should go in, yet the vision underpinning Intute was one of unification. Without managing the internal and external politics and culture of the organization we would not have been available to realize our change strategy.

It was the experience, wisdom and advice of existing leaders – the board of management and directors of hubs – within the network of institutions making up Intute that enabled the political management of the transition. We also had to handle the cultural conflicts which presented themselves. At the coal face, managers reflected on the culture of their home institutions and openly acknowledged differences. From JISC, the value-for-money agenda pushed us towards a more business-like approach to operations, yet the academic culture in which we are grounded can resist the pursuit of efficiency at the expense of providing a bespoke response to different user group needs. Cultural change has been difficult and is not yet entirely resolved, but we have made progress. As one manager puts it, 'It was knife-edge stuff. The powerful collective identity we have now was born in the most difficult times. I would like to remember the first time we all started talking about "we"; that was the turning point. "We" is one of our most frequently used words.'

Leading this transition has been the most challenging role of my career. I tried out and varied leadership styles at different points in the process, sometimes with success, other times in response to feedback from colleagues, and occasionally with results that required a quick retreat. After a period of consultation, I did have to take a top-down approach which seemed appropriate at the time, but is not my preferred way of operating. Collectively we were forced to learn the difference between consultation and consensus in decision-making as my focus on the big picture came into conflict with local needs. This proved to be demanding and psychologically taxing over a period of 18 months; it required resilience and persistence.

This experience has taught me that we can learn how to lead and that being true to ourselves in leadership gives flexibility with consistency and gains the trust of others. For me, there is no one key to success. I draw upon everything available to me, from looking at the behaviour of leaders I admire, to experimenting with the application of business models and reflecting (and seeking feedback) on my own actions and reactions so as to better understand myself. I have invested in my own leadership training and development. Throughout the transition I studied for my MBA, and benefited from courses, coaching and support from my manager, colleagues and consultants. I also read a lot; the book that gave me most food for thought was Daniel Goleman's (2002) work on emotional intelligence and the 'leadership repertoire' of the visionary, coaching, affiliative, democratic, pacesetting and commanding styles – we don't need just one style but the ability to use them all in response to our reading of any situation.

Conclusion

Transition has not been easy, but it has been successful. With the right tools and committed people the complex process has been rewarding, sustaining and reinvigorating. In 2007 Intute has a renewed commitment from JISC of five years of funding, our use statistics are rising, our project portfolio is growing and realizing other successes, e.g. the launch of Intute Informs, and as an organization we are unified and are still learning as we look to our future. We have overcome the challenges and launched our new beginning.

References

Bridges, W. (2003) *Managing Transitions: making the most of change*, 2nd edn, Nicholas Brealey.

Goleman, D. (2002) *The New Leaders: transforming the art of leadership into the science of results*, Little, Brown.

Grant, R. M. (2002) *Contemporary Strategy Analysis: concepts, techniques and applications*, 4th edn, Blackwell Business.

Johnson, G. and Scholes, K. (1993) *Exploring Corporate Strategy*, 3rd edn, Prentice Hall.

Johnson, S. (1999) *Who Moved My Cheese?: an amazing way to deal with change in your work and in your life*, Vermilion.

Lashinsky, A. (2006) Building eBay 2.0, http://money.cnn.com/magazines/fortune/fortune_archive/2006/10/16/8388658/index.htm.

Websites

Education Network Australia (EdNA), www.edna.edu.au.

Intute, www.intute.ac.uk.

Lucidus Consulting, www.lucidus.co.uk.

Mimas, www.mimas.ac.uk.

Multimedia Educational Resource for Learning and Online Teaching (Merlot), www.merlot.org.

INDEX